Start Your Own Export Business (How to Export)

Start Your Own Export Business (How to Export)

Written By :

EIRI Consultants and Engineers

ENGINEERS INDIA RESEARCH INSTITUTE

4449, Nai Sarak, Main Road, Delhi-110 006 (India)

Ph. : 91-11-23918117, 23916431, 45120361

Fax : 91-11-23916431, 23918117

* **E-Mail** : eiribooks@yahoo.com

* **Website** : www.eiriindia.org

Sole Distributor :

EIRI PROJECT CONSULTANTS & PUBLISHERS

4/54, Roop Nagar, Delhi-110007

Printed and Published by :

ENGINEERS INDIA RESEARCH INSTITUTE

4449, Nai Sarak, Main Road, Delhi-110 006 (India)
Ph. : 91-11-23918117, 23916431, 45120361
Fax : 91-11-23916431, 23918117
* **E-Mail** : eiribooks@yahoo.com
* **Website** : www.eiriindia.org

Distributed by :

EIRI PROJECT CONSULTANTS & PUBLISHERS
4/54, Roop Nagar, Delhi-110007

2nd Edition

ISBN : 9788186732571
Printed in New Delhi (India)

₹ 450

Printed and Published by Sudhir Gupta for "Engineers India Research Institute", 4449, Nai Sarak, Main Road, New Delhi-110 006 and Printed at Swastik Offset, Delhi

Preface

The book ***Start Your Own Export Business (How to Export)*** *covers almost all the basic and advanced details to setup own Export Business. The new edition of the book is covering latest methods including Rules for Successful Exporting, Brief Details for Starting Export Business, Registration of Exporters, Export of Samples, Gifts, Spares, Replacement, Repaired Goods etc., Appointing Overseas, Agents, Obtaining an Export Licence, Obtaining Export Credit Insurance, Finance Arrangement for Exports, Understanding Foreign Exchange Rates and Protection against their Adverse Movement, Procuring/Manufacturing Goods for Export and their Inspection by Government Authorities, Labelling, Packaging, Packing and Marking Goods for Export, Excise Procedure, Insuring Goods Against Marine Risks, Preparing Export Documents, Shipping and Customs Clearance of the Goods, Submitting Documents to Bank for Purchase/Collection/ Negotiation under L/C, Special Care for Negotiating Documents under L/C, Facilities of Foreign Exchange, Availing Facilities Under Export Import Policy, Availing Financial Incentives, Institutional Support for Exporters*

The book has been written for the benefit and to prove an asset and a handy reference guide in the hands of new entrepreneurs & well established industrialists.

Director

ENGINEERS INDIA RESEARCH INSTITUTE

Nai Sarak, New Delhi (INDIA)

E-Mail : eirisidi@bol.net.in

BOOKS ON PRINTINGS, OFFSET, SCREEN, FLEXO & GRAVURE TECHNOLOGY

HAND BOOK OF PRINTING TECHNOLOGY
OFFSET, SCREEN, FLEXO, GRAVURE, INKJET & DiGITAL

ISBN 81-86732-75-6 # ₹ 975/-

Typographic, Pre-Press Processes, Camera, Scanning, Offset Plate Making, Presses, Offset Press, Proof & Proofing Techniques, Newspaper Printing: Gravure & Packaging, Screen Printing, Plant Economics, Suppliers of Machineries & Raw Materials etc.

HAND BOOK OF OFFSET PRINTING TECHNOLOGY
ISBN : 81-86732-82-9

 # ₹ 500/- or US $ 50/-

Desktop Publishing Proof-Reading, Pre-Press Processes, Camera, Scanning, Offset Plate Making, Presses, Offset Press, Proof & Proofing Techniques, Newspaper Printing, Plant Economics, Suppliers of Plant & Machineries, Suppliers of Raw Materials etc.

HAND BOOK OF SCREENPRINTING WITH PROCESSES & TECHNOLOGY
ISBN. 81-86732-63-2★ ₹ 350/-

Screen Printing Methods, Screen- Process Stencils, Screen Printing Stencils, Chemicals Adhesives, Screen Printing On Glass, Colour Combination, Silk Screen Photo Stencil Preparation, Plant Economics Suppliers of Plant & Machinery & Raw Materials.

HAND BOOK OF PRINTING PROCESSES TECHNOLOGIES & INDUSTRIES
ISBN. 81-86732-07-1 # ₹ 375/-

The book covers latest technology of almost all the printing technology viz; screen, offset, velvet cloth, sheetfed offset. Project profiles on various printing industries are also provided. Suppliers of machinery are also given.

BOOKS ON PLASTIC COMPOUNDING, PROCESSING, MOULDS, POLYMER, FIBRE GLASS, PVC & PET PRODUCTS

PLASTIC COMPOUNDING MASTER BATCHES, PET & OTHER PLASTIC PROCESSING INDUSTRIES
ISBN. 81-86732-49-7 • ₹ 750/-

Extrusion, Injection, Blow & Rotational Moulding, Additives for Polymers, PVC Compounding, Colour Master Batch, PET, Suppliers of Machineries, Suppliers of Raw Materials etc.

PLASTIC PROCESSING AND PACKAGING INDUSTRIES
ISBN. 81-86732-11-X

₹ 975/- or US$ 100/-

Introduction, Plastic Processing, Injection & Blow Moulding, Compounding & Processing of PVC, PU, Project profiles and directory section. The book is covering with the 54 fully detailed chapters etc.

TECHNOLOGY OF PVC COMPOUNDING AND ITS APPLICATIONS
ISBN 81-86732-88-8

₹ 900/- or US $ 100/-

PVC Resins Processing of PVC, Additives for PVC, Compounding, Compounding of PVC, Testing of Resins and Compounds, Speciality Plastic Compounds & Masterbatches, PVC compounds, Xlpe cable compound, jelly filled telecommunication cable compound & sheating compound, Plastic Granules Applications of PVC, Suppliers of Machineries/Raw Materials etc.

MOULDS DESIGN & PROCESSING HAND BOOK
ISBN. 81-86732-23-3

 # ₹ 495/- or US$ 50/-

Classification of Moulds, Production Schedule of Plastic Injection Mould, Steel for Injection Mould,Trouble, Injection Mould Design, Compression/Transfer Mould, Blow Mould Design, Standard Mould Parts, Conversion Table etc.

Technology of PET Bottles PREFORM AND PET RECYCLING
₹ 850/-

US$ 85/-

Processing and manufacturing technology of PET Bottles, Preform and market study with Project Profiles of PET bottles, preform & others. Suppliers of Machinery & Raw Materials etc.

ENGINEERS INDIA RESEARCH INSTITUTE Mobile : 9811437895, 9811151047

4449, Nai Sarak, Main Road, Delhi - 110 006 (INDIA) Ph. 91-11- 23918117, 23916431, 23947058

CONTENTS

LIST OF PUBLICATIONS/BOOKS PUBLISHED BY

ENGINEERS INDIA RESEARCH INSTITUTE 4449, NAI SARAK, MAIN ROAD, DELHI - 6 (INDIA)

Name of Books	₹	US$
EXPORT ORIENTED INDUSTRIES/PROCEDURES		
* Hand Book of Export Oriented Industries	1300/-	130
SPICES & COLD STORAGE		
* Hand Book of Spices & Packaging with Formulaes	750/-	75
* Start Your Own Cold Storage Unit	750/-	75
TEXTILE AUXILIARIES & CHEMICALS		
* Textile Auxiliaries and Chemicals with Processes and Formulations	950/-	95
* Modern Technology of Bleaching Dyeing Printing and Finishing of Textiles	750/-	75
PHARMACEUTICALS & DRUGS		
* Pharmaceuticals and Drugs Technology with Formulations	950/-	95
LEATHER & LEATHER PRODUCTS		
* Hand Book of Leather & Leather Products Technology	850/-	85
BIOTECHNOLOGY/BIOFERTILIZERS		
* Hand Book of Biotechnology	900/	90
* Hand Book of Biofertilizers and Vermiculture	900/-	90
AYURVEDIC MEDICINES		
* Ayurvedic & Herbal Medicines with Formulaes	750/-	75
* Hand book of Ayurvedic Medicines with Formulation	900/-	90
RUBBER & RUBBER INDUSTRIES		
* Rubber Chemicals & Processing Industries	400/-	40
* Technology of Rubber & Rubber Goods Industries	900/-	90
* Modern Rubber Chemicals Compounds and Rubber Goods Technology	1500/-	150
MINERAL & MINERALS		
* Hand book of Minerals and Minerals based Industries	975/-	100
FISH FARMING		
* Hand Book of Fish Farming and Fishery Products	650/-	65
ORGANIC FARMING/FOOD		
* Hand Book of Organic Farming & Organic Foods with Vermi-Composting and Neem Products	1100/-	110
PULP & PAPER BASED TECHNOLOGY		
* Hand book of Pulp & Paper, Paper Board and Paper Based Technology	1150/-	115
STEEL / S.S./ NON FERROUS METALS		
* Modern Technology of Non Ferrous Metals and Metal Extraction	1100/-	100
* Processing Technology of Steels and Stainless Steels	1900/-	190

MULTIPLE PROJECT REPORTS IN CD-ROM AT ECONOMY COSTS

* 92 New Lucrative Project Reports in Cd	25,000/-
* 45 Infotech/IT, Hospitality, Hospital, College, School & Clubs	16,000/-
* 23 Profitable Construction Projects	16,000/-
* 56 Agro Based & Food Process Projects	16,000/-
* 52 Food, Dairy, Bakery, Confectionery & Snacks Foods	16,000/-
* 100 Profitable Plastic, Polymers & Allied Projects (100 Project Reports)	25,000/-
* 45 New Chemicals & Allied Reports	18,000/-
* 44 Textile, Garments, Hosiery & Allied	16,000/-
* 23 Dairy Farming (Buffaloe & Jersey Cows), Dairy Products and other Milk Processing Industries	16,000/-
* 42 Paper & Pulp, Paper Board and Paper Converting Industries	18,000/-
* 31 Essential Oils, Perfumes, Flavours & Aromatic Compounds	16,000/-
* 63 Profitable Packaging & Allied Projects	16,000/-
* 36 Profitable Printing & Allied Projects	16,000/-
* 28 Surgical & Disposable Medical Projects	16,000/-
* 99 Profitable Printing & Packaging Projects	25,000/-
* 42 Electroplating, Anodizing & Allied Proj.	16,000/-
* 31 Profitable Plantation, Cultivation & Farm	18,000/-
* 55 Profitable Projects from Agro and other Industrial Wastes	18,000/-
* 35 Gums, Adhesives, Sealants & Resins	18,000/-
* 43 Iron, Steel, Casting, Fabrication, Wire Drawing & Rolling Mills Projects	18,000/-
* 54 Paint, Varnish, Solvents, Lacquers, Enamels, Thinner & Powder Coating Proj.	18,000/-
* 26 Educational Projects (Schools, Colleges, Management/Training Institutes etc.)	16,000/-
* 12 Mosquitoes Preventive Projects (Coils, Mat, Liquids, Agarbatti, Nets, Spray etc.)	12,000/-
* 52 Cosmetics (Herbal & Synthetics) Technology Projects (52 Proj. Reports)	18,000/-
* 67 Rubber & Rubber Goods Industries	18,000/-
* 21 Bakery & Allied Project Reports	12,000/-
* 37 Aluminium & Aluminium Based Ind.	16,000/-
* 14 Potato & Potato Based Industries	12,000/-
* 50 Electrical, Electronic & Computer/IT Based Industries (50 Project Reports)	18,000/-
* 5 Power Plant Projects (Thermal, Hydro, Solar, Wind Energy & Lignite Coal Based)	16,000/-
* 35 New Profitable Industries (35 Reports)	16,000/-
* 10 Molasses Based Lucrative Projects	16,000/-
* 24 Fruits/Veg. & Allied Food Dehydration Proj.	16,000/-
* 24 Soap and Detergents	18,000/-
* 30 Chemicals, Mechanicals, Packaging and other Profitable Projects	16,000/-
* 43 Automobile and Automobile Based Projects	18,000/-
* 160 New Export Oriented Units & Most Profitable Projects (160 Project Reports)	30,000/-
* 5 Ginger and Ginger Based Industries	12,000/-
* 13 Fish Farming & Fishery Projects	16,000/-
* 9 Tea Plantation & Processing Industries	15,000/-
* 14 Roasted/Salted, Cashewnuts, Almonds, Namkeens and Spice Projects	15,000/-
* 28 Fruit Juice, Food Dehydration & Allied	16,000/-
* 6 Agarbatti and Allied Projects	15,000/-
* 23 Injection Moulded Plastic Projects	15,000/-
* 38 Biofertilizer, Biofuel, Enzyme, Organic Farming, Protein & Allied Projects	18,000/-
* 11 Infotech/IT Lucrative Projects	16,000/-
* 11 Solar & Solar Based Projects	15,000/-
* 42 Hospitality, Building Materials, Power, Steels, Alcohol & Other Food Products	18,000/-
* 10 Coconut & Coconut Bye Products	16,000/-
* 22 Alcohol, Beer, IMFL, Country Liquor, Wine & Other Related Projects	22,000/-
* Food Processing & Agro Proj.	30,000/-

1

Introduction

(i) General:

Now-a-days export trade is prestigious and attractive. It is such a profitable business that most of the people are interested to enter into this field. Exporters have enormous avenues in the international atmosphere and extensive scope to have a feel of the business climate and systems across the globe. At the same time, export earnings play a major role in relieving the country of adverse balance of payment situation. There is ample scope for India to increase its share in the world markets if proper initiatives are taken and competition is analysed and studied carefully. As such, special effort is being made towards export of various commodities in general and particularly in the industries where India has competitive advantage and has already reached a degree of industrial maturity. Due to massive efforts by the government, the trade and industry has been able to achieve appreciable growth in exports in recent years.

Export trade basically is to bring the producer/exporter in contact with the ultimate user by offering quality products at internationally competitive prices. This is, however, not as simple as it sounds and requires not only a thorough knowledge of product but also resources, resiliance and innovative methods of marketing. While perseverance and patience, honesty, promptitude and care of the customer's needs are necessary for the continued confidence of the customer and a reputation in the international trade.

(ii) Incentives & Facilities:

It is important to note that the international market is highly competitive. In order to achieve global competitiveness, a thrust in export is very necessary. Accordingly, the Government of India has given various incentives to the exporters who earn valuable foreign exchange for our country by which import of modern technology and essential inputs are facilitated. Apart from getting incentives from the Government like income tax, excise duty and sales tax exemption etc., the manufacturing units are able to overcome stagnation and recession in the domestic economy through export. According to the government facilities the income from export business is fully exempted under the Income Tax Act 1961. Refund of Central Excise and Customs duty on export is also made applicable under the Duty Drawback Scheme of the Government. Duty free import of raw materials is allowed under various schemes of Ministry of Commerce. Replenishment licences are also available/given against export of certain specific items. Export oriented units under the 100% EOU Scheme and units located in Free Trade/Export Processing Zones are eligble for special facilities, such as exemption from excise/custom duty, sale in domestic tariff areas and sale of rejected goods or waste materials etc. Special facilities are also available for Electronic Hardware Technology Parks (EHTP) and units under Software Technology Parks (STP) Schemes.

The Foreign Exchange Regulations have been substantially liberalised for exporters. Rupee has been made fully convertible as a result of which foreign currency proceeds of export bills are converted at the market exchange rate under the unified determined exchange rate management system. Foreign exchange is liberally released for travel abroad. Exchange rates are quoted by the bank directly instead of previous indirect quoting system. Beside, with a view to promote export of goods and services from India, the export credit has been made available to the exporters in Indian rupees as well as foreign currency at concessional rates of interest. Interest tax on export credit has been abolished. Air and rail transport subsidy has been provided. Even the Import policy has been liberalised substantially for export oriented imports.

(iii) Government Promotional Activities:

Government is seriously concerned with the development of international business and adopting various promotional activities. With a view to achieve 30% growth rate per annum for some areas, 34 extreme thrust sectors have been identified. For the purpose, the Commerce Ministry has launched a massive plan to boost the exports of agricultural and farm products. The Ministry has identified various products under constitution of thrust areas. Financial agencies are doing continuous efforts to find out the international market. EXIM Bank of India provides short term loan to the exporters, Export Houses, Trading Houses, Star-Trading House at a very nominal rate of interest in order to operate their business smoothly. Besides, there are various organisations Viz. PDHCCI, ASSOCHAM, FIEO and others who are serving as a catalyst to the growth of India's Export business all over the world. I.T.P.O. (Indian Trade Promotion Organisation) organises every year the India International Trade Fair (IITF) at Pragati Maidan, New Delhi, to Promote and Co-ordinate the business activities taking place all over world. Now a days the Government organisations are providing maximum helps to boost the India's export business and making every effort to uplift our national economy.

2

Rules for Successful Exporting

Export Business is Profitable

Export is one of the most lucrative business activities in India. The Govt also provides various incentives to the exporters for earning valuable foreign exchange for the country for meeting their requirements for importing modern technology and essential inputs. Besides the income from export business is also exempted to the specified extent under the Income Tax Act 1961. Refund of Central Excise and Custom Duty on export is also made under the Duty Drawback Scheme of the Government. There is no Sales Tax on products meant for exports Drawback payment procedures have been simplified. Duty free import of law materials is allowed under various schemes of Ministry of Commerce. These schemes have been simplified to a great extent under new Exim Policy 2002-07. Replenishment licences are also available/given against export of certain specific items. Export oriented units under the 100% EOU Scheme and units located in Special Economic Zone are eligible for special facilities, such as exemption from excise/custom duty, sale in domestic tariff area including sale of rejected goods/ wastage etc. Special facilities are also available for units in Electronics Hardware Technology Parks (EHTP) and Software Technology Parks (STP) Schemes. Foreign Exchange Regulations have been substantially liberalised for exporters. Liberal release of foreign exchange is made available for travel abroad. Norms for establishing offices abroad by the exporters have been eased. Export Credit is available to the exporters at concessional rates of interest. The same can be availed of in Indian rupees as well as in foreign currency. Interest tax on export credit has been abolished. Export Credit and Guarantee Corporation is overhauling its international operations and offers risk coverage services to exporters. Transport subsidy is given for export by Air as well as Rail. Import Policy has also been liberalised substantially for export oriented imports. Domestic Companies have been allowed to bid in any currency. Various Customs houses have introduced

EDI system of computerised processing of import and export transactions.

Rules for Successful Exporting

In order to be successful in exporting one must fully research its markets rather than try to tackle every market at once. One should identify major markets and should approach them as per priority given. Many enthusiastic persons bitten by the export bug, fail because they bite off more than they can chew. Overseas design and product requirements must be carefully considered.

Always sell as close to the market as possible. The fewer intermediaries one has the better, because every intermediary needs some percentage for his share in the business, which means less profit for the exporter and higher prices for the customer. However in the initial phase one can explore options with intermediary to keep cost of operation low.

All goods for export must be efficiently produced. They must be produced with due regard to the needs of the export markets. It is no use trying to sell windows which open outwards in a country where, traditionally, windows open inwards.

Sell Services:

If a person cannot easily export his goods, may be he can sell know-how or services which can generate revenue for them. Alternatively, a person can concentrate on supplying goods and materials to other persons who already have an export trade. Or he can concentrate on making what are termed 'own brand' products, as per requirement of buyers in overseas markets which have the manufacturing know-how or facilities. Above all, note the following four points.

Selling in Export is Tough

No one is willing to buy. Everything has to be sold as the competition today ensures that the customer always has a choice of suppliers. Selling is an honourable profession, and to be an expert salesman is an honourable calling.

Deliveries must be on Time

Late deliveries are not always the exporter's fault because dock strikes, go-slows, and so on occur almost everywhere in the world. But such difficulties can invariably be overcome, and anyone contemplating entering export for the first time must be determined to let nothing stand in the way of-fast and efficient delivery. This is the most important feature of export as compared to local business, if goods are exported in time, buyer may even refuse to accept it.

Goods must be Properly Serviced

Customers do not buy considering only the price. They buy, not only because the product is right, but also because they know that it will, if necessary, be properly serviced, both when it arrives at its destination and during its whole working life. Service is the oil of exporting and if a company gives service it can survive. Service must rank high by international standards, and must stand up to the service provided by any competitors in the world.

Communication

Communication internal and external must be far-reaching and speedy. Good communication at right time is vital in export. Failure to reply promptly to letters, using mail to answer airmail letters are everyday errors and speed is the essence of export communication. E-mail and Internet services must be used profitably to provide utmost fast momentum to the communication. When still in doubt, pick up a phone or hop on a plane to go and see the man.

To be profitable, a person must know in considerable detail how he costs his products, and what charges to apply at all stages. He must be aware of fluctuations in exchange rates and interest charges, and allow for them in its costings. He must know in advance to what extent prices can be lowered, or credit extended, without trading at a loss. Where export is additional business for a person, he must know exactly what this worth in terms of total profit, and how far he can go to get it.

A proper product strategy should be planned taking into account past trends, market penetration and level of international competition.

Finally, export staff must be carefully selected and adequately paid. They must be allowed and encouraged to travel to trade fair, exhibition and marketing tours. They must be given the suitable rank, status and pay of other similar executives in the company. They must be consulted on company policy, and made to contribute towards it.

Testing Products

While the risk of failure in export markets can he minimized by the intelligent use of research, one can never really be sure whether a given operation will succeed until it has been tried. Before committing to a large-scale operation in an overseas markets, it is sensible to try things out on a small scale, with the intention of selling on a national scale. If the test is successful, many overseas markets are so huge that to sell everywhere would be asking a great deal at the outset.

Initial Attack

Use the initial attack on a market as a test, and any mistakes can then be corrected without much harm having been done. While the test campaign may appear to cost more initially than research, remember that some of the cost will be repaid by sales, so that test marketing often turns out to be cheaper than too intensive a research programmes. This strategy has a limitation that testing should not continue long otherwise product reputation would suffer.

Attitudes

If possible some indication of the attitudes towards the product should be established, both negative and positive. This is required of any sales operation. Even if a product is successful always try to obtain reactions from the customers, because it might be that with certain minor modifications one would have in fact sold a great deal more.

3

Brief Details for Starting Export Business

1. Setting Up an Appropriate Business Organisation

The first and the foremost question you as a prospective exporter has to decide is about the kind of business organisation needed for the purpose. You have to take a crucial decision as to whether the business will be run as a sole proprietory concern or a partnership firm or a company. The proper selection of organisation will depend upon (i) your ability to raise finance, (ii) your capacity to bear the risk, (iii) your desire to exercise control over the business and (iv) nature of regulatory framework applicable to you. If the size of business is small, it would be advantageous to form a sole proprietory business organisation. It can be set up easily without much expenses and legal formalities. It is subject to only a few governmental regulations. However, the biggest disadvantage of sole proprietorship business is limited ability to raise funds which restricts its growth. Besides, the owner has unlimited personal liability. In order to avoid this disadvantage, it is advisable to form a partnership firm. The partnership firm can also be set up with ease and economy. Business can take benefit of the varied experiences and expertise of the partners. The liability of the partners though joint and several, is practically distributed amongst the various partners, despite the fact that the personal liability of the partner is unlimited. The major disadvantage of partnership form of business organisation is that conflict amongst the partners is a potential threat to the business. It will not be out of place to mention here that partnership firms are governed by the Indian Partnership Act, 1932 and, therefore they should be formed within the parameters laid down by the Act.

Company is another form of business organisation which has the advantage of distinct legal identity and limited liability to the shareholders. It can be a private limited company or a public limited company. A private limited company can be formed by just two persons subscribing to its share capital. However, the number of its shareholders cannot exceed fifty, public cannot be invited to subscribe to its capital and the members' right to transfer their shares is restricted. On the other hand, a public limited company has a minimum of seven members. There is no limit on the maximum number of its members. It can invite the public to subscribe to its capital and permit the transfer of shares. A public company offers enormous potential for growth because of access to substantial funds. The liquidity of investment is high because of easiness of transfer of shares. However, its formation can be recommended only when the size of the business is large. For small business, a sole proprietary concern or a partnership firm will be the most suitable form of business organisation.

2. Choosing Appropriate Mode of Operations

You can choose any of the following modes of operations:

(i) Merchant Exporter i.e. buying the goods from the market or from a manufacturer and then selling them to foreign buyers.

(ii) Manufacturer Exporter i.e. manufacturing the goods yourself for export.

(iii) Sales Agent/Commission Agent/Indenting Agent i.e. acting on behalf of the seller and charging commission.

(iv) Buying Agent i.e. acting on behalf of the buyer and charging commission.

(v) Service provider i.e. providing service from India to another country.

3. Naming the Business

Whatever form of business organisation has been finally decided, naming the business is an essential task for every exporter. The name and style should be soft, attractive, short and meaningful. Simple and attractive name indicating the nature of business is ideal. The office should be located preferably in a commercial complex, in clean and workable surroundings. The letter head should be simple and superb providing information concerning H.O., branches, E-mail address, telephone number, tax number, banker's name and address etc. Pick up a beautiful trade name and logo which reinforces your organisation's name and image. Open a current account in the name of the organisation in whose name you intend to export. It is advisable to open the account with a Bank which is authorised to deal in Foreign Exchange.

4. Selecting the Product

Carefully select the product to be exported. For proper selection of a product, study the trends of export of different items from India. The selected product must be in demand in the countries where it is to be exported. It should be possible to procure or manufacture the selected product at most economic cost so that it can be competitively priced. It should also be available in sufficient quantity and it should be possible to supply it repeatedly and regularly. Besides, while selecting the product, it has to be ensured that you are conversant with Government policy and regulations in respect of the product selected for export. You should also know import regulations in respect of such commodities by the importing countries. It would be preferable if you have previous knowledge and experience of commodities selected by you for export. A non-technical person should avoid dealing in high-tech products. Another important feature to be kept in mind is that product should be adapted as per market requirement.

5. Making Effective Business Correspondence

You should recognise the importance of business correspondence as it is an introduction with the buyer in proxy which may clinch his response according to the impression created by the correspondence. For creating a very favourable and excellent impression, you must use a decent letter head on airmail paper and a good envelope, nicely printed, giving full particulars of your firm's name, telephone, fax number and E-Mail address etc. Your language should be polite, soft, brief and to the point, giving a very clear picture of the subject to be put before the customer. Letters should be typed/ computer typed set, preferably in the language of the importing country. Also make sure that the full and correct address is written and the envelope is duly stamped. It should also be borne in mind that the aim of your business correspondence is not only to clinch the buyer's order but also to obtain the information on the following:

1. The specifications of the products already in use in the importing country.
2. Whether your product meets the above specifications. If not, whether your specifications offer any distinct advantages in terms of prices, quality, after-sales service, etc.
3. The import policy including import duty prevailing in the buyer's country (e.g. whether there is any import licensing, any restriction on remittances, any pre-qualification for product/supplier, etc.)
4. The trade practices in the buyers' country with special reference to your product information like whether importers import and distribute the product/high sea sales, whether agent is required to book orders from actual users, etc.
5. In case your item requires after-sales service, the manner in which it can be offered.
6. The prices at which your product sells in the retail/wholesale

market, the duty structure and any other cost element to arrive at the landed cost. Information on the margins at which the product is sold. This information will help you in evolving a pricing strategy.

7. Study of various market segments viz. Importers, Supermarkets, Government Suppliers, Institutional Sales, Tenders, Suppliers, etc.
8. The various factors that rule the market viz. Quality, Price, Delivery, Brand Name, Credit Terms etc.
9. Role of advertising and publicity and reference to the product and the country.
10. Normal mode of shipment i.e. by SEA, AIR.

A specimen export letter is given below:

Specimen of Introductory Letter to Importers Abroad

Ref: ABC/Eng 2002/ 18th April, 2002

The Manager (Purchase)

M/s XYZ Ltd.

....

....

(England)

Dear Sir,

We are exporters of a wide variety of items including .... for the last ten years.

Our major buyers are .... in .... We are one of the registered Export Houses in our country.

We represent .... the leading manufacturers of these items in India.

These items are produced in collaboration with .... the world famous company and have an understanding with them to use this technology for export production. We follow the BIS specifications.

We understand that your company imports the items we export. We are interested in expanding our trade with your company.

We are enclosing herewith a copy of our brochure and price list for your kind perusal. We shall be glad to send detailed literature/samples of items that may be of interests to you, on hearing from you.

Thanking you in anticipation,

Yours truly,
For ABC Ltd.
Manager (Exports)

End: As above.

Comments

1. The text can be suitably amended with reference to the manufacturing activity or/items dealt in by the exporter.
2. Where the manufacturing is not in collaboration with a foreign company, it need not be referred to.
3. Product literature (of the buyer's interest) and price list should invariably be sent along with the letter.
4. The price list should categorically indicate whether the prices are f.o.b., & C & for c.i.f. etc. However, discount need not be indicated in the price list.
5. The profile of your Company should generally include the following matters:

   (1) Company's name and address/E-Mail Address/Telephone/Cable/ Fax/Date of establishment/Website Address if any (2) Export Executives; (3) Status: Partnership/Company (Pvt. Ltd./Pub.Ltd) Govt. (Semi-Govt.) etc.; (4) Bank Reference; (5) Exporting Since: (6) Value of Assets; (7) No. of Employees; Manufacturing; Sales; Administration; (8) Foreign Offices/Representatives, if any; (9) Exporter; Manufacturer; Agent; (10) Main Line; (11) Technical Collaboration; (12) Standards/Specification followed; (13) Major Buyers In India; Abroad;

6. Selecting the Markets

Target markets should be selected after careful consideration of various factors like political embargo, scope of exporter's selected product, demand stability, preferential treatment to products from developing countries, market penetration by competitive countries and products, distance of potential market, transport problems, language problems, tariff and non-tariff barriers, distribution infrastructure, size of demand in the market, expected life span of market and product requirements, sales and distribution channels.

For this purpose you should collect adequate market information before selecting one or more target markets. The information can be collected from various sources like Export Promotion Councils (EPCs) / Commodity Boards, Federation of Indian Export Organisation (FIEO), Indian Institute of Foreign Trade (IIFT), Indian Trade Promotion Organisation (ITPO), Indian Embassies Abroad, Foreign Embassies in India, Import Promotion Institutions Abroad, Overseas Chambers of Commerce and Industries, Various Directories, Journals, Market Survey Reports etc.

7. Selecting Prospective Buyers

You can collect addresses of the prospective buyers of the commodity from the following sources:

1. Enquiries from friends and relatives or other acquaintances residing in foreign countries.
2. Visiting/participating in International Trade Fairs and Exhibitions in India and abroad.
3. Contact with the Export Promotion Councils, Commodity Boards and other Government Agencies.
4. Consulting International Yellow Pages (A Publication from New York) by Dun & Bradstreet. USA or other Yellow Pages of different Countries like Japan, Dubai etc.)
5. Collecting addresses from various Private Indian Publications Directories available on cost at Engineers India Research Institute, 4449 Nai Sarak, Main Road, Delhi - 110006
6. Collecting information from International Trade Directories/ Journals/ Periodicals available in the libraries of Directorate General of Commercial Intelligence and Statistics, IIFT, EPCs, ITPO etc.
7. Making contacts with Trade Representatives of Overseas Governments in India and Indian Trade and Other Representatives/ International Trade Development Authorities abroad.
8. Reading biweekly, fortnightly, monthly bulletins such as Indian Trade Journal, Export Service Bulletin, Bulletins and Magazines issued and published by Federation of Exporters' Organisations, ITPO, EPCs, Commodity Boards and other allied agencies.
9. Visiting Embassies, Consulates etc. of other countries and taking note of addresses of importers for products proposed to be exported.
10. Advertising in newspapers having overseas editions and other foreign newspapers and magazines etc.

11. Consulting ITPO, IIFT. etc.
12. Contacting authorised dealers in foreign exchange with whom exporter is maintaining bank account.
13. Visiting popular Websites by making use of Internet Services.

Overseas importers can be contacted or informed about the products by the following methods:

1. By corresponding and sending brochures and product literature to prospective overseas buyers.
2. By undertaking trips to foreign markets and establishing personal rapport with overseas buyers. The number of trips will depend on your budget and resources. But it is essential for long-term success in international marketing to establish personal rapport. Foreign trip will provide first-hand information regarding the market, overseas customers, their requirement, taste, preference and better out communication of the merits of exporters' products.
3. Participation in buyer-seller meets and meeting the members of foreign delegation invited by Export Promotion Councils concerned.
4. Participation in international trade fairs, seminars.
5. Advertisement and publicity in overseas reputed newspapers and magazines as well as in popular websites which people usually visit. Facilities of free publicity can be availed from Import Development Centres.
6. Creating Websites and making it popular on international arena.

8. Selecting Channels of Distribution

The following channels of distribution are generally utilised while exporting to overseas markets:

1. Exports through Export Consortia,
2. Export through Canalising Agencies,
3. Export through Other Established Merchant Exporters or Export Houses, or Trading Houses,
4. Direct Exports,
5. Export through Overseas Sales Agencies.
6. Exports through E-Commerce which is in developmental stage in India.

9. Negotiating With Prospective Buyers

Whatever the channel of distribution for exporting to the overseas countries is proposed to be utilized, it is essential that the exporters should possess necessary skill for negotiating with the overseas channels of distribution. The ability to negotiate effectively is needed for discussion with importers or trade agents. While conducting business negotiations, the prospective exporter should avoid conflict, controversy and criticism vis-a-vis the other party. During conversation the attitude should be to communicate effectively. There should be eight 'Cs' i.e. coherence, creativity, compromise, concessions, commonality, consensus, commitment and compensation in business negotiations.

The general problem you may face is about pricing. The buyer's contention is that prices are too high. It should be noted that though the price is only one of the many issues that are discussed during business negotiations, it influences the entire negotiating process. Since this is the most sensitive issue in business negotiations, it should be tactfully postponed until all the other issues have been discussed and mutually agreed upon. As far as the price is concerned, you should try to determine the buyer's real interest in the product from the outset, only then a suitable counter proposal should be presented. It should also be remembered that the buyer may request modifications in presentation of the product. You should show the willingness to meet such request, if possible, provided that it will result in profitable export business.

Price being the most important sales tool, it has to be properly developed and presented. Therefore, in order to create a favourable impression, minimize costly errors and generate repeated business. The following points should be kept in mind while preparing the price list:

1. Submit a computer printed list, printed on a regular bond paper and laid-out simply and clearly (with atleast an inch between columns and between groupings).
2. Prominently indicate the name of your company, its full address, telephone and fax numbers and E-Mail address, including the country and city codes.
3. Fully describe the items being quoted.
4. Group the items logically (i.e. all the fabrics together, all the made-ups together etc.).
5. Specify whether shipped by sea or by air, f.o.b. or c.i.f. and to which port.
6. Quote exact amount and not rounded-off figures.

7. Mention the dates upto which the prices quoted will remain valid.
8. Where there is an internal reference number which must be quoted, try to keep it as short as possible (the buyer has no interest in this detail and the more complex it is, the greater is the risk of error). As regards the factors determining your price, please refer to the para on 'Export Pricing and Costing' further in this chapter.
9. Clearly mention payment terms required by you.
10. Preshipment inspection should be well defined.

    One main point regarding export pricing is that while negotiating with overseas buyer, you may not remember the cost of a product. It may also be difficult for you to remember the profit margin built in various prices quoted by you. A clear jotting of this information is not free from the risk of being leaked out to the competitors or to the overseas buyers. Some coding is, therefore, essential for the prices quoted by you so that at any stage/point of time, you can always utilise the information, enabling you to profitably negotiate with the overseas buyer. This can be done by assigning codes to the cost price.

For assigning codes to the cost price, you may select an English Password consisting of 10 separate letters, each letter to represent a numerical figure. For example: 'CRAZY MOUTH' is the Password selected by you. where C = 1, R = 2, A = 3, Z = 4, Y = 5, M = 6, 0 = 7, U = 8, T = 9. H = 0. This Password can be successfully used for recognising various items of exports and their varieties. Thus, a brass candle stand which is being quoted at Rs. 100 (sale price) but whose cost price to you is Rs. 25.50 will be coded as item number 'RYYH' and then assigned with a running serial number to make it more fascinating. You can decode the word 'RYYH' to write as Rs. 25.50 so as to get an idea of the difference between the Sale Price and the Cost Price, which will provide you the range within which you can negotiate with overseas buyers.

10. Processing an Export Order

You should not be happy merely on receiving an export order. You should first acknowledge the export order, and then proceed to examine carefully in respect of items, specification, preshipment inspection, payment conditions, special packaging, labelling and marketing requirements, shipment and delivery date, marine insurance, documentation etc. and if you are satisfied on these aspects, a formal confirmation should be sent to the buyer, otherwise clarification should be sought from the buyer before confirming the order. After confirmation of the export order immediate steps should be taken for procurement/manufacture of the export goods. Meanwhile, you should proceed to enter into a formal export contract with the overseas buyer.

11. Entering Into Export Contract

In order to avoid disputes, it is necessary to enter into an export contract with the overseas buyer. For this purpose, export contract should be carefully drafted incorporating comprehensive but in precise terms, all relevant and important conditions of the trade deal. There should not be any ambiguity regarding the exact specifications of goods and terms of sale including export price, mode of payment, storage and distribution methods, type of packaging, port of shipment, delivery schedule etc. The different aspects of an export contract are enumerated as under:

1. Product, Standards and Specifications
2. Quantity
3. Inspection
4. Total Value of the Contract
5. Terms of Delivery
6. Taxes, Duties and Charges
7. Period of Delivery/Shipment
8. Packing, Labelling and Marking
9. Terms of Payment — Amount/Mode & Currency
10. Discounts and Commissions
11. Licences and Permits
12. Insurance
13. Documentary Requirements
14. Guarantee
15. Force Majeure of Excuse for Non-Performance of Contract
16. Remedies
17. Arbitration

It will not be out of place to mention here that the importance of arbitration clause in an export contract. Court proceedings do not offer a satisfactory method for settlement of commercial disputes, as they involve inevitable delays, costs and technicalities. On the other hand, arbitration provides an economic, expeditious and informal remedy for settlement of commercial disputes. Arbitration proceedings are conducted in privacy and the awards are kept confidential. The Arbitrator is usually an expert in the subject matter of the dispute. The dates for arbitration meetings are fixed with the convenience of all concerned. Thus, arbitration is the most suitable way for settlements of commercial disputes and it may invariably be used by businessmen in their commercial dealings. The Indian Council of Arbitration, Federation House, Tansen Marg, New Delhi. (Ph. 23319251 Fax. 23320714) is a specialized arbitration institution providing arbitration facilities for all types of domestic or international commercial disputes. You should use their services as far as possible.

Brief Specimen Contract Form for Sale and Purchase Transactions, Exports and Imports

1. Name and address of the parties .... (state registered and complete address of the parties)

2. We, the above named parties have entered into this contract for the sale/purchase, etc. .... (state briefly the purpose of the contract) on this .... (date) at .... (Place) .... subject to the following terms and conditions:

   (a) Goods ....

   (b) Quantity ....

   Quality ....

   (Describe the quantity, quality and other specifications of the goods precisely as per agreement. An agency for inspection/certification of quality and/or quantity may also be stipulated).

   (b) Price ....

   Mode of payment ....

   (Quote the price, terms, i.e. ex-works/FOB (free on board) CIF (cost, insurance & freight) etc. in the currency agreed upon and describe the mode of payment i.e. payment against L/C (letter of credit/DA (document against acceptance) /D/P (document against payment) etc. It is also desirable to mention the exchange rate.)

   (c) Shipment ....

   (Specify date of delivery and the maximum period upto which delivery could be delayed and for which reasons including penalty clarifications, Port of Shipment and of delivery should be mentioned).

   (d) Packing and marking ....

   (Requirements to be specified precisely).

(e) Insurance ....

(State the type of insurance cover required, i.e. FPA (free from particular average) /WA (with average)/All Risks, etc. State also the party responsible for the insurance).

(f) Brokerage/Commission ....

(if any payable may be mentioned)

(g) Passing of the property and of risk.

The property or ownership of the goods and the risk shall finally pass on to the buyer at such stage as the parties may agree, i.e. when the goods are delivered at the seller's place of work/pass the ship's rails/are covered by insurance etc. as per agreed terms).

Arbitration

Arbitration clause recommended by the Indian Council of Arbitration:

"All disputes or differences whatsoever arising between the parties out of/ relating to the construction, meaning and operation or effect of this contract or the breach thereof shall be settled by arbitration in accordance with the rules of Arbitration of the Indian Council of Arbitration and the award made in pursuance thereof shall be binding on the parties." (or any other arbitration clause that may be agreed upon between the parties).

3. Any other special condition, prevalent in or relevant to the particular line of trade or transaction, may also be specified.

Sd/- Seller

Sd/- Buyer

Notes: The above specimen contract form, drawn up in brief essentials, is meant for simple small scale transactions and is intended to draw the attention of the parties to important aspects of the trade deal in drafting the contract. The parties are free to add to or modify the terms as per the peculiar nature of their trade transaction. They may also consult with advantage, experienced commercial or arbitration bodies for the purpose or study published literature on the subject. The use of arbitration clauses in commercial contracts is becoming increasingly common, particularly in export-import transactions, with a view to promoting smooth and swift flow of business. The Indian Council of Arbitration (ICA) which is partly founded by the Government of India, provides comprehesive institutional arbitration service to all government departments and public undertakings as well as private traders, exporters and importers in India for amicable and quick settlement of all types of commercial disputes. It has been suggested by the Ministry of Commerce that all commercial organisations should make use of the arbitration clause of the Council in their commercial contracts with Indian and foreign parties.

12. Export Pricing and Costing

Export pricing should be differentiated from export costing. Price is what we offer to the customer. Cost is the price that we pay/incur for the product. Price includes our profit margin, cost includes only expenses we have incurred.

Export pricing is the most important tool for promoting sales and facing international competition. The price has to be realistically worked out taking into consideration all export benefits and expenses. However, there is no fixed formula for successful export pricing. It will differ from exporter to exporter depending upon whether the exporter is a merchant exporter or a manufacturer exporter or exporting through a canalising agency.

You should also assess the strength of your competitor and anticipate the move of the competitor in the market. Pricing strategies will depend on various circumstantial situations. You can still be competitive with higher prices but with better delivery package or other advantages. Your prices will be determined by the followings factors:

1. Range of products offered.
2. Prompt deliveries and continuity in supply.
3. After-sales service in products like machine tools, consumer durables.
4. Product differentiation and brand image.
5. Frequency of purchase and total Annual Requirement.
6. Presumed relationship between quality and price.
7. Speciality value goods and gift items.
8. Credit offered.
9. Preference or prejudice for products originating from a particular source.
10. Aggressive marketing and sales promotion;
11. Prompt acceptance and settlement of claims.
12. Unique value goods and gift items.

Export Costing is basically Cost Accountant's job. It consists of fixed cost and variable cost comprising various elements. It is advisable to prepare an export costing sheet for every export product.

As regards quoting the prices to the overseas buyer, the same are quoted in the following internationally accepted terms:

Ex-works (EXW)

'Ex-works' means that the seller's responsibility is to make the goods available to the buyer at works or factory. The full cost and risk involved in bringing the goods from this place to the desired destination will be borne by the buyer. This term thus represents the minimum obligation for the seller. It is mostly used for sale of plantation commodities such as tea, coffee and cocoa.

Free Carrier (FCA)

'Free Carrier' means the seller's obligations are fulfilled when the goods are delivered to the carrier named by the buyer at the named place. The term may be used for all modes of transport including multimodal transport.

Free Alongside Ship (FAS)

Once the goods have been placed alongside the ship, the seller's obligations are fulfilled and the buyer notified. The seller has to contract with the sea carrier for the carriage of the goods to the destination and pay the freight. The buyer has to hear all costs and risks of loss or damage to the goods hereafter.

Free on Board (FOB)

The seller's responsibility ends the moment the contracted goods pass the ship's rail at the port of shipment named in the sales contract. This means that the buyer has to bear all costs and risks of loss or of damage to the goods from that point. The seller is required to clear the goods for export.

Cost and Freight (CFR)

'Cost and Freight' means that the seller delivers when the goods pass the ship's rail in the port of shipment. The seller must on his own risk contract for the carriage of the goods to the port of destination named in the sale contract and pay the freight. This being a shipment contract, the point of delivery is fixed to the ship's rail and the risk of loss or of damage to the goods is transferred from the seller to the buyer at that very point. As will be seen though the seller bears the cost of carriage to the named destination, the risk is already transferred to the buyer at the port of shipment itself.

Cost Insurance Freight (CIF)

The term is basically the same as CFR, but with the addition that the seller has to obtain insurance at his cost against the risks of loss or of damage to the goods during the carriage.

Carriage Paid to (CPT)

'CPT' means that the seller delivers the goods to the carrier nominated by him but the seller must in addition pay the cost of carriage necessary to bring the goods to the named destination. The buyer bears all risks and any other costs after the point of delivery. The seller is required to clear the goods for export.

Carriage and Insurance Paid to (CIP)

CIP is the same as CPT, with the addition that the seller is also required to procure insurance against the buyer's risk of loss or of damage to the goods during the carriage.

Delivered at Frontier (DAF)

The term is primarily intended to be used when the goods are to be carried by rail or road. The seller's obligations are fulfilled when the goods have arrived at the frontier, but before the 'Customs border' of the country named in the sales contract.

Delivered Ex-ship (DES)

This is an arrival contract and means that the seller makes the goods available to the buyer in the ship at the named port of destination as per sales contract. The seller has to bear the full cost and risk involved in bringing the goods there. The seller's obligation is fulfilled before the Customs border of the foreign country and it is for the buyer to obtain necessary import licence at his own risk and expense.

Delivered Ex-Quay (DEQ)

Ex-Quay means that the seller makes the goods available to the buyer at a named quay. As in the term 'Ex-ship' the points of division of costs and risks coincide, but they have now been moved one step further-from the ship into the quay or wharf i.e. after crossing the Customs border at destination. Therefore, in addition to arranging for carriage and paying freight and insurance the seller has to bear the cost of discharging the goods on the quay.

The buyer is required to clear the goods for import and to pay for all formalities, duties, taxes and other charges upon import.

Delivered Duty Unpaid (DDU)

'DDU' means that the seller delivers the goods to the buyer, at the port of destination. The seller has to bear the costs and risks involved in bringing the goods thereto. The buyer has to get the goods unloaded and cleared for import, by paying the applicable duty.

Delivered Duty Paid (DDP)

This term may be used irrespective of the type of transport involved and denotes the seller's maximum obligations as opposed to 'Ex-Works'. The seller has not fulfilled his obligation till such time that the goods are made available at his risk and cost to the buyer at his premises or any other named destination. In the latter case necessary documents (e.g., transport document or Warehouse Warrant) will have to be made available to the buyer to enable him to take delivery of the goods.

13. Understanding Risks in International Trade

While selling abroad, you undergo the following risks:

1. Credit risk
2. Currency risk
3. Carriage risk
4. Country risk

These risks can be insured to a great extent by taking appropriate steps. Credit risk against the buyer can be covered by insisting upon an irrevocable letter of credit from the overseas buyer. An appropriate policy from Export Credit Guarantee Corporation of India Ltd. can also be obtained for this purpose. Country risks are also covered by the ECGC. As regards currency risk, i.e. possible loss due to adverse fluctuation in exchange rates, you should obtain forward cover from your bank authorised to deal in foreign exchange. Alternatively, you should obtain export order in Indian rupees. Carriage risk, i.e. possible loss of cargo in transit can be covered by taking a marine insurance policy from the general insurance companies.

4

Registration of Exporters

I. Registration with Reserve Bank of India No More Required

Prior to 1.1.1997 it was compulsory for every exporter to obtain an exporters' code number from the Reserve Bank of India before engaging in export. This has since been dispensed with and registration with the licensing authorities is sufficient before commencing export or import.

II. Registration with Regional Licensing Authorities (Obtaining IEC Number)

The Customs Authorities will not allow you to import or export goods into or from India unless you hold a valid IEC number. However, if you are exporting goods to Nepal or Myanmar through Indo-Myanmar Border areas, you are not required to obtain IEC number provided the CIF value of a single consignment does not exceed Indian Rs. 25000/-. For obtaining IEC number you should apply to Regional Licensing Authority (list given in Appendix II) in duplicate in the prescribed form given. Before applying for IEC number it is necessary to open a bank account in the name of your company/firm with any commercial bank authorised to deal in foreign exchange. The duly signed application form should be supported by the following documents:

1. Bank Receipt (in duplicate) /Demand Draft for payment of the fee of Rs. 1,000/-.
2. Certificate from the Banker of the applicant firm as per Annexure 1 to the form given in Appendix I of this Book.
3. Two copies of Passport size photographs of the applicant duly attested by the banker to the applicants.
4. A copy of Permanent Account Number issued by Income Tax Authorities duly attested by the applicant.
5. In case the application is signed by an authorised signatory, a

copy of the letter of legal authority may be furnished.

6. If there is any non-resident interest in the firm and non-resident investment is to be made with repatriation benefits, full particulars thereof with photocopy of RBI approval must be submitted. If there is non-resident investment without repatriation benefits, a simple declaration indicating whether it is held with the general/ specific permission of the RBI on the letter head of the firm should be furnished. In case of specific approval a copy may also be furnished. Indian Companies issuing shares to foreign nationals/ NRIs under automatic route, 100% scheme or 24/40% scheme are not required to obtain prior approval of RBI.

7. Declaration by the applicant that the proprietor/partners/directors as the case may be of the applicant firm/company, are not associated as proprietor/partners/directors in any other firm/ company which has been cautionlisted by the RBI. Where the applicant declares that they are associated with a firm/company cautionlisted by the RBI they will be allotted IE Code No. but with an additional condition that they can export only with RBIs prior approval and they should approach RBI for the purpose.

8. Each importer/exporter shall be required to file importer/exporter profile once with the licensing authority in the form given in Appendix-2. Licensing authority shall enter the information furnished in Appendix-2 in their database so as to dispense with the need for asking the repetitive information. In case of any change in the information given in Appendix-2, importer/exporter shall intimate the same to the licensing authority.

   The Regional Licensing Authority concerned will on merits grant an IEC number to the applicant. The number should normally be given within 2 working days provided the application is complete in all respects and is accompanied by the prescribed documents.

   An IEC number allotted to an applicant shall be valid for all its branches/divisions/units/factories as indicated on the IEC number.

III Registration with Export Promotion Councils

In order to enable you to obtain benefits/concession under the export-import policy, you are required to register yourself with an appropriate export promotion agency by obtaining registration-cum-membership certificate (RCMC). For this purpose you should apply in the prescribed form, given at Appendix III of this Book to the Export Promotion Council relating to your main line of business. However, a status holder has the option to obtain RCMC from FIEO. The service exporters (except software service exporters) shall be required to obtain RCMC from FIEO. In addition an exporter has the option to obtain an RCMC from FIEO or any other EPC if the products exported by him relate to those EPCs. If the export product is that it is not covered by any EPC, RCMC in respect thereof may be issued by FIEO.

For list of Registering Agencies, please refer to Appendix IV of this Book.

An application for registration should be accompanied by a self certified copy of the Importer-Exporter Code Number issued by the Regional Licensing Authority concerned and bank certificate in support of the applicant's financial soundness. If the applicant is already registered with any other EPC, a copy of RCMC should be furnished. In case an exporter desires to get registration as a manufacturer exporter, he should furnish evidence to that effect. In the case of a manufacturer exporter the licensing authority may seek copy of registration with SSI/any other sponsoring authority in addition to the application in the prescribed form. Membership fee should be paid in the form of cheque/draft after ascertaining the amount from the EPC concerned. If the application for registration is granted, the EPC or FIEO shall issue the RCMC indicating the status of the applicant as merchant exporter or manufacturer exporter. The RCMC shall be valid for five years ending 31st March of the licensing year. The certificate shall be deemed to be valid from 1st April of the licensing year in which it was issued.

IV. Registration with Sales Tax Authorities

Goods which are to be shipped out of the country for export are eligible for exemption from both Sales Tax and Central Sales Tax. For this purpose, you should get yourself registered with the Sales Tax Authority of your State after following the procedure prescribed under the Sales Tax Act applicable to your State.

V. Registration with Excise Authorities

Goods meant for exports are exempt from Excise duty. For this purpose the manufacturer and merchant exporters have two options. Either they can deposit excise duty at the time of clearance from factory and later on take refund or can establish a bond with maritime Collector of Central Excise. A running bond account is maintained which is credited after proof of exports including Bill of Lading, Shipping Bill and AR-4 are submitted with Excise Authorities.

5

Export of Samples, Gifts, Spares, Replacement, Repaired Goods etc.

As the overseas buyers generally insist for the samples before placing confirmed orders, it is essential that the samples are attractive, informative and have retention and reminder value. Besides, the exporter should know the Government policy and procedures for export of samples from India. He should also be aware about the cheapest modes of sending samples. In this connection, it is advised that the postal channel is comparatively cheaper than sending samples by air. While sending samples through postal channel due regard should be given to weight and dimension of the post parcels as postal authorities have prescribed maximum weight and dimension for the post parcels handled by them. Where it is not possible to send the samples by post parcels, the same may be sent by air.

Export of Items as Gift

So far as the Government policy regarding export of samples is concerned, distinction has been made between export of commercial samples and gift parcels.

In terms of Para 2.32 of the Import Export Policy 2002-07, goods including edible items of value not exceeding Rs. 1, 00, 000 in a licensing year may be exported as a gift. However, items mentioned as restricted for exports in the ITC (HS) Classifications of Export & Import items shall not be exported as a gift without a licence/certificate/permission except in the case of edible items. For export of gifts in excess of the ceiling prescribed above, an application may be made to the DGFT.

Export of Bonafide Trade and Technical Samples

Export of bonafide trade and technical samples of freely exportable items are allowed without any limit.

An application for export of samples or exhibits which are restricted for export may be made to the DGFT.

Export of Garment Samples

Special provisions have been made for export of garment samples. Garment samples are allowed to be exported only by exporters who are registered with the Apparel Export Promotion Council (AEPC) or the Wool and Woollen Export Promotion Council for woollen knitwears.

Declaration on GR/PP Form

As per Regulation 4 of Foreign Exchange Management (Export of Goods and Services) Regulations 2000. (i) trade samples of goods and publicity material supplied free of payment can be sent abroad without furnishing the declaration on GR/PP form. (ii) for export of goods/software not exceeding Rs. 25000 in value declaration on GR etc. form is not required provided the goods or software are accompanied by a declaration by the exporter that they are not more than twenty five thousand rupees in value.

Export of Trade Samples against Payment

Trade samples against which the foreign buyer agrees to make payment can be exported in the same manner in which normal exports are effected. Samples can also be carried personally by you while travelling abroad provided these are otherwise permissible or cleared for export as explained earlier. However, in case of precious jewellery/stone items, you should declare the same to the customs authorities while leaving the country and obtain necessary endorsement on export certificate issued by the Jewellery Appraiser of the Customs.

Export of Samples by EOU/EHTP/STP Units

(a) EOU/EHTP/STP units may, on the basis of records maintained by them, and on prior intimation to Customs authority supply or sell samples in the DTA for display/market promotion on payment of applicable duties.

(b) Remove samples without payment of duty, on furnishing a suitable undertaking to Customs authorities for bringing the samples back within a stipulated period.

(c) All EOUs may export free samples, without any limit, including samples made in wax moulds, silver moulds and rubber moulds through all permissible mode of export including through courier agencies/post.

Export of Samples by SEZ

(a) SEZ units may, on the basis of records maintained by them, and on prior intimation to Customs authority supply or sell samples in the DTA for display/market promotion on payment of applicable duties.

(b) SEZ units may also remove samples without payment of duty, under prior intimation to the Customs authorities subject to the condition that the goods shall be brought back within a stipulated period.

(c) SEZ units may export free samples, without any limit including samples made in wax moulds, silver moulds and rubber moulds through all permissible mode of export including through courier agencies/post.

Free of Cost Exports by Status Holders

The Status holders shall be entitled to export freely exportable items on free of cost basis for export promotion subject to an annual limit of Rs. 5 lakh or 2% of the average export realisation during the preceding three licensing years whichever is higher.

Export of Passenger Baggage

Bonafide personal baggage may be exported either along with the passenger or, if unaccompanied, within one year before or after the passenger's departure from India. However, items mentioned as Restricted in ITC (HS) shall require a licence/certificate/permission, except in the case of edible items.

Export of Spares

Warranty spares, whether indigenous or imported, of plant, equipment. machinery, automobiles or any other goods may be exported alongwith the main equipment or subsequently but within the contracted warranty period of such goods subject to approval of RBI.

Export of Imported Goods

Goods imported, in accordance with the Exim Policy, may be exported in the same or substantially the same form without a licence/certificate/ permission provided that the item to be imported or exported is not mentioned as restricted for import or export in the ITC (HS) Classification of Import & Export Items'. Exports of such goods imported against payment in freely convertible currency would be permitted against payment in freely convertible currency.

Goods, including those mentioned as restricted item for import (except prohibited items) may be imported under Customs Bond for export in freely convertible currency without a licence/certificate/ permission provided that the item is freely exportable without any conditionally/requirement of licence/ permission as may be required under ITC (HS) Schedule II.

Export of Replacement Goods

Goods or parts thereof on being exported and found defective/damaged or otherwise unfit for use may be replaced free of charge by the exporter and such goods shall be allowed clearance by the customs authorities provided that the replacement goods are not mentioned as restricted items for exports in ITC (HS) Classification of Imports and Exports.

Export of Repaired Goods

Goods or parts thereof on being exported and found defective, damaged or otherwise unfit for use may be imported for repair and subsequent re-export. Such goods shall be allowed clearance without a licence/certificate/ permission and in accordance with customs notification issued in this behalf.

6

Appointing Overseas Agents

Selling through the overseas agents is an effective strategy for export marketing, as these agents serve as a source of market intelligence, regularly feeding the exporter with the latest trends in demand, fashion, taste and price in the overseas market. Being a man on the spot, the agent is in a position to render his advice to exporter on new methods and strategy for pushing up sales of your products. He also provides you support in the matter of transportation, reservation of accommodation, appointment with the government departments as and when required by you. In some countries it is compulsory under their law to sell through local agents only. It is, therefore, essential that you should carefully select overseas agent. A check list for careful selection of agent is given as under :

1. Size of the agent's company.
2. Date of foundation of the agent's company.
3. Company's ownership and control.
4. Company's capital, funds available and liabilities.
5. Name, age and experience of the company's senior executives.
6. Number, age and experience of the company's salesmen.
7. Other agencies that the company holds, including those of competing products and turn-over of each.
8. Length of company's association with other principals,
9. New agencies that the company obtained or lost during the past year.
10. Company's total annual sales and the trends in its sales in recent years.

11. Company's sales coverage, overall and by area.
12. Number of sales calls per month and per salesmen by company staff.
13. Any major obstacles expected in the company's sales growth.
14. Agent's capability to provide sales promotion and advertising services.
15. Agent's transport facilities and warehousing capacity.
16. Agent's rate of commission; payment terms required.
17. References on the agent from banks, trade associations and major buyers.

Some sources of information on agents are:

1. Government Departments
2. Trade Associations, both in India and Abroad
3. Chambers of Commerce
4. Banks
5. Independent Consultants/Credit Rating Agencies
6. Export Promotion Councils, Commodity Boards etc.
7. Advertisement Abroad.
8. Your own friends, associates etc.

A specimen Agency Agreement is given below:

Specimen Agency Agreement

An agreement made this the .... day .... of between .... (name and address) hereinafter called the exporters of the first part and .... (name and address) hereinafter called the importers of the second part, wherein the exporters grant to the importers the importation and selling right in the territory of .... (fill name of country) for .... (names and brief description of product) subject to the terms and conditions given below:

(1) The exporter agrees that during the term of the agreement he will not correspond or in any way deal with any part in the territory specified unless requested to do so by the importers.

(2) The exporter agrees that any orders or enquiries relating to the specified territory received by him during the term of this agreement will be passed on to the importers to deal with.

(3) The exporter agrees that he will make shipment of all orders received from the importers by earliest shipping opportunity unless prevented from so doing by circumstances beyond the former's control.

(4) The exporter agrees to charge the importers for all goods ordered during the term of this agreement the prices detailed in Price List No. .... appended to this agreement unless any order is received atleast one month after notification of price changes by the exporter to the importer.

(5) The exporter agrees to pay the importer commission on .... (fill in the dates of each year during the currency of this agreement) at the rate of .... per cent of .... the F.O.B. value of all orders satisfactorily completed during the .... months preceding the dates specified.

(6) The exporter agrees that he will allow to the importers .... per cent .... of the value of all business satisfactorily completed with the importers during the term of this agreement as contribution towards the importer's costs in publicising the products covered by this agreement. This allowance is to be settled by deduction from the manufacturer's invoices to the importers.

(7) The importers agree that during the term of this agreement they will not sell, recommend or in any other way deal with any competing or rivalling lines in the territory specified.

(8) The importers agree that they will use their best efforts and endeavours at all times during the currency of this agreement to promote the sales of products covered by this agreement.

(9) The importers agree that they will make net and full payment for all goods ordered through confirmed and irrevocable letter of credit established in .... (name of manufacturer's town or city).

OR

The importers agree that they will make net and full payment for all goods ordered against presentation of draft and shipping documents in .... (name of importer's town or city).

OR

The importers agree that they will immediately upon presentation at .... and retire such drafts net and in full upon maturity.

(10) The importers agree that they will write to the manufacturer atleast once each calendar month and will send to the manufacturer a full market report on the prospects for sale of the products covered by this agreement every six months.

(11) The importer agrees that they will place regular and adequate orders with the manufacturer amounting in total, not less than Rs. .... during the first calendar year and not less than Rs. .... in each and every subsequent calender year during the currency of this agreement.

(12) This agreement shall become valid with effect from the date of shipment of the substantial order amounting in value of not less than Rs. .... and remain in force for a period of twelve calendar months therefrom subject to either party being at liberty to terminate this agreement without notice in the event of the other party being in breach of any of the térms and conditions stated herein.

(13) Notwithstanding anything herein aforesaid if during the first twelve calendar months the importers have placed satisfactory orders with the exporters amounting to not less than Rs. .... this agreement shall be automatically renewed year after year provided that in the twelve calendar months immediately preceding the expiry date satisfactorily business amounting in total to not less than Rs. .... has been placed by the importers with the exporters.

(14) Any disputes arising under this agreement shall be settled in accordance with Indian Law in (......................)

Witness .... (Exporter)

Witness .... (Importer)

7

Obtaining an Export Licence

Exports free unless regulated

The current Export Licensing Policy of the Government of India is contained in the Import Export Policy and Procedures. However, for the sake of information of the prospective exporters, it may be stated that all goods may be exported without any restriction except to the extent such exports are regulated by the ITC (HS) Classifications of Export and Import items or any other provisions of this Policy or any other law for the time being in force. The Director General of Foreign Trade may, however, specify through a Public Notice such terms and conditions according to which any goods, not included in the ITC (HS) Classifications of Export and Import items may be exported without a licence/certificate/permission.

Application for an Export Licence/Certificate/Permission

An application for grant of export licence/certificate/permission in respect of items mentioned in Schedule 2 of ITC (HS) Classifications of Export and Import items may be made in the form given in Appendix-16 or 16A of Handbook of Procedures, as the case may be, to the Director General of Foreign Trade and shall be accompanied by the documents prescribed therein. The EXIM Facilitation Committee shall consider such applications on merits for issue of export licences/ certificate/permissions.

An Inter-Ministerial working group in Directorate General of Foreign Trade shall consider applications for export of Special Chemicals, Organism, Materials, Equipments and Technologies (SCOMET) as specified in Schedule 2, Appendix-3 of ITC (HS) on the basis of guidelines issued in this regard from time to time.

DGFT may also issue on application, Free Sale Certificate as per guidelines in force on medical and surgical equipments.

Export of Items under State Trading Regime

An application for export of items mentioned in ITC (HS) Classifications of Export and Import Items under State Trading Regime may be made to the Director General of Foreign Trade.

Export through Courier Service

Import/Export through a registered courier service is Permitted as per the Notification issued by the Department of Revenue. However importability/exportability of such items shall be regulated in accordance with the Policy.

8

Obtaining Export Credit Insurance

Export credit insurance protects you from the consequences of the payment risks, both political and commercial. It enables you to expand your overseas business without fear of loss. Further, it creates a favourable climate for you under which you can hope to get timely and liberal credit facilities from the banks at home. You can obtain Export Credit Insurance from the Export Credit Guarantee Corporation of India Limited.

In order to provide you Export Credit Insurance, the following covers are issued by the ECGC:

(i) Standard policies to protect you against the risk of not receiving payment while trading with overseas buyers on short-term credit.

(ii) Specific policies designed to protect you against the risk of not receiving payment in respect of: (a) exports on deferred payment terms, (b) services rendered to foreign parties, and (c) construction work, including turnkey projects undertaken abroad. The policies are either:

1. Whole Turnover Policies in the form of 'Open Cover' in respect of shipments made during 24 months period DP, DA & open delivery terms. You have to obtain credit limit on each one of your buyers to enable ECGC to approve a limit on the basis of credit worthiness of the buyer. Further you have to declare the details of shipments on monthly basis.
2. Specific Policies for exports of capital goods on medium or long-term credit, turnkey projects, civil construction works and technical services. These policies are basically similar to whole turnover policies but only apply to specific contracts.

(iii) Financial guarantees issued to hanks against risk involved in providing credit or guarantee facilities to you, both at the pre-shipment or post-shipment stages and

(iv) Special schemes viz. transfer guarantee issued to protect banks which add confirmation to letters of credit, Insurance cover for Buyers' Credit, Lines of Credit, Overseas Investment Insurance, and Exchange Fluctuation Risk Insurance.

The other guarantees which banks can offer to you through ECGC schemes are :

- Bid Bonds,
- Advance payments guarantee,
- Bank guarantee for due performance of the contract by the exporter,
- Bank guarantee for payment of retention money,
- Bank guarantee for loans in foreign currencies.

Details of these schemes can be obtained from your own banker or local office of the Export Credit Guarantee Corporation of India Ltd.

The Shipments (Comprehensive Risks) Policy is the one ideally suited to cover risks in respect of goods exported on short-term credit.

Shipments to associates or to agents and those against letters of credit can be covered for only political risks by suitable endorsements to the Shipments (Comprehensive Risks) Policy. Premium is charged on such shipments at lower rates. Normally insurance value is calculated as 110% of invoice value.

For obtaining a policy you should apply to the nearest office of the ECGC in the prescribed Form (obtainable from ECGC). You should also confirm your acceptance of the premium rates, which will be intimated to you at the time of obtaining the prescribed proposal form from the ECGC office. You should also remit Minimum Premium of Rs. 7,500/-

As commercial risks are not covered in the absence of a credit limit, you are advised to apply to ECGC for approval of credit limit on buyer in the prescribed Form No. 144 (obtainable from ECGC) before making shipment. Credit Limit is the limit upto which claim can be paid under the policy for losses on account of commercial risks.

If no application for Credit Limit on a buyer has been made, ECGC accepts liability for commercial risks upto a maximum of Rs. 5,00, 000 for D.P./C.A.D. transactions on a particular buyer subject to the condition that the claims will be limited to two buyers during the currency of the policy or commercial risks upto a maximum of Rs. 3, 00, 000 for DA transactions and Rs. 10, 00, 000 for DP/CAD transactions provided that atleast three shipments have been effected to the buyer during the preceding two years on similar payment terms and atleast one of them was not less than the discretionary limit availed of by the exporter and the buyer had made payment on the due dates.

9

Finance Arrangement for Exports

Financial assistance to the exporters is generally provided by the Commercial Banks before shipment as well as after shipment of the goods. The assistance provided before shipment of goods is known as pre-shipment finance and that provided after the shipment of goods is known as post-shipment finance. Pre-shipment finance is given for working capital for purchase of raw material, processing, packing, transportation, ware-housing etc. of the goods meant for export. Post-shipment finance is provided for bridging the gap between the shipment of goods and realisation of export proceeds. The later is done by the Banks by purchasing or negotiating the export documents or by extending advance against export bills accepted on collection basis. While doing so, the Banks adjust the pre-shipment advance, if any, already grafted to the exporter.

I. Preshipment Finance

An application for pre-shipment advance should be made by you to your banker alongwith the following documents:

1. Confirmed export order/contract or L/C etc. in original. Where it is not available, an undertaking to the effect that the same will be produced to the Bank within a reasonable time for verification and endorsement, should be given.

2. An undertaking that the advance will be utilised for the specific purpose of procuring/manufacturing/shipping etc. of the goods meant for export only, as stated in the relative confirmed export order or the L/C.

3. If you are a sub-supplier and want to supply the goods to the Export/ Trading/Star Trading House or Merchant Exporter, an undertaking from the Merchant Exporter or Export/Trading/Star Trading House stating that they have not/will not avail themselves

of packing credit facility against the same transaction for the same purpose till the original packing credit is liquidated,

4. Copies of Income Tax/Wealth Tax Assessment Order for the last 2/3 years in the case of sole proprietory and partnership firm.
5. Copy of Importer's Exporter's Code Number.
6. Copy of a valid RCMC (Registration-cum-Membership Certificate) held by you and/or the Export/Trading/Star Trading House Certificate.
7. Appropriate policy/guarantee of the ECGC.
8. Any other document required by the Bank.

For encouraging exports, R.B.I. has instructed the banks to grant preshipment advance at a concessional rate of interest. Under the new Monetary and Credit Policy announced by the Reserve Bank of India in September, 2001, interest rates on preshipment advances have been revised with effect from 26th September, 2001, as under:

Category	*Revised w.e.f. 26.9.2001*[1]
(i) Upto 180 days	Not exceeding PLR minus 2.5 percentage points
(ii) Beyond 180 days and upto 270 days	Not exceeding PLR plus 0.5 percentage points

Note: Since these are ceiling rates banks would be free to charge any rate below the ceiling rates.

Following special schemes are also available in respect of preshipment finance:

1. Exim Bank's Scheme for grant of foreign currency presh[illegible] credit to exporters for financing cost of importe[illegible] manufacture of export products.
2. Scheme of export packing credit to [illegible] order.
3. Packing credit for deemed exports.
4. Preshipment Credit in Foreign Currency (PCFC).

II. Post-Shipment Finance in Indian Rupees

Post-shipment finance is the finance provided against shipping

1. Three rates have been further extended w.e.f. 1.10.2002 vide RBI DBOD No. BC-26 dated 23.9.2002.

documents. It is also provided against duty drawback claims. It is provided in the following forms:

(a) Purchase of Export Documents drawn under Export Order

Purchase or discount facilities in respect of export bills drawn under confirmed export order are generally granted to the customers who are enjoying Bill Purchase/Discounting limits from the Bank. As in case of purchase or discounting of export documents drawn under export order, the security offered under L/C by way of substitution of credit-worthiness of the buyer by the issuing bank is not available, the bank financing is totally dependent upon the credit worthiness of the buyer, i.e. the importer, as well as that of the exporter or the beneficiary. The documents drawn on DP basis are parted with through foreign correspondent only when payment is received while in case of DA bills documents (including that of title to the goods) are passed on to the overseas importer against the acceptance of the draft to make payment on maturity. DA bills are thus unsecured. The bank financing against export bills is open to the risk of non-payment. Banks, in order to enhance security, generally opt for ECGC policies and guarantees which are issued in favour of the exporter/banks to protect their interest on percentage basis in case of non-payment or delayed payment which is not on account of mischief, mistake or negligence on the part of exporter. Within the total limit of policy issued to the customer, drawee-wise limits are generally fixed for individual customers. At the time of purchasing the bill bank has to ascertain that this drawee limit is not exceeded so as to make the bank ineligible for claim in case of non-payment.

(b) Advances against Export Bills Sent on Collection

It may sometimes be possible to avail advance against export bills sent on collection. In such cases the export bills are sent by the bank on collection basis as against their purchase/discounting by the bank. Advance against such bills is granted by way of a 'separate loan' usually termed as 'post-shipment loan'. This facility is, in fact, another form of post-shipment advance and is sanctioned by the bank on the same terms and conditions as applicable to the facility of Negotiation/Purchase/Discount of export bills. A margin of 10 to 25% is, however, stipulated in such cases. The rates of interest etc. chargeable on this facility are also governed by the same rules.

This type of facility is, however, not very popular and most of the advances against export bills are made by the bank by way of negotiation/ purchase/ discount.

(c) Advance against Goods Sent on Consignment Basis

When the goods are exported on consignment basis at the risk of the exporter for sale and eventual remittance of sale proceeds to him by the agent/consignee, bank may finance against such transaction subject to the customer enjoying specific limit to that effect. However, the bank should ensure while forwarding shipping documents to its overseas branch/ correspondent to instruct the latter to deliver the documents only against Trust Receipt/Undertaking to deliver the sale proceeds by specified date, which should be within the prescribed date even if according to the practice in certain trades a bill for part of the estimated value is drawn in advance against the exports.

(d) Advance against Undrawn Balance

In certain lines of export it is the trade practice that bills are not to be drawn for the full invoice value of the goods but to leave small part undrawn for payment after adjustment due to difference in rates, weight, quality etc. to be ascertained after approval and inspection of the goods. Banks do finance against the undrawn balance if undrawn balance is in conformity with the normal level of balance left undrawn in the particular line of export subject to a maximum of 10% of the value of export and an undertaking is obtained from the exporter that he will, within 6 months from due date of payment or the date of shipment of the goods, whichever is earlier surrender balance proceeds of the shipment. Against the specific prior approval from Reserve Bank of India the percentage of undrawn balance can be enhanced by the exporter and the finance can be made available accordingly at higher rate. Since the actual amount to be realised out of the undrawn balance, may be less than the undrawn balance, it is necessary to keep a margin on such advance.

(e) Advance against Retention Money

Banks also grant advances against retention money, which is payable within one year from the date of shipment, at a concessional rate of interest upto 90 days. If such advances extend beyond one year, they are treated as deferred payment advances which are also eligible for concessional rate of interest.

(f) Advances against Claims of Duty Drawback

Duty drawback is permitted against exports of different categories of goods under the 'Customs and Central Excise Duty Drawback Rules, 1995'. Drawback in relation to goods manufactured in India and exported means a rebate of duties chargeable on any imported materials or excisable materials used in the manufacture of such goods in India or rebate on excise duty chargeable under Central Excise Act, 1944 on certain specified goods. The Duty Drawback Scheme is administered by Directorate of Duty Drawback in the Ministry of Finance. The claims of duty drawback are settled by Custom, House at the rates determined and notified by the Directorate.

As per the present procedure, no separate claim of duty drawback is to be filed by the exporter. A copy of the shipping bill presented by the exporter at the time of making shipment of goods serves the purpose of claim of duty drawback as well. This claim is provisionally accepted by the customs at the time of shipment and the shipping bill is duly verified. The claim is settled by customs office later.

As a further incentive to exporters, various Customs Houses in India have evolved a simplified procedure under which claims of duty drawback are settled immediately after shipment and no funds of exporter are blocked. However, where settlement is not possible under the simplified procedure exporters may obtain advances against claims of duty drawback as provisionally certified by customs.

(g) Negotiation of Export Documents Drawn under L/C

This aspect has been discussed in the chapter on Special Care for Negotiation of Export Documents under Letter of Credit.

Rates of Interest

The rate of interest depends on the nature of the Bills, i.e. whether it is a demand bill or usance bill. Like preshipment, post-shipment finance is also available at concessional rate of interest. Under the new Monetary Credit Policy announced by the RBI in September 2001 interest rates on post shipment credit have been revised with effect from 26.9.2001 as under:

Category	*Revised*† *(With effect from September 26, 2001*[1]*)*
1. On demand bills for transit period (as specified by FEDAI)	Not exceeding PLR minus 2.5 percentage points
2. Usance Bills (for total period comprising usance period of export bills, transit period as specified by FEDAI and grace period, wherever applicable):	
(i) Upto 90 days	Not exceeding PLR minus 2.5 percentage points
(ii) Beyond 90 days and upto 6 months from date of shipment	Not exceeding PLR Plus 0.5 percentage points

† Since these are ceiling rates, banks would be free to charge any rate below the ceiling rates.

* Free: The banks are free to decide the rate of interest to be charged in view PLR and spread guidelines.

Category	Revised[†] (With effect from September 26, 2001[1])
3. Against incentives (duty drawback etc.) receivable from Government covered by ECGC guarantees (upto 90 days)	Not exceeding PLR minus 2.5 percentage points
4. Against undrawn balance (upto 90 days)	-do-
5. Against retention money (for supplies portion only) payable within one year from the date of shipment (upto 90 days)	-do-
6. Deferred credit for period beyond 180 days	Free*
7. Export credit not otherwise specified:	
(a) Preshipment	Free
(b) Post-shipment	Free*

Normal Transit Period

Foreign Exchange Dealers Association of India (FEDAI) has fixed transit period for export bills drawn on different countries in the world. The concept of this transit period is that an export bill should normally be realised within that period. The transit period so fixed by FEDAI is known as 'Normal Transit Period' and mainly depends on geographical location of a particular country.

Direct and Indirect Bill

If the currency of the bill is the same as the currency of the country on which it is drawn, it is termed as direct bill, e.g. an export bill in US $ drawn on a place in USA. However, if the currency of the bill in which it is drawn is different than the currency of the country on which it is drawn, it is termed as indirect bill, e.g. an export bill in US $ drawn on a place in Japan. The normal transit period fixed for indirect bill is on higher side as compared to transit period fixed for direct bills.

Notional Due Date

To determine the due date of an export bill we have to consider the following three components:

(i) Normal transit period as fixed by FEDAI.

(ii) Usance period of the bill.

(iii) Grace period if applicable in the country on which the Bill is drawn. Grace period is applicable only in case of usance bills.

The notional due date of an export bill may thus be calculated after adding all the above three components.

The concessional rate of interest is chargeable upto the notional due date subject to a maximum of 90 days.

III. Forfaiting Finance By Authorised Dealers

Reserve Bank has now permitted the authorised dealers (Banks) to arrange forfaiting of medium term export receivables on the same lines as per the scheme of EXIM Bank and many International forfaiting agencies have now become active in Indian market. Forfaiting may be usefully employed as an additional window of export finance particularly for exports to those countries for which normal export credit is not intended by the commercial banks.

It must be noted that charges of forfaiting are eventually to be passed on to the ultimate buyer and should, therefore, be so declared on relative export declaration forms.

IV. External Commercial Borrowings

Proposals for raising foreign currency loans/credits viz Buyer's Credits. Supplier's Credits or Lines of Credits by firms/companies/lending institutions. banks, etc. for financing cost of import of goods, technology or for any other purposes, other than short-term loans/credits maturing within one year should first be submitted to Government of India, Ministry of Finance (Department of Economic Affairs). ECB Division, New Delhi for necessary clearance. The proposals are considered by the Government on merits of each case and in the light of prevailing Government policy.

V. Exim Bank Finance

Besides commercial banks, export finance is also made available by the EXIM Bank. The EXIM Bank provides financial assistance to promote Indian exports through direct financial assistance, overseas investment finance, term finance for export production and export development, pre-shipment credit, buyer's credit, lines of credit, re-lending facility, export bills re-discounting, refinance to commercial banks, finance for computer software exports, finance for export marketing and bulk import finance to commercial banks. The EXIM Bank also extends non-funded facility to Indian exporters in the form of guarantees. The diversified lending programme of the EXIM Bank now covers various stages of exports, i.e. from the development of export markets to expansion of production capacity for exports, production for exports and post shipment financing. The EXIM Bank's focus is on export of manufactured goods, product exports, exports of technology, services and export of computer software.

Forfaiting Finance from EXIM Bank

A new financing option for the Indian exporters is available under the Forfaiting Finance Scheme introduced by the EXIM Bank. Forfaiting is a form of trade finance involving discounting of medium-term export receivables with or without recourse to the exporter. The arrangement envisages discounting by Indian exporters of bill of exchange/promissory notes relating to export transactions which are "avalised" or guaranteed by the buyer's bankers with overseas forfaiting agencies on "without recourse" basis.

Briefly, the procedure involved in the scheme of forfaiting finance by the Exim Bank is as follows:

1. Exporter initiates negotiations with the prospective overseas buyer with regard to the basic contract price, period of credit, rate of interest, etc.
2. After successful negotiations, he furnishes the relevant particulars such as name and country of overseas buyer, contract value, nature of goods, tenure of credit, name and country of guaranteeing bankers to the Exim Bank and requests for an indicative discounting quote. Exim Bank obtains the indicative quote of forfaiting discount together with commitment fee and other charges, if any, to be paid by the exporter, from an overseas forfaiting agency.
3. On receipt of the indicative quote from the Exim Bank, the exporter finalises the terms of the contract, loading the discount and other charges in the value and approaches Exim Bank for obtaining a firm quote. Exim Bank arranges to get the same from an appropriate overseas forfaiting agency and furnishes the same to the exporter. At this stage, exporter would be required to confirm acceptance of the arrangement to Exim Bank within a specific period as stipulated by that Bank.
4. The export contract should clearly indicate that the overseas buyer shall prepare a series of avalised Promissory Notes in favour of the exporter and hand them over against the shipping documents to his banker. The Promissory Notes will be endorsed with the words without recourse by the exporter and handed over to his banker in India for onward transmission to the Exim Bank.
5. Alternatively, the export contract may provide for exporter to draw a series of Bills of Exchange on the overseas buyer which will be sent with the shipping documents through latter's banker for acceptance by the overseas buyer. Overseas buyer's banker will handover the documents against acceptance of Bills of Exchange by the buyer and signature of 'aval' or the guaranteeing bank. Avalised and accepted bills of exchange will be returned to the

exporter through his banker. Exporter will endorse avalised Bills of Exchange with the words 'without recourse' and return them to his banker for onward transmission to the Exim Bank.

6. Exim Bank will forward the Bills of Exchange/Promissory Notes after verification to the forfaiting agency for discounting by the latter.

7. Exim Bank will arrange to collect the discounted proceeds of Promissory Notes/Bill of Exchange from the overseas forfaiting agency and effect payment to the nostro account of the exporter's bank as per the latter's instruction.

8. The exporter's bank in turn will pass the proceeds to the exporter.

10

Understanding Foreign Exchange Rates and Protection against their Adverse Movement

I. Exchange Rates

Export contracts are concluded either in Indian rupee or in foreign currency. Where the contracts are in Indian rupee, the related documents are also prepared in Indian rupees and no conversion is involved. However, where the bill is drawn in foreign currency, like US \$, £, DM etc., you will get Indian rupees only after the conversion of foreign currency at the appropriate exchange rate. Thus the exchange rates become very important to determine the Indian rupees payable. A favourable exchange rate will fetch you more rupees and vice-versa. It, therefore, becomes essential for you to gain some basic knowledge about exchange rate, the working out of its quotation by the banks, the factors determining the exchange rates in the market and the precautions you should take so as to avoid possible losses in future, due to adverse movement of exchange rates. In the following paragraphs we shall endeavour to explain these issues.

The rates applied by the banks for converting foreign currency into Indian rupees and vice versa are known as exchange rates. In other words, exchange rate is the rate at which one currency can be exchanged for another. There are two systems of quoting exchange rates:

(i) Direct Quotation. Where the price of foreign currency is quoted in terms of home or local currency. In this system variable units of home currency equivalent to a fixed unit of foreign currency is quoted.

For example: US \$ 1 = Rs. 47.00.

(ii) Indirect Quotation. Where exchange rates are quoted in terms of variable units of foreign currency as equivalent to a fixed number of units of home currency. For example: US \$ 2.1275 = Rs. 100.

Till 1.8.1993 banks were required to quote all the rates on indirect basis as foreign currency equivalent to Rs. 100 except in case of sale/ purchase of foreign currency notes and traveller cheques where exchange rates on direct quotation basis were quoted. From 2.8.1993 banks are quoting rates on direct basis only.

There is a distinction between inter-bank exchange rates and merchant rates. Merchant rates are the exchange rates applied by the bankers for transactions with their customers for various purposes, such as import, export, travel, remittances etc. These rates are calculated by the banks as per the guidelines issued by the Foreign Exchange Dealers Association of India (FEDAI). On the other hand inter-bank rates are the rates for transactions amongst the authorised dealers in foreign exchange. These rates depend on the market conditions. It is not out of place to mention here that exchange rates are volatile and, therefore, you should make sincere efforts to choose appropriate time for tendering your export documents to the bank for purchase/negotiation. Therefore, plan your affairs in such a way that the documents are delivered to the bank when the exchange rates are favourable enabling you to get more Indian rupees after conversion of foreign currency amount of the bill into Indian rupees.

A distinction is also made between spot rates and forward rates. Spot rates are applicable on the day of transaction, i.e. the same day, whereas forward rates are the rates fixed in advance for a transaction which will mature at a specified date or during a specified period in future. Quotations for spot rates only are generally available and the customers have to enter into specific contracts for forward rates.

Foreign exchange rates are always quoted as two way price i.e., a rate at which the bank is willing to buy foreign currency (buying rate) and a rate at which the bank sells foreign currency (selling rate). Banks do expect some profit in exchange operations and there is always some difference in buying and selling rates. However, the maximum spread available to banks is restricted in terms of ceilings imposed by Reserve Bank of India.

All exchange rates by authorised dealers are quoted in terms of their capacity as buyer or seller.

Different sets of exchange rates are applied for various types of foreign exchange transactions as under:

TT Selling Rate

This rate is applied for all clean remittances outside India i.e., for selling foreign currency to its customer by the bank such as for issuance of bank drafts, mail/telegraphic transfers etc.

Bill Selling Rate

This rate is applied for all foreign remittances outside India as proceeds of import bills payable in India. This rate is a little worse than TT selling rate.

TT Buying Rate

This rate is applied for purchase of foreign currency by banks where cover is already obtained by banks in India. Thus all foreign inward remittances which are made payable in India are converted by applying this rate. A mail transfer issued by a bank in Dubai for US $ 10, 000 drawn on (say) Oriental Bank of Commerce, New Delhi, will be converted into rupees at TT buying rate as the bank in Dubai would have already paid the US $ in bank a/c of Oriental Bank of Commerce in New York.

Bills Rate

This rate is applied for purchase of sight export bills which will result in foreign remittance to India after realisation. This rate is worse than TT buying rate and, in addition, interest will also be recovered by the bank for the period for which the bank is out of funds.

II. Forward Contracts

As regards elimination of exchange risk due to unfavourable movement in the exchange rate, the same can be avoided by the following methods:

1. By invoicing in Indian rupees.
2. By fixing the foreign exchange contract.

First alternative is possible only when the buyer agrees to it. He may have his own reasons for not agreeing to invoicing in Indian rupees. The second alternative is commonly resorted to. This alternative involves booking of forward exchange contract with your bank. This means that pending submission of documents to the bank for purchase/negotiation, you have made firm commitment with the bank under which you agree to sell to the bank foreign exchange at a future date/period and the bank agrees to purchase at the firm rate the foreign exchange to be tendered by you on that date/ during the agreed period. Thus you are in a position to know in advance the exchange rate you are going to get on submission of your export documents. Thus, though you have to pay some charge for booking a forward contract, you are certain about the rupee amount of the bill on conversion of foreign currency at a future date.

For booking a forward contract, you should approach your bank with whom you are enjoying a credit limit. The bank will book a forward contract only against a firm export order showing description and quantity of the goods to be supplied, aggregate price and approximate date of shipment. The bank can accept telex, cable order/fax in this regard, provided you give an undertaking to produce the original one. Where shipment has already been completed, forward contract will be booked on the basis of export bill tendered by you. It can also be booked against an irrevocable Letter of

Credit provided L/C is complete in all respects and you give a declaration to the bank that you have not booked any forward contract against the underlying sale contract covering shipments under the L/C.

Forward Contract

A person resident in India may enter into a forward contract with an authorised dealer in India to hedge an exposure to exchange risk in respect of a transaction for which sale and/or purchase of foreign exchange is permitted under the Act, or rules or regulations or directions or orders made or issued thereunder, subject to following terms and conditions—

(a) the authorised dealer through verification of documentary evidence is satisfied about the genuineness of the underlying exposure or as otherwise permitted by the Reserve Bank from time to time,

(b) the maturity of the hedge does not exceed the maturity of the underlying transaction,

(c) the currency of hedge and tenor are left to the choice of the customer,

(d) where the exact amount of the underlying transaction is not ascertainable, the contract is booked on the basis of a reasonable estimate,

(e) foreign currency loans/bonds will be eligible for hedge only after final approval is accorded by the Reserve Bank where such approval is necessary,

(f) in case of Global Depository Receipts (GDRs) the issue price has been finalised,

(g) balances in the Exchange Earner's Foreign Currency (EEFC) accounts sold forward by the account holders shall remain earmarked for delivery and such contracts shall not be cancelled. They may, however, be rolled-over,

(h) contracts involving rupee as one of the currencies, once cancelled shall not be re-booked although they can be rolled over at ongoing rates on or before maturity. This restriction shall not apply to contracts covering export transactions which may be cancelled, rebooked or rolled-over at on-going rates,

(i) substitution of contracts for hedging trade transactions may be permitted by an authorised dealer on being satisfied with the circumstances under which such substitution has become necessary. Authorised dealers may enter into forward contracts with residents in accordance with the provisions contained in paragraph 1 of Schedule I to Reserve Bank Notification No. FEMA 25/RB-2000 dated 3rd May, 2000.

While booking contracts for their constituents, authorised dealers should verify suitable documentary evidence, irrespective of the underlying transaction being a current account transaction or a capital account transaction, to ensure that an exposure exists, to the extent of the amount of cover sought. Full particulars of contract should be marked on such documents under proper authentication and copies thereof retained for verification.

Authorised dealers may also allow importers and exporters to book forward contract on the basis of a declaration of an exposure and based on past performance subject to the conditions prescribed by Reserve Bank of India in this regard.

Early Delivery, Extension and Cancellation of Forward Contracts

You must ensure delivery of the related documents within the agreed period of the contract. In case you fail to deliver the documents within the specified period, the forward contract needs to be cancelled and fresh contract booked for which your bank will levy cancellation charges as per the FEDAI Rules. In case the documents are delivered before the stipulated period, it will involve early delivery and bank will levy charges for the early delivery, as per FEDAI Rules. Where the-documents are not delivered at all, contract has to be cancelled either at your request or by the bank itself under certain circumstances, and this will entail cancellation charges as per the FEDAI Rules. It, therefore becomes extremely important that the period of delivery of the export documents is carefully chosen and strictly adhered to, so as to avoid unnecessary charges on account of early delivery or cancellation of forward contracts. However, facility for substitution of contracts covering trade transactions is permitted, if the authorised dealer is satisfied after verification of suitable documentary evidence, with the circumstances under which such substitution has become necessary.

A forward contract cancelled with one authorised dealer can be rebooked with another authorised dealer subject to the following conditions:

(a) the switch is warranted by competitive rates on offer, termination of banking relationship with the authorised dealer with whom the contract was originally booked, etc.

(b) the cancellation and rebooking are done simultaneously on the maturity date of the contract.

(c) the responsibility of ensuring that the original contract which has been cancelled rests with the authorised dealer who undertakes rebooking of the contract.

A strategic policy should be adopted for forward contracts. Exporters can improve profitability by properly blending forward and open position anticipating the expected trend of currency behaviour. For commodity exports where turnover is high and profitability is low, this strategy is specially useful.

11

Procuring/Manufacturing Goods for Export and their Inspection by Government Authorities

I. Procuring/Manufacturing Goods

Once you are ready with the infrastructure for exporting goods and have obtained necessary finance, you should proceed to procure the goods for export. Procuring the goods should be done with extreme care and caution as to the quality and cost. However, procuring the raw materials etc. and manufacturing the goods for export will need extra efforts on your part. If you are an established exporter, you can have the facility of procuring raw materials under the Duty Exemption Scheme. You can be issued Duty Free Replenishment Certificate (DFRC) for the import of inputs used in the manufacture of goods without payment of customs duty but additional customs duty equal to the excise duty shall be paid at the time of import of inputs.

II. Compulsory Quality Control & Preshipment Inspection

An important aspect about the goods to be exported is compulsory quality control and preshipment inspection. Under the Export (Quality Control and Inspection) Act, 1963, about 1000 commodities under the major groups of Food and Agriculture, Fishery, Minerals, Organic and Inorganic Chemicals, Rubber Products, Refractories, Ceramic Products, Pesticides, Light Engineering Steel Products, Jute Products, Coir and Coir Products, Footwear and Footwear Products/Components are subject to compulsory preshipment inspection. At times, foreign buyers lay down their own standards/ specifications which may or may not be in consonance with the Indian standards. They may also insist upon inspection by their own nominated agencies. These issues should be sorted out before confirmation of order. In addition to that buyers have their own preference for third party and independent inspection agencies. Many agencies are operational in this service sector.

Products having ISI Certification mark or Agmark are not required to be inspected by any Indian agency. These products do not fall within the purview of the export inspection agencies network. The Customs Authorities allow export of such goods even if not accompanied by any pre-shipment inspection certificate, provided they are otherwise satisfied that the goods carry ISI Certification Mark or the Agmark.

Depending upon the nature of products, goods meant for export are inspected for quality in the following manner:

Consignment to Consignment Inspection

Each individual consignment is inspected by the Export Inspection Agency. Commodity Board and certificate of inspection is issued.

The application for inspection for goods has to be submitted well in advance before the expected date of shipment of the consignment. Inspection of the consignment is generally carried out either at the premises of the exporter, provided adequate facilities exist therein for inspection, or at the port of shipment. The export inspection agency has a right to exercise supervision of inspected consignment(s) at any place or time.

The application should be made in duplicate in the new prescribed form 'Intimation for Inspection' as per standardised pre-shipment export documents, to the nearest office of the respective Export Inspection Agency along with the following documents:

1. Particulars of the consignment intended to be exported.
2. A crossed cheque/draft for the amount of requisite inspection fees or an Indian Postal Order.
3. Copy of commercial invoice.
4. Copy of letter of credit.
5. Details of packing specifications.
6. Copy of the export order/contract, indicating inter alia the buyer's requirement that goods are strictly according to the prescribed specifications, or as per samples etc.

After satisfying itself that the consignment of exportable goods meets the requirements stipulated in the export contract/order, the inspection agency issues, generally within four days of receipt of intimation for inspection, the necessary certificate of inspection to the exporter in the prescribed proforma in five copies. The certificate is issued in the standardised form which is an aligned pre-shipment export document. (Three copies for exporter, original copy for customs use, the second copy for the use of the foreign buyer and the third copy for the exporter's use, fourth copy for Data Bank, Export Inspection Council, New Delhi and the fifth copy is retained with the agency for their own office record).

In-Process Quality Control (IPQC)

Certain products like chemicals or engineering goods are subject to this control. The inspection is done at various stages of production. The exporter has to get his unit registered as "Export Worthy" and keep record of processing and production. Inspection by the officers of Export Inspection Agency is done from time to time. The certification of inspection on the end-products is then given without in-depth study at the shipment stage.

Under this system, export is allowed on the basis of adequacy of in-process quality control and inspection measures exercised by the manufacturing units themselves. The certificates of inspection in favour of the units approved under the scheme are issued by the Export Inspection Agencies (EIAs) in the normal course. However, these units are kept under surveillance by the EIAs and random spot checks of the consignments are carried out by them.

Units approved under this system of in-process quality control may themselves issue the certificate of inspection, but only for the products for which they have been granted IPQC facilities. However, these units have the option either to get the certificate from the Export Inspection Agencies (EIAs) or issue the same themselves. Consequently, the manufacturer-exporters of products approved under the IPQC have been recognised as an agency for pre-shipment inspection for export of engineering products for which they have been approved by the Export Inspection Agencies at Mumbai, Calcutta, Cochin, Delhi and Chennai.

Self Certification Scheme

Large manufacturers/exporters, export houses/trading houses are allowed the facility of Self-Certification on the theory that the exporter himself is the best judge of the quality of his products and will not allow his reputation to be spoiled in the international market by compromising on quality. The industrial units having proven reputation and adequate testing facilities have to apply to the Director (Inspection and Quality Control), Export Inspection Council of India, 11th Floor, Pragati Tower, 26 Rajendra Place, New Delhi-110008. They are granted a certificate valid for a period of one year, allowing them self-certification facility. The facility is available to manufacturers of engineering products, chemical and allied products and marine products. During this period the exporter can issue a certificate signed by himself or by a person authorised by him. The certificate has to indicate the number and date of EIA's reference for registration under

Self-Certification Scheme. It has to be issued in the aligned format as per new standardised pre-shipment documents. The approval of an industrial unit under this scheme is notified in the Gazette of India and the exporter has to pay a lump sum fee to the export inspection agencies depending upon his export turnover. Minimum Quality Norms prescribed by the Export Inspection Council should be maintained and achieved for the grant of facility under Self-Certification Scheme.

III. Fumigation

Commodities like de-oiled rice bran, crushed bones, hooves and horns are prone to insect infestation in storage and transit. They are subject to compulsory fumigation so that the product reaches destination in sound condition. This is another device to preserve quality.

IV. ISO 9000

The discussion on quality control and preshipment inspection will be incomplete without saying a few words about ISO 9000.

The ISO-9000 Series of Standards evolved by the International Standards Organisation has been accepted worldwide as the norm assuring high quality of goods. The ISO-9000 is also the hallmark of a good quality-oriented system for suppliers and manufacturers. It identifies the basic principles underlying quality, and specifies the procedures and criteria to be followed to ensure that what leaves the manufacturer/supplier's premises fully meets the customer's requirements.

The ISO-9000 series of standards are basically quality assurance standards and not product standards.

ISO-9000 spells out how a company can establish, document and maintain an effective and economic quality control system which will demonstrate to the customer that the company is committed to quality. The series of Standards aims at the following:

- increased customer confidence in the company,
- a shift from a system of inspection, to one of quality management,
- removing the need for multiple assessments of suppliers,
- gaining management commitment,
- linking quality to cost-effectiveness,
- giving customers what they need.

The implementation of ISO-9000 Standards involves:

- management education,

- writing a quality policy,
- nominating a quality representative,
- identifying responsibilities,
- identifying business processes,
- writing a quality manual,
- writing procedures,
- writing work instructions.

It is thus clear that the ISO-9000 series of standards constitute of concept of Total Quality Management (TQM).

12

Labelling, Packaging, Packing and Marking Goods for Export

An important stage after manufacturing of goods or their procurement is their preparation for shipment. This entails labelling, packaging, packing and marking of export consignments.

Labelling requirements differ from country to country and the same should be ascertained well in advance from the buyer. The label should indicate quality, quantity, method of use etc. Special international care labels have been specified for the textile items by GINETEX. and the same should be scrupulously adhered to. As per latest requirement bar code labelling is proposed to be made compulsory for many products.

Packaging fulfills a vital role in helping to get your export products to the market in top condition, as well as in presenting your goods to the overseas buyer in an attractive way. While packaging, quality should not be compromised merely to cut down costs. Packaging should also be in conformity with the instructions issued by the importer.

Packing refers to the external containers used for transportation. The shape of packing cases plays a very important role in packing the cargo, and the nature of packing material to be used will depend upon the items exported. As regards specification for the size, weight and strength, care must be taken to ensure that the weight of standard case does not exceed 50 kg. for easy handling of the cargo. The size of packs should be designed in such a way that maximum cargo can be loaded in containers.

Before packing and sealing the goods, it should be ensured that all the contents are properly placed in the case and the list of contents of packing notes should be prepared so that the buyer, the Customs authorities and the Insurance authorities can easily check the contents of each and every case. The consolidated statement of contents for a number of case is called the Packing List, which should be prepared in the prescribed standardised format.

Marking means to mark the address, number of packages etc. on the packets. It is essential for identification purpose and should provide information on exporters' mark, importers' mark, port of destination, place of destination, order number and date, gross, net and tare weight and handling instructions. It should also be ensured that while putting marks, the law of buyer's country is duly complied with.

All shipping cases should be marked a number with special symbols selected by the exporters or the importers, so that competitors are not in a position to find out the details of the customers and the country of destination or supplier's country of despatch. Care should also be taken to ensure that the marking conforms to those written in the invoice, insurance certificate, bill of lading and other documents. The International Cargo Handling Coordination, Association has set out for the use of exporters a number of recommendations for the marking of goods carried by ocean-going vessels. They are equally useful for sending goods by other modes of transportation. Some of these recommendations are as under:

1. The marks should appear in a certain order. Essential data should be placed in oblong frames with lines 1.5 centimeters thick, and subsidiary information should be placed in another type of frame.

2. Declaration on large packages should be placed on two continuous sides, and for consignments bound together on a pallet, also on the top. Handling instructions should be placed on all four sides. Similar packages, such as goods in sacks, should be marked on two opposite sides;

3. Lettering should be atleast 7.5 centimeters high for essential data, and at least 3.5 centimeters for subsidiary data. If the package is too small for such letter, other sizes may be used, but in the same ratio. The sizes of the symbols should also be in proportion to the size of the package and of the other markings.

4. Only fast dyes should be used for lettering. Essential data should be in black and subsidiary data in a less conspicuous colour; red and orange lettering should be reserved for dangerous goods only. For food packed in sacks, only harmless dyes should be employed, and the dye should not come through the packing in such a way as to affect the goods.

5. Stick-on labels should only be used on individual package or parcel and all old labels should be removed.

6. Marking should be made by stencil or by branding or by pencil

or brush without a stencil. If stencils are used, care should be taken that the letters and figures are perfectly legible to prevent confusion. This is especially true of the letters and figures — B.R.P, 0, G-G-D-C, H.N; 3-8: 6-9 and 1-7.

7. The surface to be marked should be smooth and clean. If packages are to be bonded, they can be marked before this is done; the hoops should not however, cover the markings.
8. The figure should indicate the total number of packages making up the consignment and the consecutive number of the individual package. For example, 1520/15/1 identifies the first package of a total number of 15 packets and 1520/15/15 the last one.
9. The name of the ship and the bill of lading number should be shown when this is possible. Handling instructions must appear in the language of exporter and importer, and also, if possible, in the language of the countries where goods are to be handled en route or transshipped.

13

Excise Procedure

All excisable goods exported out of India are exempt from payment of Central Excise duties, for which two different procedures have been prescribed.

1. Rebate of Duty on Goods Export Procedure

Under the first procedure, known as 'Rebate of Duty on Goods Export' the manufacturer has first to pay the excise duty on goods meant for export and then claim refund of the same after exportation of such goods to countries except Nepal and Bhutan. This is done under Rule 12 of Central Excise Rules. Under this rule, rebate of duty is granted for the finished stage as well as input stage. Rebate of duty in respect of the excisable materials used in the manufacture of exported goods shall not be allowed if the exporter avails of drawback allowed under the Customs and Central Excise Duties Drawback Rules, 1995 or CENVAT. The following procedure should be followed while exporting under rebate of duty.

Removal of goods under claim of rebate from a factory or warehouse without examination by the Central Excise Officers—

The exporters are allowed to remove the goods for export on their own without getting the goods examined by the Central Excise Officers. Form AR4 in such cases should be prepared in sixtuplicate, giving all particulars and declarations. The exporter shall deliver triplicate, quadruplicate, quintuplicate and sixtuplicate copies of AR4 to the Superintendent of Central Excise having jurisdiction over the factory or the warehouse, within twenty four hours of the removal of the consignment and would retain the original and duplicate copies for presenting along with the consignment to the Customs Officer at the point of export.

The jurisdictional Superintendent of Central Excise examines the information contained in AR4 and verifies the facts of payment of duty and other certificates/declarations made by the exporter. After he is satisfied that the information contained in the AR4 is true, he signs at appropriate places in the four copies of AR4 submitted to him and puts his stamp with his name and designation below his signature. He would then dispose of the triplicate, quadruplicate, quintuplicate and sixtuplicate copies of AR4 as under:

(i) Triplicate : To the rebate sanctioning authority viz. Maritime Commissioner of Central Excise or the Assistant Commissioner of Central Excise declared by the exporter on the AR4. This copy on the request of exporter may be sealed and handed over to the exporter/his authorized agent for presenting to the rebate sanctioning authority.

(ii) Quadruplicate : To the Chief Accounts Officer in the Commissionerate Headquarters.

(iii) Quintuplicate : Office copy to be retained by the Central Excise Officer.

(iv) Sixtuplicate : To be given to the exporter.

Procedure for exports under Central Excise Seal

Where the exporter desires the sealing of the goods by the Central Excise Officers so that the export goods may not be examined by the Customs Officers at the Port/Airport of shipment, he should present an AR4 application in sixtuplicate to the Superintendent of Central Excise having jurisdiction over the factory/warehouse atleast twenty four hours before the intended removal of the export goods from the factory/warehouse.

The Superintendent of Central Excise may depute an Inspector of Central Excise or may himself go for sealing and examination of the export consignment. Where the AR4 indicates that the export is in discharge of an export obligation under a Quantity-based Advance Licence or a Value-based Advance Licence issued under the Duty Exemption Scheme, in such cases the consignment is invariably examined and sealed by the Superintendent of Central Excise himself.

The Central Excise Officer examining the consignment would draw samples wherever necessary in triplicate. He would hand over two sets of samples, duly sealed, to the exporter or his authorized agent, for delivering to the Customs Officers at the point of export. He would retain the third set for his records.

The export consignment is carefully examined vis-a-vis the description of goods, their value and other particulars/declarations on the AR4. The Central Excise Officer verifies the facts of payment of duty and other certificates/declarations made by the exporter. After he is satisfied that the information contained in the AR4 is true he would allow the clearances and also sign all the six copies of the AR4 at appropriate places and put his stamp with his name and designation below his signature.

The copies of AR4 are disposed of as under:

Original & Duplicate:To the exporter for presenting to Customs Officer at the point of export along with the export consignment.

Triplicate: To the rebate sanctioning authority i.e. Maritime Commissioner of Central Excise or the jurisdictional Assistant Commissioner of Central Excise, as declared by the exporter on the AR4. The Central Excise Officer may handover this copy under a sealed cover on exporter's request.

Quadruplicate: To the Chief Accounts Officer at his Commissionerate Headquarters.

Quintuplicate: To be retained for records.

2. Export under Bond Procedure

Under the second procedure known as 'Exports Under Bond' goods can be exported out of India except to Nepal or Bhutan without prior payment of duty subject to the execution of the Bond with security/security for a sum equivalent to the duty chargeable on (the goods to be exported. This is done under Rule 13 of Central Excise Rules which deals with export of goods in Bond as well as utilisation of raw materials etc. without payment of duty for manufacture and export of excisable goods. The following procedure has been prescribed in this regard.

Removal of goods without payment of Central Excise duty from a factory or warehouse without examination by the Central Excise Officers—

The exporters are allowed to remove the goods for export on their own without getting the goods examined by the Central Excise Officers in respect of all commodities other than those covered under physical control. The AR4 in such cases should be prepared in sixtuplicate, giving all particulars and declarations. The exporter shall deliver triplicate, quadruplicate, quintuplicate and sixtuplicate copies of AR4, to the Superintendent of Central Excise having jurisdiction over the factory or the warehouse, within twenty four hours of the removal of the consignment and would retain the original and duplicate copies for presenting alongwith the consignment to the Customs Officer at the point of export. However, the exporters may ensure before clearances that the necessary bond has been executed for this purpose.

Exporters, whether manufacturer exporter or merchant exporter may be cautioned that unless they execute the necessary bond before the Competent Authority they should not clear the goods under the relaxed procedure. They should without fail indicate the Bond Number and the authority before whom the relevant bond is executed in the relevant columns provided in Form AR4.

The jurisdictional Superintendent of Central Excise examines the information contained in AR4 and verifies the fact of execution of bond and other certificates/declarations made by the exporter. After he is satisfied that the information contained in the AR4 is true, he will sign at appropriate places in the four copies of AR4 submitted to him and put his stamp with his name and designation below his signature. He would then dispose of the triplicate, quadruplicate, quintuplicate and sixtuplicate copies of AR4 as under —

(i) Triplicate :To the authority before whom the bond is executed and who will accept the proof of export i.e. Maritime Commissioner of Central Excise or the Assistant Commissioner of Central Excise declared by the exporter on the AR4. This copy on the request of exporter may be sealed and handed over to the exporter/his authorized agent for presenting to the authority.

(ii) Quadruplicate : To the Chief Accounts Officer in the Commissionerate Headquarters.

(iii) Quintuplicate : Office copy to be retained by the Central Excise Officer.

(iv) Sixtuplicate : To be given to the exporter or his authorized agent in the sealed cover.

Procedure for exports under Central Excise seal

Where the exporter desires the sealing of the goods by the Central Excise Officers so that the export goods may not be examined by the Customs Officers at the Port/Airport of shipment, he should present an AR4 application in sixtuplicate to the Superintendent of Central Excise having jurisdiction over the factory/warehouse atleast twenty four hours before the intended removal of the export goods from the factory/warehouse.

The Superintendent of Central Excise may depute an inspector of Central Excise or may himself go for sealing and examination of the export consignment. Where the AR4 indicates that the export is in discharge of an export obligation under a Quantity-based Advance Licence or a value based Advance Licence issued under the Duty Exemption Scheme, in such cases the consignment is invariably examined and sealed by the Superintendent of Central Excise himself.

The Central Excise Officer examining the consignment would draw samples wherever necessary in triplicate. He would hand over two sets of samples, duly sealed to the exporter or his authorized agent, for delivering to the Customs Officer at the point of export. He would retain the third set for his records.

The export consignment is carefully examined vis-a-vis the description of goods, their value and other particulars/declarations on the AR4. The Central Excise Officer shall verify the facts, certificates/declaration made by the exporter. The value declared on AR4 should be as per Section 4 of Central Excises Act, 1944. After Central Excise Officer is satisfied that the information contained in the AR4 is true and after verifying that necessary bond has been executed by the exporter, he would allow the clearances and also sign all the six copies of the AR4 at appropriate places and put his stamp with his name and designation below his signature.

The copies of AR4 would be disposed of as under:

Original & Duplicate : To the exporter for presenting to Customs Officers at the point of export along with the export consignment.

Triplicate : To the authority competent to accept the proof of exports i.e. Maritime Commissioner of Central Excise or the Jurisdictional Assistant Commissioner of Central Excise, as declared by the exporter on the AR4. The Central Excise Officer may handover this copy under a sealed cover on exporter's request.

Quadruplicate : To the Chief Accounts Officer at his Commissionerate Headquarters.

Quintuplicate : To be retained for records. Sixtuplicate: To be given to (the exporter or his authorized agent, in a sealed cover, for handling over to Customs Officer. After shipment proof of export i.e. documents like bill of lading, shipping bill are submitted to the Maritime Collector of Central Excise who after verification credit the running bond account and the excise duty liability is discharged.

Simplified Export Procedure for Exempted Units

Manufacturers having value of clearances for consumption within exemption limit and who are availing full exemption can avail simplified export procedure.

14

Insuring Goods Against Marine Risks

In order to cover yourself against various risks while the goods are in transit, you should obtain a marine insurance policy. For banks extending finance to you this policy also works as a collateral security, the cargo constituting the primary security.

Cargo can be got insured either by the seller or the buyer depending the type of sale contract. In case of C.I.F. contract and in the absence of any specific advice from the buyer, you should arrange insurance of the c.i.f. value of the goods plus 5 to 10% towards incidental charges. Where the contract is C & F the responsibility of arranging insurance is on your buyer. For C & I contract, you should arrange insurance. For F.O.B. contract, the buyer is obliged to arrange insurance. As soon as you fix up the ship you should advise the buyer immediately so that he could arrange for insurance before commencement of the risk (before the vessel sails). In case of F.A.S., your obligation is to bring the goods at the shore of the side of the ship. It is the responsibility of the buyer to arrange for shipment and insurance of the goods. The buyer should be properly and timely notified above movement of cargo so that risks can be insured.

You should obtain marine insurance policies from GIC or any of its four subsidiaries in India. You are not permitted to take marine insurance cover with insurance companies in foreign countries without prior permission of RBI/Govt. of India.

Payment of premium on marine insurance policies can be made in Indian rupees on your furnishing a certificate (i) that insurance charges on shipment in question have to be borne by you in terms of the contract with the overseas buyer and that you are not making the payment on behalf of any non-resident or (ii) that you are defraying insurance charges on account of the overseas buyer of the goods and undertake to add the amount on the invoice and recover the payment so made from the buyer in an approved manner.

The different types of marine insurance policies can be divided into three broad groups (1) Individual Shipment Policy, (2) Open Policy and (3) Floating Policy. Individual shipment policy is taken for every individual shipment. Under an open policy or open cover, you have the automatic protection for all shipments. Generally a maximum limit of cover is set for a shipment on any vessel. Under this cover you are duly bound to declare to the insurer all shipments. Big exporters prefer this method as it saves them the trouble of having to arrange for protection before shipment is made. It also enables their competitiveness by obtaining special premium rates. Floating policy describes the insurance in general terms and leaves the name or names of the ship or ships and other particulars to be stated by subsequent declaration.

The risks covered in a marine insurance policy are represented by special clauses inserted for this purpose. These are Institute Cargo Clauses (C), Institute Cargo Clauses (B), Institute Cargo Clauses (A). Extraneous Perils. Trade Clauses War and SRCC Cover, etc.

It is important to note that marine insurance policies are freely assignable, the sum insured indicated in the policy is value agreed between the insured and the insurer and the duration of cover is subject to the transit clause of the respective policy.

The commonly used documents in marine insurance are Letter of Insurance. Broker's Certificates, Insurance Certificate. Insurance Policy and Marine Insurance Declaration. The Marine Insurance Declaration and Marine Insurance Certificate are prepared in the Standardised Aligned Forms.

In case of any damage to cargo the insurance agency should be notified immediately. A surveyor is deputed by agency to assess the loss and on the basis of response of surveyor the damages are paid.

15

Preparing Export Documents

Export documents have to be prepared for various purpose viz.

1. Declaration of exports as per exchange control regulations of the country.
2. Transportation of the goods.
3. Customs clearance of the goods.
4. Other purposes.

Some of the forms for preparing documents have been standardised under the Aligned Documentation System introduced w.e.f. 1.10.1991.

I. Documents For Declaration of Goods under Foreign Exchange Regulations

The Statutory Control

Section 7 of the Foreign Exchange Management Act, 1999 lays down the statutory control concerning exports. Under the provision of this section, RBI has issued Foreign Exchange Management (Export of Goods & Services) Regulations, 2000 w.e.f. 1.6.2000.

Under Regulation 3 every exporter of goods or software in physical form or through any other form, either directly or indirectly, to any place outside India other than Nepal and Bhutan shall furnish to the specified authority a declaration in prescribed form and supported by such evidence as may be specified.

Export of goods or services may be made without furnishing the declaration in the following cases, namely —

(a) trade samples of goods and publicity material supplied free of payment.

(b) personal effects of travellers whether accompanied or unaccompanied;

(c) ship's stores, transhipment cargo and goods supplied under the orders of Central Government or of such officers as may be appointed by the Central Government in this behalf or of the military naval or air force authorities in India for military, naval or air force requirements;

(d) goods or software accompanied by a declaration, by the exporter that they are not more than twenty-five thousand rupees in value;

(e) by way of gift of goods accompanied by a declaration by the exporter that they are not more than one lakh rupees in value[1];

(f) aircrafts or aircraft engines and spare parts for overhauling and/or repair abroad subject to their re-import into India after overhauling/repairs, within a period of six months from the date of their export;

(g) goods imported free of cost on re-export basis;

(h) goods not exceeding US $ 1000 or its equivalent in value per transaction exported to Myanmar under the Barter Trade Agreement between the Central Government and the Government of Myanmar;

(i) the following goods which are permitted by the Development Commissioner of the Export Processing Zones, Electronic Hardware Technology Parks, Electronic Software Technology Parks or Free Trade Zones to be re-exported, namely:

  (1) imported good found defective, for the purpose of their replacement by the foreign suppliers/collaborators,

  (2) goods imported from foreign suppliers/collaborators on loan basis,

  (3) goods imported from foreign suppliers/collaborators free of cost found surplus after production operations;

(ia) goods listed at items (1) (2) and (3) of clause (i) to be re-exported by units in Special Economic Zones, under intimation to the Development Commissioner of Special Economic Zones/concerned Assistant Commissioner or Deputy Commissioner of Customs;

(j) replacement goods exported free of charge in accordance with the provisions of Exim Policy in force for the time being;

(k) goods sent outside India for testing subject to re-import into India;

---

1. Gifts of goods exceding rupees one lakh in value require approval of reserve Bank of India.

(l) defective goods sent outside India for repair and re-import provided the goods are accompanied by a certificate from an authorised dealer in India that the export is for repair and re-import and that the export does not involve any transaction in foreign exchange;

(m) exports permitted by the Reserve Bank, on application made to it subject to the terms and conditions, if any, as stipulated in the permission;

Declaration Forms

All exports to which the requirement of declaration applies must be declared on appropriate forms as indicated below

GR Form : To be completed in duplicate for exports otherwise than by post including export of software in physical form i.e. magnetic tape/ discs and paper media.

SDF Form : To be completed in duplicate and appended to the Shipping Bill for exports declared to customs offices notified by the Central Government which have introduced EDI system for processing shipping bill.

PP Form : To be completed in duplicate for export by post.

SOFTEX : To be completed in triplicate for export of software otherwise than in physical form i.e. magnetic tapes/ discs and paper media.

It may be noted that under the new Regulations form VP/COD has been dispensed with.

GR/PP forms are printed in distinctive colour and each set bears a printed number which appeals on both copies of the form. They are available for sale with Reserve Bank of India. However, exporters can get these forms through authorised dealers also.

Export declaration forms have utmost importance and are binding on the exporter. It is, therefore, necessary that enough care is taken while declaring exports on these forms with special reference on the following points:

(i) Name and address of authorised dealer through whom proceeds of exports have been or will be realised should be specified in the relevant column of the form.

(ii) Details of commission and discount due to foreign agent or buyer should be correctly declared otherwise difficulties may arise at the time of remittance of such commission.

(iii) It should be clearly indicated in the form whether the export is on 'outright sale basis' or 'on consignment basis' and irrelevant clauses must be struck out.

(iv) Under the item 'Analysis of full export value', a break up of the full export value of goods under f.o.b. value, freight and insurance should be furnished in all cases, irrespective of the terms of contract.

(v) All documents relating to export of goods from India must pass through the medium of an authorised dealer in foreign exchange in India within 21 days of shipment.

(vi) The amount representing the full export value of goods must be realised within six months from date of shipment.

Disposal of Copies of Export Declaration Forms

Copies of export declaration forms should be disposed of as under:

(a) GR forms should be completed by the exporter in duplicate and both the copies submitted to the Customs at the port of shipment along with the shipping bill. Customs will give their running serial number on both the copies after admitting the corresponding shipping bill. The Customs serial number will have ten numerals denoting the code number of the port of shipment, the calendar year and a six digit running serial number. Customs will certify the value declared by the exporter on both the copies of the GR form at the space earmarked and will also record the assessed value. They will then return the duplicate copy of the form to the exporter and retain the original for transmission to Reserve Bank. Exporters should submit the duplicate copy of the GR form again to Customs along with the cargo to be shipped. After examination of the goods and certifying the quantity passed for shipment on the duplicate copy, Customs will return it to the exporter for submission to the authorised dealer for negotiation or collection of export bills.

(b) Within twenty-one days from the date of export, exporter should lodge the duplicate copy together with relative shipping documents and an extra copy of the invoice with the authorised dealer named in the GR form. After the documents have been negotiated/sent for collection, the authorised dealer should report the transaction to Reserve Bank in statement ENC under cover of appropriate R-Supplementary Return. However, the duplicate copy of the form together with a copy of invoice etc. will henceforth be retained by the authorised dealer and may not be submitted to Reserve Bank.

NOTE:

(i) In the case of exports made under deferred credit arrangement or to joint ventures abroad against equity participation or under rupee credit agreement, the number and date of Reserve Bank approval and/or number and date of the relative RBI circular should be recorded at the appropriate place on the GR form.

(ii) Where Duplicate copy of GR form is misplaced or lost, authorised dealer may accept another copy of duplicate GR form duly certified by Customs.

(c) On account of introduction of Electronic Data Interchange (EDI) System at certain Customs offices where shipping bills are processed electronically, the existing declaration in GR form is replaced by a declaration in form SDF (Statutory Declaration Form). The SDF form should be submitted in duplicate (to be annexed to the relative shipping bill) to the concerned Commissioner of Customs. After verifying and authenticating the declaration in form SDF, the Commissioner of Customs will hand over to the exporter, one copy of the shipping bill marked 'Exchange Control Copy' in which form SDF has been appended for being submitted to the authorised dealer within 21 days from the date of export. The authorised dealer should accept the Exchange Control (EC) copy of the shipping bill and form SDF appended thereto, submitted by the exporter for collection/negotiation of shipping documents. The manner of disposal of EC copy of shipping bill (and form SDF appended thereto) is same as that for GR forms.

(d) In cases where ECGC initially settles the claims of exporters in respect of exports insured with them and subsequently receives the export proceeds from the buyer/buyer's country through the efforts made by them, the share of exporters in the amount so received is disbursed through the bank which had handled the shipping documents. In such cases, ECGC will issue a certificate to the bank which had handled the relevant shipping documents after full proceeds have been received. The certificate will indicate the number of declaration form, name of the exporter, name of the authorised dealer, date of negotiation, bill number, invoice value and the amount actually received by ECGC.

(e) The authorised dealer should ensure by random check of the relevant duplicate forms by their internal/concurrent auditors to confirm that non-realisation or short realization allowed, if any, is within the powers delegated to them or has been duly approved by Reserve bank, wherever necessary.

(f) Where a part of export proceeds are credited to EEFC account, the export declaration (duplicate) form may be certified as under:

"Proceeds amounting to ....

representing .... % of the export realisation

credited to EEFC account maintained by the exporter with ...."

(ii)The manner of disposal of PP forms is same as that for GR forms. Postal authorities will allow export of goods by post only if the original copy of the form has been countersigned by an authorised dealer. Therefore, PP forms should be first presented by the exporter to an authorised dealer for counter-signature. Authorised dealer will countersign the forms in accordance with directions given later in this Chapter and return the original copy to the exporter, who should submit the form to the post office with the parcel. The duplicate copy of the PP form will be retained by the authorised dealer to whom the exporter should submit relevant documents together with an extra copy of invoice for negotiation/collection, within the prescribed period of twenty-one days.

Counter signature on PP Forms

PP forms will be presented by the exporter to an authorised dealer for counter signature. Authorised dealers should countersign the PP forms after ensuring that the parcel is being addressed to their branch or correspondent bank in the country of import. The concerned overseas branch or correspondent should be instructed to deliver the parcel to consignee against payment or acceptance of relative bill. Authorised dealers may, however, countersign PP forms covering parcels addressed direct to the consignees, provided:—

(a) an irrevocable letter of credit for the full value of the export has been opened in favour of exporter and has been advised through authorised dealer concerned;

or

the full value of the shipment has been received in advance by the exporter through an authorised dealer;

or

the authorised dealer is satisfied, on the basis of the standing and track record of the exporter and the arrangements made for realisation of the export proceeds, that he could do so.

In such cases, particulars of advance payment/letter of credit/ authorised dealer's certification of standing, etc., of the exporter should be furnished on the form under proper authentication. Any alteration in the name and address of consignee on the PP form should also be authenticated by the authorised dealer under his stamp and signature.

Terms of Payment - Invoicing - (Software)

(i) In respect of long duration contracts involving series of transmissions, the exporters should bill their overseas clients periodically, i.e., at least once a month or on reaching the 'milestone' as provided in the contract entered into with the overseas client and the last invoice/bill should be raised not later than 15 days from the date of completion of the contract. It would be in order tor the exporters to submit a combined SOFTEX form for all the invoices raised on a particular overseas client, including advance remittances received in a month.

(ii) In respect of contracts involving only 'one shot operation', the invoice/ bill should be raised within 15 days from the date of transmission.

(iii) The exporter should submit declaration in Form SOFTEX in triplicate in respect of export of computer software and audio / video / television software to the concerned designated official of Government of India at STPI / EPZ /FTZ / SEZ for valuation/ certification not later than 30 days from the dale of invoice / the date of last invoice raised in a month, as indicated above. The designated officials may also certify the SOFTEX Forms in respect of EOUs which are registered with them.

(iv) The invoices raised on overseas clients as at (i) to (iii) above will be subject to valuation of export declared on SOFTEX form by the concerned designated official of Government of India and consequent amendment made in the invoice value, if necessary.

Disposal of SOFTEX forms

As for disposal of SOFTEX forms the procedure indicated in Regulation 6 of Export of Goods and Services Regulations 2000 is to be observed. However, the duplicate copy of the form together with a copy of invoice etc. will henceforth be retained by the authorised dealer and may not be submitted to Reserve Bank.

II. Documents For Transportation of Goods

The following documents are connected with transportation of the goods:

Airway Bill/Air Consignment Note

The receipt issued by an airline company or its agent for carnage of goods is called airway bill or air consignment note. It is not a document of title and it is not issued in a negotiable form. The goods are delivered to the consignee mentioned in the AWB after identifying himself as the party named in the airway bill as consignee/receiver against payment of charges, if any. It is therefore, desirable to consign the goods in the name of a foreign correspondent bank as it will enable you to retain the control over goods until the payment is made/ documents are accepted for payment.

The airway bill consists of three originals and six to eleven copies. It is a non-negotiable document. Original 1 (Green) is retained by the carrier issuing the AWB for accounting purposes. Original 2 (Pink) accompanies the consignment to final destination. Original 3 (Blue) is given to shipper as proof of receipt of the goods for shipment.

Bill of Lading

The bill of lading is a document issued by the shipping company or its agent acknowledging the receipt of goods mentioned in the bill for shipment on board the vessel and undertaking to deliver the goods in the like order and condition as received to the consignee or his order provided the freight and other charges specified in the bill of lading have been duly paid. Bill of Lading is issued in the standardised aligned document format.

For preparation of bill of lading the exporter should submit the complete sets of bill of lading together with mate receipt in the standardised aligned form to the shipping company which will calculate the freight amount on the basis of measurement or weight as certified by the recognised Chamber of Commerce. On payment of the freight, the shipping company returns the Bill of Lading duly signed and supported by requisite adhesive stamps.

A bill of lading is generally made out in the sets of two or three originals. All originals are duly signed by the master of the ship or the agent of the steamship company and all the originals are equally valid for taking the delivery of the goods and once one original is utilised the other originals become null and void. Utmost care is, therefore, required to be exercised to ensure that full set of original B/L is obtained by the exporter from the Shipping Company and no original copy goes in the wrong hand. Few extra copies of B/L are also issued generally marked as 'Non Negotiable Copy' which cannot be utilised for taking the delivery of the goods.

The type of bill of lading required will depend upon the terms of Letter of Credit (L/C). The following are the various types of Bills of Lading, some of which are not acceptable under L/C unless specifically permitted:

(a) Received for Shipment B/L certifying only receipt of goods — not acceptable under L/C unless specifically permitted.

(b) On deck B/L containing a remark that goods are shipped on deck — not acceptable unless specifically permitted.

(c) On board B/L certifying goods received on board the ship.

(d) Combined B/L covering several modes of transport.

(e) Custody B/L issued by American warehouses pending arrival of carrying vessel in port— acceptable.

(f) Forwarding agent B/L issued by forwarding agents not accepted unless specifically authorised — a single B/L covering a group of several consignments meant for different consignees — delivery achieved by issuing delivery orders relating to specified portions of the whole consignment.

(g) House B/L unacceptable as either evidence of title or contract of carriage.

(h) B/L — one on which the detailed conditions of transportation are not printed — not acceptable unless specifically permitted.

(i) Through B/L covering goods being transhipped en route. It covers the whole voyage and is acceptable if transhipment is permitted.

(j) Charter Party B/L covering shipment on chartered ship — issued subject to charter party agreements which supersede the usual memorandum of conditions of carriage appearing on the reverse of B/L not acceptable unless specifically authorised.

(k) Ocean/Liner B/L covering shipment by sea from port of shipment to — usually covering shipment made under letter of credit.

(l) Third party B/L acceptable if third party shipper endorses it in favour of the beneficiary (seller) who in turn either endorses it in blank or as stipulated in letter of credit.

A clause B/L is a B/L containing additional clauses limiting the responsibility of the shipping company and indicating defective conditions of the goods. Such a B/L is not acceptable under L/C unless specifically authorised. A clean B/L is one which does not bear any superimposed clause or annotation which expressly declares a defective condition of the goods and/or the packaging. A stale B/L is one which is tendered to the paying bank at so late a date, that though within validity of letter of credit it is impossible for it to be despatched to the consignee in time to reach him before the goods themselves arrive at destination port.

Mate Receipt

It is issued by the Chief of Vessel after cargo is loaded and it contains the name of shipper, place of receipt and voyage No., port of loading, port of discharge, place of delivery, marks and Nos., container No., description of goods, gross weight and other details as per the standardised aligned document format. The receipt is of transferable nature and must be presented at the shipping company's office to be exchanged into Bill of Lading.

Combined Transport Document

Inland Container Depots have been set up at various centres in the country. These dry ports have made it possible to cover the entire movement of goods from ICD to destination under the transport document called Combined Transport Document.

III. Documents For Customs Clearance of Goods

Shipping Bill/Bill of Export

Shipping Bill is the main document required by the Customs Authority for allowing shipment. Basically, shipping bills are of four types. The major distinction between one type and another Shipping Bill lies with regard to the goods being subject to: (a) export duty/cess, (b) free of duty/cess. (c) entitlement to duty drawback, (d) entitlement of credit of duty under DEPB Scheme and (e) re-export of imported goods.

Free Shipping Bill is used for export of goods which neither attracts any duty/cess nor entitled to duty drawback on their exportation. Dutiable Shipping Bill is used in case of goods subject to export duty/cess but may or may not be entitled to duty drawback. Drawback Shipping Bill or Bill of Exports is the document to be filed with the land Customs Authorities for export of goods which are entitled to drawback. DEPB Shipping bill is used when the goods are exported under DEPB scheme. Shipping Bill for Shipment Ex-Bond is for use in case of imported goods for re-exports and which are kept in bond.

Following documents are required for processing of Shipping Bill:

(a) GR forms in duplicate for shipments to all countries.

(b) Four copies of packing list giving contents, quantity, gross and net weight of each package.

(c) Four copies of invoices indicating all relevant particulars such as No. of packages, quantity, unit rate, total f.o.b./c.i.f. value, correct and full description of goods etc. (One copy of this invoice is to be pasted on the duplicate copy of Shipping Bill).

(d) Contract, Letter of Credit, Purchase Order.

(e) Inspection/Examination Certificate.

The formats presented for the shipping bill are as under:

1. White shipping bill for export of duty free goods prepared in triplicate in the standardised format.

2. Green shipping bill for export of goods under claim for duty drawback prepared in quadruplicate.
3. Yellow shipping bill for export of dutiable goods prepared in triplicate.
4. Pink shipping bill for export of duty free goods ex-bond prepared in triplicate.
5. Blue Shipping bill for exports under the DEPB scheme prepared in seven copies.

Where the goods are to be cleared by the Land Customs. Bill of Export is prepared instead of Shipping Bill. Bill of Exports are also of four types i.e. White, Green, Yellow and Pink for the purpose stated above:

Appraisal by the Custom Authorities

The Customs Appraiser/Examiner examines shipping documents and appraises the value having regard to the following considerations:

1. That the value and the quantity declared in the shipping Bill is the same as in the export order/letter of credit.
2. That the formalities regarding exchange control, pre-shipment quality control inspection etc. have been duly completed. After examination of documents and appraisement of value, the Customs Examiner/ Appraiser makes an endorsement on the duplicate copy of the Shipping Bill giving directions to the Dock Appraiser about the extent of physical examination of the cargo to be conducted at the docks. All the documents, except GR (Original) Form, the original Shipping Bill and a copy of the Commercial Invoice are returned to the Forwarding Agent to be presented to the Dock Appraiser.

After taking delivery of documents from the Export Department, Forwarding Agent presents the Port Trust Documents to the Shed Superintendent of the port and obtains carting order for bringing the export cargo to the transit shed for physical examination by the Dock Appraiser and for the shipment. After bringing the cargo into the shed he presents the following documents to the Dock Appraiser for conducting physical examination of the Cargo:

1. Duplicate, triplicate and export promotion copies of the Shipping Bill
2. Commercial Invoice
3. Packing List
4. AR4 (Original and Duplicate) and Invoice

5. Inspection Certificate (Original)

6. GR Form (Duplicate)

The Dock Appraiser after conducting physical examination records examination report and makes "Let Export" endorsement on the duplicate copy of the Shipping Bill and hands it over to the Forwarding Agent alongwith all other documents to be presented to the Preventive Officer of the Customs Department who supervises the loading of cargo on board the vessels.

The Preventive Officer makes an endorsement "Let Ship" on the duplicate copy of the Shipping Bill. The duplicate copy of the Shipping Bill is then handed over to the agent of the Shipping Company. This constitutes an authorisation by the Customs to the Shipping Company to accept the cargo on board the vessel.

After the goods are loaded on board the vessel the Captain of the ship issues a receipt called "Mate's Receipt" to the Shed Superintendent of the Port.

The Forwarding Agent then makes a payment of the port charges and takes delivery of the Mate Receipt. He presents the Mate Receipt first to the Preventive Officer who records the Certificate of Shipment on all the copies of Shipping Bill, original and duplicate copies of AR-4 form and returns the Export Promotion copy, a copy of Drawback Shipping Bill and duplicate AR-4 to the Forwarding Agent. The latter then presents the Mate Receipt to the Shipping Company and requests it to issue the Bill of Lading (2/3 negotiable and a few non-negotiable copies as required).

Exports by land/river are effected either by lorry transport or rail or in boats usually to three countries only i.e. Bangladesh, Pakistan and Nepal. Exports to Bhutan and Nepal though made by land route are not considered as exports except in specified circumstances. The procedure to export by land/river is by and large the same as outlined for shipment by sea or air except that the goods must pass through the specified Border (Customs) Check posts. Instead of Shipping Bill, Bill of Export is used which is also of four types like shipping bill.

Separate procedure is prescribed for export of containerised freight from Container Freight Stations/Internal Container Depots.

IV. Other Documents

Other important documents used in export business are briefly explained as under:

Commercial Invoice

It is one of the most important document issued by the seller in the standardised format. The invoice is usually made out for the full realisable amount of goods as per trade term, the exception being the undrawn balance which is shown as a deduction from the full amount.

If the export documents are drawn under L/C, unless otherwise stated in L/C, commercial invoice must be made out in the name of the applicant for the credit and the description of the goods in the commercial invoice must correspond with the description in the credit. Similarly, it should be noted that unless otherwise stipulated in the credit, banks may refuse commercial invoice issued for amount in excess of the amount permitted by the credit.

The invoice should be strictly according to the contract of sale and should be on the paper of the seller and must be signed by him or by the person acting on his behalf.

Consular Invoice

Consular Invoice is a document required mainly by the Latin American countries like, Kenya, Uganda, Tanzania, Mauritius, New Zealand, Burma, Iraq, Australia, Fiji, Cyprus, Nigeria, Ghana, Zanzibar etc.. This invoice is most important document which needs to be submitted for certification to the Embassy of the Country concerned. The exporter has to pay to the Embassy concerned some fees for the certification of this invoice.

A consular invoice is required to be prepared in a prescribed format and it should be signed/certified by the consul of the importing country located in the country of export. The main purpose of a consular invoice is to enable the importer's country to collect accurate and authenticated information about the value, volume, quality, source etc. of the import for assessing import duties and for other statistical purposes. It helps the importer to get cleared the goods through the customs without any undue delay. The consular invoice forms are generally available at the importing country's consuls and is certified against payment of some fees.

Consular invoices should be made in multiple copies as per the buyer's requirements.

Customs Invoice

Countries like U.S.A., Canada etc. need custom's invoice. It is generally made out on a special form presented by the customs authorities of the importing country and helps for allowing entry of goods in the importing country at preferential tariff rates. The invoice forms are generally available at the consular office of the importing country and are required to be signed and witnessed after duly filling the same.

Legalised/Visaed Invoice

These are the invoices sworn for their genuineness by the seller as being correct before the appropriate consulate/chamber of commerce/ embassy as the case may be and they bear the stamp and authentication of the consulate/chamber of commerce/embassy as being in order. A nominal charge is collected by them from the seller for doing this. These invoices are required by some of the Latin American countries. There is no prescribed form of this invoice.

Certified Invoice

At times exporter is called upon to certify on the invoice that the goods are of particular origin or manufactured/packed at a particular place and in accordance with specific contract. When certificates as such appear on the invoice it is called as a certified invoice.

Bill of Exchange/Draft

A bill of exchange also known as draft contains an order from the creditor to the debtor to pay a specified amount to a person mentioned therein. The maker of a bill is called the "drawer", the person who is directed to pay is called the "drawee". The person who is entitled to receive payment is called the "payee".

When it is drawn on a foreign firm it is termed as a foreign draft or bill of exchange. It is prepared either in an international currency or Indian rupees depending on the terms of contract. Accordingly, the bill is known by the name of currency in which it is drawn. For example, a bill drawn in US dollars is known a 'Dollar Bill' and when prepared in rupees, being termed as 'Rupees Bill'.

When the goods are shipped by sea, the bills are drawn in sets and two sets of documents including drafts are mailed to the foreign correspondent through an authorised dealer for presentation to the drawee (importer). Each one bears a reference to the other.

A bill of exchange or draft is of two types: (i) 'Sight Draft' or 'Draft at Sight' and (ii) Usance Draft or Usance Bill.

When the drawer i.e. exporter expects the drawee i.e. importer to make payment immediately after the draft presented to him, it is called a 'Sight Draft'. Unless and until the draft is retired, the negotiating/collecting bank does not hand over the shipping documents and the buyer cannot take delivery of goods.

Where the exporter has agreed to give credit to the foreign buyer, he draws a 'Usance Bill' i.e. draft is drawn for payment at a date later than the date of presentation. A draft may be drawn according to the period of credit such as 30 days sight, 60 days sight and so on, implying thereby, that the drawee i.e. importer is to retire the draft 30 days or 60 days or as the case may be, after it is presented to the drawee who will retire it by writing upon it "Accepted' with his signature and date. Thereafter, the documents are handed over to him enabling him to take the delivery of goods.

As there is no aligned document for draft, the same can be prepared by the exporter in the usual format.

Packing List

It is a list showing details of goods contained in each parcel/shipment. It shows item-by-item the contents of the containers or parcels shipped to enable the buyer/receiver of the shipment to check the shipment Packing list has to be prepared in the aligned document form.

Certificate of Inspection

Inspection certificate, indicating that goods have been inspected before shipment is needed under some contracts or by some countries. This certificate is generally required to be issued by one of the authorised independent inspection agencies/surveyors in the exporter's country. The certificate is issued in the aligned document form.

Black List Certificate

This is to certify that the ship/aircraft carrying the goods has not touched a particular country on its journey or that the goods are not of a particular country. This certificate is usually called for where countries have strained political relations with another.

Weight Note

This document is used to confirm that the packets/bales etc. are of a particular weight and not more than the stipulated weight as per contract. It may at times give the gross weight and net weight of the whole consignment.

Manufacturer's/Supplier's Quality/Inspection Certificate

This is a certificate to the effect that the goods which have been manufactured/supplied are as per the requirement of the contract of sale.

GSP Certificate/Certificate of Origin

The EEC member Countries have adopted the Generalised System of Preferences. Under GSP, manufacturers and semi-manufacturers from developing countries including India will be entitled to a concessional rate of import duty in these countries.

The Govt. of India has authorised the Export Inspection Council of India and its various agencies to issue the Certificate of Origin. The Export Promotion Offices at Bombay, Calcutta, Madras and Cochin, FIEO, Chambers of Commerce and the heads of the licensing offices have also been authorised to issue the Certificate of Origin.

Languages Certificate

Importers in the European Economic Community Countries require a Languages Certificate along with the GSP Certificate in respect of handloom cotton fabrics classifiable under NEMEX Code 55.09. Indian exporters should apply for this certificate simultaneously or separately with the GSP Certificate and application for pre-shipment inspection. The Language Certificate is issued in quadruplicate, three copies of which are given to the exporter. He should transmit one copy to his overseas importer, along with the documents for realisation of export proceeds.

The Languages Certificate is issued by the Textile Committee against a small fee.

Manufacturer's Certificate

In addition to the Certificate of Origin, some countries require a manufacturer's certificate to the effect that goods shipped have actually been manufactured and are available.

Certificate of Chemical Analysis

To ensure that the quality and grade of items like metallic ores, pigments, etc. is the same as specified in the sale contract, importers may require the exporters to send a certificate of chemical analysis from a recognised analyst.

Certificate of Shipment

Certificate of shipping agent that a certain lot of goods have been shipped.

Health/Veterinary /Sanitary Certificates

When the goods that are exported are foodstuffs, marine products, hide, livestock etc.. usually depending upon the goods which are being imported, a certificate from the health/veterinary/sanitary authorities is called for by the overseas buyers or their custom department. This is because the importing country desires to know if the goods are fit for human consumption and are free from any decease which can later on create a problem.

Certificate of Conditioning

Certificate issued by a competent office in which, on the basis of the ascertained humidity factor, the dry weight of wool or, silk is reckoned and certified.

Antiquity Certificate

This certificate is issued by the Archaeological Survey of India in the case of antiques.

Certificate of Measurement

Freight can be charged either on the basis of weight or measurement. When it is charged on weight basis, the weight declared by exporter is accepted. However, certificate of measurement from the Indian Chamber of Commerce or any other approved organisation may be obtained by the exporter and given to the shipping company for calculation of necessary freight. This certificate contains the name of vessel, the port of destination, description of goods, quantity, length, breadth, depth etc. of packages.

Transhipment Bill

This document is used for goods imported into a customs port/airport intended for transhipment.

Transhipment Permit

The Transhipment Permit is the permission for transhipment of goods from the vessel on which the same are hooked originally to another for export.

Shipping Order

Shipping Order is issued by the Shipping (Conference) Line intimating the exporter about the reservation of space of shipment of cargo through a particular vessel from a specified port and on a specified date.

Cart/Lorry Ticket

This ticket is prepared for admittance of cargo through the port gate. This is also known as 'Vehicle Ticket or Gate Pass'. This includes the details of export cargo i.e. Shipper's name, Cart/Lorry number, marks on packages, quantity and description.

Shut Out Advice

It is a statement of packages shut out by a ship and is prepared by the shed concerned and sent to the exporter showing the particulars of packages, for disposal arrangement.

Short Shipment Form

Short shipment form is an application to the customs authorities at port advising the short shipment of goods and for claiming the return of the duty and/ or cess paid on such short shipping goods.

Shipping Advice

A shipping advice is used to inform the overseas customer about the shipment of goods. The shipping advice is prepared in aligned document. The exporter only advises his importer about the invoice number, bill of lading/ airway bill number and date, name of the vessel with date, the port of export, description of goods and quantity and the date of sailing of the vessels.

Preparing Documents under The Aligned Documentation System

The Aligned Documentation System (ADS), based on the UN layout key, is a methodology of creating information on a set of standardised forms printed on paper of the same size and in such a way that items of identical information occupy the same position on each form.

Under this system the documents are aligned to one another in a manner that the common items of information are given the same relative slots in each of the documents. This enables to prepare one 'Master Document' embodying the information common to all documents included in the aligned system, and to zerox all the aligned documents from the same Master Document with the help of suitable masking and reproduction technique. The mask consists of a transparent polyester film with white opaque patches to blank out such information as is not required in a particular document. Separate mask is required for each document. Any information which is specific to a document can either be preprinted or added as and when required.

For the purpose of aligned documentation system documents have been classified as Commercial Documents and Regulatory Documents. Commercial documents are those which by customs of trade are required for effecting physical transfer of goods and their title from the exporter to the importer and the realisation of export sale proceeds. Out of the 16 commercial documents in the export documentation framework as many as 14 have been standardised and aligned to one another. These are proforma invoice, commercial invoice, packing list, shipping istructions, intimation for inspection, certificate of inspection of quality control, insurance declaration certificate of insurance mate receipt, bill of lading/ combined transport document application for certificate of origin, certificate of origin shipment advice and letter to the bank for Collection/Negotiation of documents. As per govt indications all documents will have single common number and it would be PAN.

Regulatory preshipment export documents are those which have been prescribed by different Govt Deptts /bodies in compliance of the requirements of various rules and regulations under relevant laws governing export trade such as export inspection, foreign exchange regulation, export trade control, customs etc. Out of 9 regulatory documents four have been standardised and aligned. These are (i) shipping bill/bill of export, (ii) exchange control declaration, (GR Form), (iii) export application dock challan/port trust copy of shipping bill and (iv) receipt for payment of port charges.

Following points must be noted carefully, while preparing the export documents under the new system:

General

1. The export documents shall be prepared on pre-printed forms available in the market and/or provided by the concerned authority. Pre-printed shipping bills will be provided by Freight Forwarders/ Customs House Agents.
2. The documents must only be typewritten to ensure clarity and legibility.
3. The new system is amendable to photocopy and computerisation. Photocopy can be done by using the Master Document-1 or the appropriate Master Document II, as the case may be. However use of a photocopier is not a must. Documents can also be prepared manually. In that case the exporters shall not get the benefits of Aligned Documentation System.
4. The documents can also be prepared with the help of a computer Software package has been developed by the Indian Institute of Foreign Trade, New Delhi and National Informatic Centre, New Delhi. However, the sizes and layout of each form shall be strictly as prescribed.
5. The exporters will have to strictly adhere to the prescribed size layout and box wise space.
6. Exporters who do not have access to computer or photocopier can type out the relevant data in the appropriate boxes.

16

Shipping and Customs Clearance of the Goods

Shipping the Goods

The following steps are involved in the shipment of goods :

1. Submitting the documents to the forwarding agent and indicating to him the steamer/airline. Simultaneously space has to be booked on the steamer/airline after negotiating freight with them as discount is generally given on amount of freight.
2. Based on the documents submitted by you the forwarding agent prepares the Shipping Bill/Bill of Export and gets it passed by the Customs Authorities.
3. Moving the goods in the Docks/Air Cargo Complex. For in house stuffing the goods are offered for inspection within factory premises.
4. Offering the goods for Customs examination. The Customs official (Appraiser) examines the goods and certifies the same for loading.
5. Handing over the cargo/container to Port Authorities/Shipping Company/Airline Company for loading on the steamer/aircraft.
6. Certificate on the GR form by the Customs and handling over the duplicate copy of the same to the forwarding agent. The consignment is now said to be out of charge.
7. Once the goods are loaded you should demand a Bill of Lading/ Airway Bill, GR form, Export Promotion copy of the Shipping Bill, Freight Certificate etc.
8. Small consignments (approx upto 70 kgs) can be shipped by Air Post Parcel. Shipments are permitted by Sea Post Parcel as well.

If necessary you should avail the facility of container services provided by some companies Containerisation is a method of distributing merchandise in a unitized form thereby permitting an intermodal transport system providing a possible combination of rail, road, canal and maritime transport.

For the purpose of shipment of goods, selection of a good freight forwarding agent is very important. While selecting a freight forwarding agent, you should take into account various factors like location, facilities, rates, service flexibility and efficiency of the agent.

After the goods have been shipped you should send Shipment Advice in aligned format to the importer intimating the date of shipment of the consignment by a named vessel and its expected time of arrival at the destination port. Where the goods are sent by air the shipment advice should be faxed to the importer.

Customs Clearance of Exports by Air

The phases involved in the customs clearance of export cargo by air are the same as for customs clearance of export cargo going by ship, which has already been discussed in the preceding Chapter.

However, suitable adjustments have been made in these phases to suit the requirements of expeditious movement of cargo by air. These are mentioned below :

(i) Actual booking by the flight concerned is done in advance. Even Airway Bill is obtained before arrival of the flight.

(ii) All the documents required for customs clearance i.e. the Shipping Bill, the appropriate type, and all the supporting documents as required in connection with the shipment by a vessel are to be brought along with the cargo for which booking has already been done. The documents are first submitted to the section meant for checking them at the Air Cargo complex. After the documents have been checked and physical examination order has been given, physical examination is conducted in quick succession.

(iii) Physical examination is conducted on a much larger scale in respect of export by air, as compared to export by vessel i.e. 50 to 25 per cent of the total in respect of air cargo, as against 1 to 2 per cent of the total in respect of cargo moving by vessel. Each packet is to be passed for shipment — whether examined and passed for shipment or passed for shipment.

(iv) The export cargo examined and passed for shipment is kept under the charge of Customs in the control of GROUND HANDLING AUTHORITIES.

Usually some cooling period is observed. 24 to 48 hrs. before the cargo is to be loaded on board the aircraft.

(v) Before arrival of the flight Export General Manifest (EGM) whether provisional or final, is to be prepared by the airline concerned and is to be handed over to the Customs Authority.

(vi) With the help of EGM, goods are to be moved from the storage under Customs charge to the place where from they are to be moved alongside the aircraft for being loaded on board.

(vii) In the case of air flights, no entry inward permit is required for each flight. There is standing facility granted to the airline concerned for landing and taking off specified flight. Hence, non-rotation number is allotted in advance. This number is allotted by the station-officer on duty when the flight has landed.

(viii) The Customs Officer who has to supervise the loading operation with reference to the EGM has to write Rotation Number on the Shipping Bill — the copies available at that stage and the EGM.

(ix) Unlike the practice followed in the case of ship, there is no arrangement for associating a Preventive Officer right from the stage when entry inward permit is granted. The Customs Officer in-charge of the duty routine for the period when the flights are scheduled to land, assigns the task of supervision of unloading and loading operation to customs official on duty.

(x) After the loading of the cargo on board the aircraft, the captain does not issue Mate's Receipt. He signs the Duplicate and Triplicate copy of the Shipping Bill against contents received. He may initial the copy of the Shipping Bill.

This flexibility is provided in keeping with requirement of air-cargo's expeditious movement.

(xi) In case of export by air, every cargo is checked for non-hazardous and non–dangerous cargo. Few items like special chemicals are not allowed by customs for export by air.

Customs Clearance of Post Parcel

Post parcels can be sent from any part of the country even without completing customs clearance before the booking of the parcel. As such, employment of customs house agent can be easily dispensed with. However, it should not be construed that the post parcel can be despatched to foreign destinations without customs check. In fact the booking post office cannot prepare the final bag for destination. The parcel has to be routed through the foreign post office having the destination within its jurisdiction, where customs check and clearance are arranged. At each foreign post office there are two wings — Customs Wing and Postal Wing. The latter has to get customs examined parcels received from different post offices of the country for despatch to foreign destinations.

In the case of post parcel there is no Shipping Bill required. Instead a Customs Declaration Form, prescribed by the Universal Postal Union (UPU) — an international apex body coordinating activities of national postal administration to facilitate movement of postal articles among different countries of the world is required. This document, popularly known by its code number CP2/CP3 has to be prepared in quadruplicate duly signed by the sender. One copy is to be pasted on the parcel and two copies are to be placed inside the parcel alongwith two copies of Invoice. One copy is to be retained by the sender for record and future reference.

Another document prescribed by the Universal Postal Union (UPU) is the Despatch Note, popularly known by its code number, CP2. It has to be filled in by the sender to specify the action to be taken by the postal authority at destination if the address is not traceable or the addressee refuses to accept the parcel. It has to be safely tagged to the parcel.

The other prescriptions of the UPU are regarding the minimum and maximum sizes of the parcel and its maximum weight.

Minimum size: Total surface area not to be less than 140 mm X 90 mm.

Maximum size: Lengthwise not more than 1.05 M. Measurement of any other side of circumference 0.9M./2.00M — the two taken together

Maximum Weight: 10 kg for most destinations. 20 kg for some destinations.

Computerised Processing of Export Documents

In order to ensure increased automation in the processing of import and export documentation for expeditious clearance of import and export Cargo through the Air Cargo Unit at the IGI Airport. Delhi Customs has introduced electronic processing of export documents relating to export of goods w.e.f. 1.11.1996. The New Delhi Customs have issued Public Notice No. 56/96 dt. 26.10.1996. Later on Public Notice Nos. 42/98 dt. 3.9.1998, 40/98 dt. 21.9.1998 and 3/99 dt. 28.1.1999 have also been issued in this regard. After its success at Air Cargo Complex of Delhi Customs House, the Indian Customs EDI system has been extended to Mumbai and ICD Tughlakabad and is implemented in a phased manner to cover other Customs Houses.

17

Submitting Documents to Bank for Purchase/ Collection/ Negotiation under L/C

Documentary Collection of Export Bills — Legal Requirements

As slated earlier in this Book, it is obligatory for you that after shipping the goods, you must hand over the relative documents within 21 days of shipment to your bank for onward despatch to the overseas correspondent bank who will arrange payment of the same to your banker. Thus, the legal requirement is that the payment against exports should be realised through an authorised dealer in foreign exchange within six months of date of shipment (12 months in case of status holder exporters). Status holders have also been permitted to despatch shipping documents direct to the consignee.

Payment for export in certain cases

Payment for export may also be received by the exporter as under, namely:

(i) The amount representing the full export value of the goods exported shall be received through an authorised dealer in the manner specified in the Foreign Exchange Management (Manner of Receipt & Payment) Regulations, 2000 notified vide Notification No. FEMA 14/2000-RB, dated 3rd May, 2000.

(ii) Payment for export may also be received by the exporter in the following manner:

(a) In the form of bank draft, pay order, banker's or personal cheques.

(b) Foreign currency notes/foreign currency travellers' cheques from the buyer during his visit to India.

(c) Payment out of funds held in the FCNR/NRE account maintained by the buyer.

(d) Through International Credit Cards. When payment, in respect of goods sold to overseas buyers during their visits is received in this manner the GR/SDF (duplicate) should be released by the authorised dealers only on receipt of funds in their Nostro account or on production of a certificate by the exporter from the Credit Card servicing bank in India to the effect that it has received the equivalent amount in foreign exchange, if the authorised dealer concerned is not the Credit Card servicing bank. ADs may also receive payment for exports made out of India by debit to the credit card of an importer where the reimbursement from the card issuing bank/organisation will be received in foreign exchange.

(e) All transactions between a person resident in India and a person resident in Nepal may be settled in Rupees. However, in case of export of goods to Nepal, where an importer resident in Nepal has been permitted by the Nepal Rashtra Bank to make payment in free foreign exchange, such payments shall be routed through the ACU mechanism.

Once the goods are despatched to foreign destination whether by land, sea or post, the exporter should approach his bank (authorised dealer in foreign exchange) with a formal letter requesting the bank to realise the Export Bills from the overseas buyer.

The letter of request to the bank has to be in the aligned form called Letter to Bank.

Negotiation/Collection through Banks

It is pertinent to note that documents are handed over to the bank with a request either to negotiate the documents if the same are drawn under the letter of credit or to purchase the documents where the bank has granted pre-shipment facility to the exporter or has sanctioned post-shipment limit for purchase of export bills or to collect the bills with or without any advance against the security of these bills.

Authorised dealers may permit the Status Holder Exporters to despatch the export documents direct to the consignees outside India subject to the conditions that (a) the export proceeds are repatriated through the authorised dealer named in the GR form and (b) the duplicate copy of the GR form is submitted to the authorised dealer for monitoring purposes, by the exporters within 21 days of the date of shipment of export.

Besides, number of other instructions are required to be given to the banker handling the documents.

Documents Required

Where the documents are drawn under a letter of credit, the letter to the bank should be enclosed with the documents as prescribed in the letter of credit, if any or stipulated in the export order or such documents which enable the buyer to take delivery of goods and the documents required by the exporter to claim export assistance, if any. Following documents are generally required by bank to negotiate or collect necessary payment from abroad and by the exporter:

(i) Bills of exchange

(ii) Full set of Bill of Lading/Airway Bill (all negotiable copies plus one non-negotiable copy) /Post Parcel Receipt/Combined Transport Document, as the case may be.

(iii) Commercial invoice including one copy duly certified by the Customs. The number of copies should be the same as specified by the buyer plus two additional copies. Invoice not certified by the Customs may also be acceptable, in cases where the particulars furnished in the GR form agree with those indicated in the copy of invoice produced by the exporter and the value of the invoice agrees with the value of goods passed for shipment by Customs. However, Customs Certified invoice is necessary where the RBI has specifically stipulated such a requirement viz., for countersigning GR form for export of precious stones and jewellery by air.

(iv) Original letter of credit, if any.

(v) Customs invoice/Consular invoice.

(vi) Certificate of origin, GSP/APR Certificate, etc.

(vii) Insurance policy/certificate with complete set. (brokers cover note should not be sent).

(viii) Packing list.

(ix) Foreign exchange declaration forms i.e. GR/PP Forms.

(x) Bank certificate of export realisation in the prescribed form (in triplicate).

(xi) Other documents like certificate of analysis/inspection certificate. declaration to ECGC, etc.

Discrepancies in Documents — To be Avoided

As documentary credit operations cover only documents and not goods it is of utmost importance that the beneficiary tenders documents in conformity with the terms of credit. Discrepancies, howsoever, negligible result in nullification of the opening bank's engagement to pay. Discrepant documents can be paid only if the buyer agrees to accept them, but the seller runs a great risk in time of recession when slight default in the documents can result in their total rejection by the buyer. Therefore, importance of complying with the terms of credit cannot be over-emphasised. For full details regarding tendering and negotiation of documents under L/C please refer to chapter 'Special Care for Negotiating Documents under Letter of Credit'.

Time Limit

It is obligatory for the exporters to submit the shipping documents to an authorised dealer within 21 days of the date of shipment of goods.

The authorised dealers may accept the documents after the prescribed period of 21 days, provided they are satisfied that the delay has been on account of reasons beyond the control of exporter.

Checklist for Exporters at the time of Submitting Documents to Authorised Dealers for Negotiation or Collection of Export Bills

1. It is obligatory that all shipping documents must be routed only through an authorised dealer except where Reserve Bank of India has allowed despatch of shipping documents direct to the consignees by authorised dealers/exporters provided (i) advance remittance for the full value of the consignment has already been received or an irrevocable letter of credit covering the full export value has been received or the authorised dealer is satisfied on the basis of the standing and track record of the exporter and the arrangements made for realisation of export proceeds, that he could do so, (ii) the exporter is a Status Holder as per the EXIM Policy of the Govt. of India.
2. It should be ensured that the airway bill is drawn in favour of overseas bank for self (exporters) unless (i) an advance payment has been received from the buyer or an irrevocable letter of credit has been opened, (ii) the exporter is a status holder as per the EXIM Policy of the Govt. of India.
3. Exporters cannot accept payments directly from their overseas buyers. However, exporters are permitted by the Reserve Bank of India to accept demand draft, banker's cheques and pay orders etc. directly from their overseas buyers without any monetary limit.
4. Usuance bills, should not be drawn for payment 6 months after

sight, since this will result in realisation of export proceeds beyond the prescribed period.

5. Amount for which bill is drawn should tally with the amount declared on GR forms, etc.
6. Invoices should also be raised for the same amount as declared on GR, etc. forms. If any reduction, other than towards trade discount is shown, Reserve Bank of India's approval should be obtained.
7. For allowing trade discount from the invoice value, exporters should have declared the same on GR etc. forms at the time of shipment and the Customs authorities should have accepted the same.
8. If the export has been made on FOB basis where the freight is to the account of overseas buyers and the exporters have paid the Freight amount, the freight amount should be included in the invoice for recovery from overseas buyers.
9. In cases of bills involving part drawings i.e. where undrawn balances will be paid by overseas buyer only after arrival of goods and inspection, the exporter should furnish an undertaking on the duplicate of GR/SDF/PP that he will surrenders/account for the balance proceeds of the shipment within the prescribed period for realisation.
10. If the exporter wants to transfer the goods to some other buyer, the authorised dealers can themselves (i.e. without Reserve Bank of India approval) draw fresh bill of exchange on the new buyer provided the terms of export contract (i.e. outright or consignment sale) are the same, reduction in value, if any, involved does not exceed 10% and realisation of export proceeds is not delayed beyond the period of six months from the date of shipment.
11. In case of loss of the duplicate copy of the forms after they are approved by the Customs, fresh set of forms can be used provided the printed number on the fresh set of forms is scored off and the number of lost form is prominently written on the duplicate copy of the fresh set. The original of fresh set can be destroyed.
12. Shipping documents should be presented to authorised dealer within 21 days from the date of shipment. If presented after 21 days, authorised dealers will accept the documents if explanation given by exporter with supporting documentary evidence for the delay in submission of documents is satisfactory.
13. In case of reimport of exported goods due to rejection by overseas buyer, exporter should arrange for the same on freight to pay in rupees in India. If freight has to be paid in free foreign exchange, prior approval of Reserve Bank of India should be obtained.

18

Special Care for Negotiating Documents under L/C

Mechanism of a Letter of Credit

A letter of credit is a very common and familiar instrument in settling payments between the buyer and the seller. Buyers and sellers negotiate for purchase and sale of goods, sellers demanding cash or the buyer's banker's letter of credit as guarantee for payment before they undertake shipment. A letter of credit reinforces the buyer's integrity by adding to it his banker's undertaking. A documentary credit is a signed instrument embodying an undertaking by the banker of a buyer to pay his seller a certain sum of money on presentation of documents evidencing shipment of specified goods and subject to compliance with the stipulated terms and conditions. In order to bring uniformity in matters pertaining to documentary credits, the International Chamber of Commerce (ICC) have published a set of Rules (called UCPDC), wherein a documentary credit has been defined as any arrangement, however, named or described, whereby a bank (the issuing bank) acting at the request and on the instructions of a customer (the applicant for the credit) or on its own behalf is to make payment to or to the order of a third party (the beneficiary) or to accept and pay bills of exchange drawn by the beneficiary: authorises another bank to effect such payment or to accept and pay such bills of exchange or authorises another bank to negotiate against stipulated documents and compliance with stipulated terms and conditions. Banks handling documents under a credit are guided by the UCPDC Rules.

A documentary credit generally requires that drafts drawn thereunder (representing only claim) must be accompanied by other documents as stipulated therein, giving title to the goods, providing protection against loss or damage to the goods, and furnishing other information and particulars. Bills of Lading, Marine Insurance Policies or Certificates, Commercial

Invoice, Customs Invoice, Certificate of Origin, Weight List, Packing List, Inspection Certificate, Certificate of Analysis and/or other documents as may be stipulated, are such documents.

When a person who ships goods in reliance on a letter of credit issued by a bank, does so in exact compliance with its terms, the bank concerned is bound to honour his draft if drawn and presented in strict accord with the credit as opened. The paying or the confirming bank can claim indemnity if the terms and conditions of the credit are strictly observed, for which it must examine all the documents with care.

The parties to a Letter of Credit are the importer or the opener, the opening bank, the advising bank, the negotiating bank (also known as paying bank), the confirming bank (if the advising bank adds its confirmation to the credit at the request of the opening bank) and the beneficiary or the exporter.

Uniform Customs and Practice for Documentary Credit

In the course of time, a number of practices, expressions and terms have evolved between banks dealing with documentary credits. To ensure uniformity of interpretation in international trade, the International Chamber of Commerce in Paris has worked out the "Uniform Customs and Practice for Documentary Credits". These have been revised and brought up to date several times in the past. They are now applied by the banks in nearly all countries. The latest in the line of revisions is the UCP 500 (w.e.f. January 1, 1994) which updates and consolidates the previous UCP 400.

The new UCPDC has since been subscribed to by India.

Revocable or Irrevocable Letters of Credit

Basically, the credits are either (i) revocable or (ii) irrevocable.

All credits should, therefore, indicate whether they are revocable or irrevocable, but in the absence of any indication, the credit will be treated as irrevocable as per Article 6 (c) of UCP 500. Under UCP 400 the position was just the opposite i.e., in the absence of any indication, the Credit was deemed to be revocable.

The inherent weakness of revocable credit is that it may be cancelled or modified without prior notice by the issuing banker to the beneficiary. However, the opening bank is responsible for any operation on the revocable credit effected prior to the receipt by the negotiating bank of any cancellation or modification advice.

An irrevocable letter of credit does not suffer from such disadvantage and it is, therefore, widely accepted.

Confirmed Credit

If an irrevocable credit is opened by a bank in the buyer's country, the seller may require the credit to be confirmed by a bank in his own country as he may be unaware of the standing of the opening bank, or may otherwise like to ask for additional protection of his interest. In such cases, the opening bank requests its correspondent in the seller's country to add its confirmation which in effect means that the confirming bank undertakes the liability to honour the seller's drafts drawn under the credit. It bcars an unequivocal undertaking that drafts conforming to the terms of the credit will be honoured notwithstanding any charge in the position between the person or the bank opening the credit and the bank confirming the same. It ensures double protection to the seller since it is already irrevocable on the pan of the opening bank and additionally on the pan of the confirming bank in his own country. Although a confirmed letter of credit is irrevocable an irrevocable credit is not necessarily a confirmed one.

An unconfirmed credit may be a credit not even confirmed by the opening bank and if so, it is in fact a revocable credit. It is normally, however, a credit which is irrevocable on the pan of the opening bank but not confirmed by the advising bank in the seller's (beneficiary) country.

Transferable Credit

A letter of credit is not a negotiable instrument and is not transferable by delivery or endorsement except under the express authority of the opener. When business is transacted through a middleman, credits are sometimes marked transferable. This enables the middleman, in whose favour the original credit is issued, to ask for a transfer of the credit to another party who may be manufacturer or actual supplier. Transferable, assignable and transmissible are terms which normally convey the same meaning.

A transferable credit should be clearly designated as 'transferable' by the opening bank which will of course be acting on the instructions of the opener (buyer). A transferable credit permitting part shipments may be 'divisible' in which case the amount of the credit can be split in favour of more than one beneficiary against separate shipments.

With or Without Recourse Credit

If a credit is marked 'without recourse', no recourse can be had against the drawer. The addition of the words 'without recourse' to the seller's drafts (bills of exchange) would negative his liability which normally attaches to the drawer of a bill of exchange, as in case of, with recourse' or in the absence of any specific mention of the words 'without recourse'.

Revolving Letter of Credit

Such a credit stipulates automatic restoration of the amount already drawn (under the credit) — as soon as the bills are paid, thus obviating the necessity of opening a fresh credit for each despatch/shipment. A revolving credit may revolve with reference to either its amount or validity period, and if the latter, it may be either cumulative or non-cumulative.

There may be three types of revolving credits as commonly used: (a) credit providing for the drawing of a fixed amount by one draft at any one time, (b) credit under which a limit is placed on the drawings, outstanding at any one time, and (c) credit stipulating that the drawings are limited to an agreed total figure within a specified period (say, upto a limit of Rs. 10,000/- in any one month).

Transit Credit

It is issued in one foreign country with the beneficiary in another but is advised through and usually confirmed by a bank in London.

Back to Back Credit

Such credits are also called countervailing credits. These are usually opened to finance an intermediary who is short of capital but is not willing to divulge to his overseas buyer the name of the actual supplier. A banker issues such a credit in favour of the actual supplier on the strength of a credit established by the overseas buyer in favour of the intermediary. A back-to-back credit naturally stipulates an earlier validity date and a smaller amount to enable the beneficiary (intermediary) to replace the actual supplier's invoice by his own and earn a margin of profit. While granting such facilities, a banker requires to ensure itself that the documents to be submitted by the actual supplier and the substituted ones conform precisely to the terms of the credit established by the overseas buyer.

The Sight Credit

The amount is payable as soon as the prescribed documents have been presented and the bank has checked them. So the proceeds are normally at the immediate disposal of the beneficiary.

In some cases (e.g. foreign currencies) a few days may pass between presentation of the documents and actual transfer of the funds. As a rule, it is the time required by the banks to remit the amount of the credit.

In the case of unconfirmed credits, situations can arise where the advising bank delays payment to the beneficiary until it has received the amount specified by the documents from the issuing bank.

The Credit Available Against Time Drafts (Usance Credit)

In addition to presenting the documents, the beneficiary is required to draw a time draft on a specific bank (issuing, advising, or a third bank). After the documents have been found to be in order, the exporter receives back the draft after it has been accepted by the drawee bank, if he so wishes.

It is possible to discount this bank acceptance. So the draft can be cashed in immediately by the seller, while the buyer will be charged with the draft amount only upon maturity.

The Deferred Payment Credit

The payment is not initiated immediately upon presentation of the documents, but only after a period of time specified in the credit.

A deferred payment credit allows the buyer a grace period, and ensures the seller that payment will be made on the due date.

Acceptance Credit

When a credit stipulates that drafts are to be drawn at a certain usance i.e., payable after a certain number of days/months after sight, it is regarded as an acceptance credit, the undertaking to accept, guaranteeing payment of such a draft at maturity being given by a bank. A bank may grant this facility-to an exporter whereby it agrees to accept bills drawn by him against specific shipment of goods. The bills drawn on the overseas buyers together with the documents of title, are handed to the bank and at the same time an additional bill is drawn on the bank itself under the acceptance credit granted by it.

Anticipatory Credits

Under these credits the seller is assisted by receiving an advance before acquiring goods or despatching them. Under this, there are RED CLAUSE and GREEN CLAUSE credits. Red Clause Credits bear a clause in RED authorising negotiating bank to make an advance to the seller prior to shipment and tender of documents. The advance will be liquidated from the proceeds of the bill negotiated. This advance is granted against exporters undertaking to tender documents in terms of credit within the validity. Green clause credits in addition to permitting preshipment advance also entail sorting of goods in the name of the bank, Green clauses are extensively used in Australian wool credits.

Credits Available by Instalments

These credits specify shipments and/or drawing by instalments stipulating specified period for each instalment of shipment and/or drawings. In case any instalment of shipment is missed, credit will not be available for that and the subsequent instalments except when credits permit such lapse.

Restricted and Unrestricted Credits

Credits which do not specify any particular bank who is authorised to negotiate, etc. are unrestricted or open or general credits. If a specified bank is designated to pay, accept or negotiate the credit is termed as restricted or special.

Accepting a Letter of Credit

When the letter of credit is received the proper verification and study of the same by the exporter is of utmost importance. The points to note are as under:

Revocable or Irrevocable Letter of Credit. It is highly dangerous to get a revocable letter of credit in export trade as the name itself suggests the party opening the letter of credit in export trade can revoke the same at any time. It might be revoked before the goods are produced by the manufacturer or seller procuring the goods or before the goods are despatched to the place of destination or after the goods are despatched or when the goods are in transit or when the goods arrived at the destination. Hence, it is always wise to ask for an irrevocable letter of credit to avoid all the risk in the export trade.

Name of the beneficiary and address. The next important factor is that the name and address of the exporter should be correctly mentioned on the letter of credit. Even a slight variation in the name of the exporter or exporting company or address may lead to undesired results in export trade where the buyer may reject the goods after goods reach the destination on the plea that the goods have not been exported by the company to whom he had placed the order or letter of credit opened. The rejection may be genuine or a mischief to gain time or to get the goods free of payment. Hence, utmost care should be taken to see that letter of credit contains the correct name of the business and address. Sometimes, it may so happen that the letter of credit may contain the address of the Registered Office of the Company from where the agreements and contracts conclude, but the goods may be despatched by the factory and the factory address will obviously be printed on the documents prepared at the time of despatch of goods like Invoice. Bill of Lading, Insurance Policy, G.R. Form, Certificate of Origin etc., and may be vice-versa.

Similarly, where a branch is involved, it may also lead to rejection of goods by the buyer.

Whether the letter of credit is transferable or not: If the letter of credit is transferable then the transfer by the bank has to take place correctly on the letter of credit in favour of the seller.

Other clauses and terms and conditions of letter of credit to be watched are:

(i) Expiry date of letter of credit. If the expiry date is not appearing on the letter of credit, the last date for negotiation of documents should be considered as the expiry date of the letter of credit. The last date of negotiation should be clearly mentioned and should give you enough time to submit documents.

(ii) Value of the letter of credit should cover the full value of goods ordered and currency as per the quotation.

(iii) Correct quality and quantity of goods quoted and ordered should appear on the letter of credit.

(iv) Other terms and conditions like:

(a) Shipping particulars. The letter of credit may sometimes contain that the partial shipment and transhipments during the transit are not permitted. If this is not feasible then the exporter should ask for amendment to the letter of credit before taking any further action.

(b) Legalised invoice. The letter of credit may require a legalised invoice which means that the Embassy of the particular country of destination where the buyer resides should discharge the invoice. The Embassy might have their own norms which they would like to follow before discharging the invoice like the inspection of goods before packing etc.

(c) Consular invoice. The letter of credit may require a consular invoice prepared by the consulate of that particular country to which the goods are being despatched and the consular invoice should be duly signed by the consul.

(d) Customs invoice. The invoice of the exporter should be certified by the customs authorities for having inspected the goods before loading into the ship or aircraft.

Local Confirmation of the Letter of Credit

One should know the difference between having simply a letter of credit only and having a letter of credit from a recognised bank on whom one should have faith. Bank should be sound and should be in a position to honour the letter of credit on due date. In such circumstance the exporter will have two options:

(i) to seek alternative bank when the bank who has opened the letter of credit has not kept up its commitments earlier;

(ii) to have local confirmation of the letter of credit from the local bank or advisory bank or from the exporter's bank.

For turbulant markets like Russia and central Asia, internationa institutions offer confirmation through EBRD & IRDA. (EBRD-Europear Bank for Reconstitution and Development.)

Usually the confirming bank will take the responsibility on behalf o the letter of credit opening bank to honour the commitment and thi confirmation is on a separate letter and not on the letter of credit. Th confirming bank would like to see in such cases the original contract o sale as the letter of credit is only an offshoot of the original contract o sale.

Payment terms. One should also see that how the letter of credi opening bank proposes to pay and on what date and within reasonable time

Banks do not encourage letters of credit with too much of technica and excessive details. Exporters should ensure that by fulfilling any of th conditions the letter of credit would not violate the regulations prevailin in India, such as requiring the exporter to mail negotiable copies of bill o lading directly to the buyer or handing over by the exporter of a negotiabl copy of the bill of lading to the Master of Vessel, etc. If such condition are incorporated, necessary permission from the authorities should b obtained, just as they need to obtain export licence in respect of good which are subject to such licence. Failure to act in advance on suc conditions would entail unnecessary frustration if the exporters were t approach the bank to negotiate documents with the onerous conditions

The terms of the credit should not contradict one another and instruction contained therein should be precise and unambiguous, e.g. if letter of credi calls for shipment in one or more lots, it cannot prohibit part shipment i another place in the same letter of credit, or if the contract price is on FO terms, the credit cannot call for a hill of lading evidencing freight prepai amount under the letter of credit. If the exporter finds it difficult to understan any of the implications of the letter of credit, he should seek the assistanc of the bank.

After the exporter is satisfied that the letter of credit terms do nc in any way contradict the contract terms, and that the conditions in th letter of credit are such as could be conveniently fulfilled by the exporte he should go ahead with shipment within the validity period and obtai shipping documents drawn in the exact manner as called for in the lette of credit.

In letter of credit business, there is no distinction between a majo and a minor discrepancy, as for refusal of documents by credit openin bank. even a discrepancy which is of most minor nature from the point c view of the exporter is a sufficient ground. If the documents submitted ar not a perfect tender, the exporter runs the risk of the buyer using suc discrepancies as an excuse to delay or default payment for the documents. It should be remembered that buyers abroad often reject documents on very flimsy and extraneous grounds by pointing out even minor discrepancies.

It is of vital importance that the exporters should first ascertain the means, standing and business morality of the buyer by calling for credit reports from banks. For large-sized transactions, even contacts at personal level would be necessary to obtain complete information about the buyer.

Letter of Credit Checklist and Guide for Exporters

Detailed Checks to be made immediately after the Letter of Credit is received:

1. Does the type of Letter of Credit gives you the security of payment you wanted?
    - Irrevocable, but carrying only the undertaking of your customer's bank in his country.
    - Irrevocable and Confirmed, carrying the extra undertaking of a bank.

    or

    - Revocable, which can be cancelled, without your agreement at any time before documents have been accepted by the paying bank.
2. Is it payable when and where you wanted?
    - At sight,
    - or
    - at a later date
    - in India with little or no delay or
    - Abroad
3. Is the value of the Letter of Credit correct?
    - Any extra agreed costs, such as freight or inspection fees.
    - Unplanned variations — upto 5 per cent is sometimes allowed in quantity. The value of Letter of Credit must permit a corresponding drawing to be made.
    - Planned variations — "About" in a Letter of Credit permits upto a 10 per cent variation in whatever it refers to e.g. value or quantity and as specified.

4. Are the terms of delivery the same as you quoted? (e.g. FOB, CIF), and do they and the price match properly?
5. Are your company's name and address spelled correctly and shown exactly as on your invoice heading? And are the buyer's details similarly correct?
6. Are partial shipments prohibited?
7. Can you meet the expiry date and also present documents within transport document time limit? Allowing time for —
   - Production and packing
   - Inspection, if required
   - Shipment - check sailing frequencies
   - Chamber of Commerce and/or Consular work
   - Obtaining the inspection certificate
   - Assembling and checking documents
   - Presenting them to the bank.

   Note. That the last four stages must be completed within 21 days of the issue of the transport document in order to present documents in time — unless the Letter of Credit specifies a different period, which could be less.
8. Has any export or import licence been obtained ?
9. Are the goods described accurately enough to identify them properly and are the quantities and other units correct ?
10. Can you provide the transport document called for?
    - "On deck" shipment must be authorised if the goods are dangerous or for any reason cannot be stored under deck.
    - "Claused" transport documents must be permitted if your products legitimately attract such clauses — such as superficial rust on steel. The Letter of Credit must state which clauses are acceptable.
11. Can you obtain insurance cover for the risks specified?
12. Can you supply all other documents in the way called for ? Remembering that some — such as Inspection Certificate or Consular Documents — may take some time to arrange.
13. Are there any contradictions in the Letter of Credit such as requiring bills of lading for air freight?

14. If any of the above points fail to check out, prompt decision and action is necessary on.
    - Whether you can change your plans or paper-work to meet the requirement.
    - Whether to ask the customer to amend the Letter of Credit and who pays for the amendment.
    - Whether to let things stand and very possibly not be paid.

    If in doubt, consult your own bank and/or the paying bank for advice, but remember that only the buyer can authorise amendments or extensions.
15. If the Letter of Credit has been telexed or cabled — check that it provides details of the Letter of Credit that you can act on and is not just a pre advice.
16. Watch out for forgeries — rare but dangerous. Letter of Credit are normally sent through an advising bank. Any departure from this routine should be viewed with suspicion, for example if it comes to you direct from overseas.

When assembling documents for presentation to the bank —

1. Check that the documents match the Letter of Credit and ensure that,
    - You have the correct number of copies of each; they carry the information called for and the name of each is correct. The document name must match exactly what the Letter of Credit calls for.
    - They are consistent, for example, the shipping marks, quantities/ weights, transport details, references and in general terms the description must tally.
    - The description of goods is correct. They may be described in general terms, not inconsistent with the Letter of Credit, in all documents except the invoice, where the exact Letter of Credit description must be reproduced. Letter of Credit details should preferably not be repeated in full in transport documents.
    - Documents are authenticated where necessary — import regulations in some countries still make it essential to sign, and possibly witness documents and any alterations or additions to them.

- Any restrictions in the Letter of Credit are catered for.

2. Check each document to ensure it is in order

Transport document

(i) Type of transport document

(ii) Consignor — can be different from beneficiary

(iii) Consignee's name and spelling

(iv) Places and ports

(v) Clauses

(vi) On-deck shipment

(vii) "intended", "received", "on-board", or "transshipment", notations (if the Letter of Credit calls for Marine Bills of Lading).

(viii) "Freight paid" notation — authenticated if an addition

(ix) Full set of originals — unless otherwise permitted

(x) Date of shipment (on board or despatch or taking in charge date, as applicable) and date of issue — watch the time limit for presentation.

Insurance document

(i) Type e.g. a Certificate

(ii) Correct amount e.g. CIF plus 10 per cent

(iii) Same currency as the Letter of Credit unless otherwise stipulated in the Letter of Credit

(iv) Risks covered

(v) Date — not later than date of issue of the transport document

(vi) Endorsed if necessary.

Invoice

(i) Invoice heading in your Company's name, expressed and spelled as in the Letter of Credit.

(ii) Made out in name of buyer, expressed and spelled exactly as in the Letter of Credit.

(iii) Description of goods — including import licence or proforma details; price and terms of delivery — worded and spelled exactly as set out in the Letter of Credit.

(iv) Clauses or statements — word for word identically spelled.

(v) Value not more than the Letter of Credit permits and the same as Bills of Exchange — you can under certain conditions sometimes underdraw by up to 5 per cent.

(vi) Quantity — a 5 per cent variation is sometimes permitted — see Uniform Customs on variations — but only where the value of the Letter of Credit allows for this.

(vii) Reproduced and authenticated as necessary in a way allowed for by Uniform Customs and in the Letter of Credit e.g. copier, computer, carbons.

Other Documents

(i) Correct issuer

(ii) Correct wording or content

(iii) Clearly relates to the goods invoiced

(iv) Letters, telexes to the buyer correctly set out and addressed, and dated Certificates to cover any other Letter of Credit requirement

Bills of Exchange (if any)

(i) Date

(ii) Signature

(iii) Endorsement

(iv) Clause

(v) Letter of Credit number

(vi) Term-sight or usance dates

(vii) Amount and currency

(viii) Words and figures tally

(ix) Drawn on correct party

(x) Correct number e.g. "sole" or "1st and 2nd of exchange"

Importance of Complying with L/C Terms

As documentary credit operations cover only documents and not goods it is of utmost importance that the beneficiary tenders documents in conformity with the terms of credit. Discrepancies howsoever negligible result in nullification of the opening bank's engagement to pay. Discrepant documents can be paid only if the buyer agrees to accept them, but the seller runs a great risk in time of recession when slight default in the documents can result in their total rejection by the buyer. Therefore, importance of complying with the terms of credit cannot be over-emphasised.

However, in the event of documents not complying with the terms of credit the following alternatives are available to the negotiating bank:

1. Return the documents to the beneficiary who can then arrange to have them sent for collection.
2. Payment under reserve against beneficiary's indemnity provided he is of undoubted and of highest financial standing and if he is the customer of negotiating bank.
3. If he is not the customer, payment under reserve against beneficiary's banker's indemnity.
4. Cable for opening bank's authority to pay. In this case complete disclosure of all discrepancies must be made.

Tender of Documents

While presenting the documents under the L/C to the negotiating bank the following aspects are to be specifically looked into apart from the general observance of completeness, conformity with terms of credit, consistency of documents with one another, compliance with exchange control/trade control requirements and the Uniform Customs & Practices for Documentary Credits.

1. The documents should be presented within the validity date for presentation under the L/C. If, however, the expiry date of the credit falls on a day when banks are closed on account of holiday, the expiry date is extended to the first following business day on which the bank is open. If documents are discrepant and the credit expires before all the discrepancies are rectified, the exporter cannot claim that the documents were submitted within the expiry period. Under restricted L/Cs, it should particularly be noted that sufficient time is available to the exporter's bankers to present the documents to the bank to whom negotiation is restricted since presentation at the latter's counters within validity will only amount to valid presentation.
2. It should be checked that all documents as called for in the L/C are being presented for negotiation. These documents should be subjected to a detailed check vis-a-vis L/C terms before presentation.
3. The documents should be presented in required numbers as per L/C terms.
4. Apart from the documents required to be presented as per L/C terms, there are certain additional documents like GR/PP forms, customs certified copy of the invoice, etc. which are to be submitted to the bank as per exchange control provisions. It should be ensured that these requirements are complied with.
5. The original Letter of Credit alongwith all amendments thereto should also be presented to the negotiating bank.

19

Facilities of Foreign Exchange

The following foreign exchange facilities are available to the exporters as per Foreign Exchange Management (Export of Goods and Services) Regulations, 2000 as amended from time to time read with RBI Master Circular No. EC.CO.PCD.No. 29/15.02.76/2002-03, dt. 24.1.2003.

Counter Trade Arrangements [Refer Para A.7[1]]

(i) Counter Trade proposals involving adjustment of value of goods imported into India against value of goods exported from India in terms of an arrangement voluntarily entered into between the Indian party and the overseas party through an Escrow Account opened in India in U.S. dollar is considered by Reserve Bank. All imports and exports under the arrangement should be at international prices in conformity with the EXIM Policy and Foreign Exchange Management Act, 1999 and the Rules and Regulations issued thereunder. No interest will be payable on balances standing to the credit of the Escrow Account but the funds temporarily rendered surplus may be held in a short-term deposit upto a total period of three months in a year (i.e. in a block of 12 months) and the banks may pay interest at the applicable rate. No fund based/or non-fund based facilities would be permitted against the balances in the Escrow Account.

(ii) Application for permission for opening an Escrow Account may be made by the overseas exporter/organisation through the authorised dealer with whom the account is proposed to be opened, to the office of Reserve Bank of India under whose jurisdiction the authorised dealer is functioning.

RBI vide A.P. (DIR Series) Circular No. 4 dated 27th August, 2001

1 These paras are as per Annexure to RBI Master Circular No. EC.CO.PCD. No. 29/15.02.76/2002-03, dated 24.1.2003.

has allowed counter-trade arrangements between Indian and Romanian parties in which exports from India to Romania may precede imports into India and the U.S. Dollar Escrow Accounts may be opened and maintained by the Indian parties with banks in Romania, subject to the condition, among others, that the Indian exporter should utilise the funds for imports of goods from Romania into India within six months from the date of credit to such Escrow Accounts. Authorised dealers may forward such proposals to the concerned Regional Office of Reserve Bank under whose jurisdiction the exporter is situated. The concerned authorised dealer shall monitor the transactions in the U.S. Dollar Escrow accounts with banks in Romania through a mirror account.

Foreign Currency Accounts

In terms of Regulation 7 of Foreign Exchange Management (Foreign Currency Accounts by a Person Resident in India) Regulations, 2000, an exporter who has undertaken, a construction contract or a turnkey project outside India or who is exporting services or engineering goods from India on deferred payment terms may open, hold and maintain a Foreign Currency Account with a bank outside India provided that:—

(a) approval as required under the Foreign Exchange Management (Export of Goods and Services) Regulations 2000 has been obtained for undertaking the contract/project/export of goods or services, and

(b) the terms and conditions stipulated in the letter of approval have been duly complied with.

Project Exports and Service Exports [Refer Para A. 10[1]]

(i) Export of engineering goods on deferred payment terms and execution of turnkey projects and civil construction contracts abroad are collectively referred to as 'Project Exports'. Indian exporters offering deferred payment terms to overseas buyers and those participating in global tenders for undertaking turnkey/civil construction contracts abroad are required to obtain approval of Authorised dealer/Exim Bank/Working Group at post-award stage before undertaking execution of such contracts. Regulations relating to 'Project Exports' and 'Service Exports' are laid down in the Memorandum on Project Exports (PEM).

(ii) Pure supply contracts (contracts for export of goods) where at least 90 per cent of the export value is realised within the prescribed period i.e. six months from the date of export and the

1 These paras are as per Annexure to RBI Master Circular No. EC.CO.PCD. No. 29/15.02.76/2002-03, dated 24.1.2003.

balance amount within a maximum period of two years from the date of export are not treated as deferred payment exports, provided the exporter does not require/avail of any funded or non-funded facilities for such exports from authorised dealers.

(iii) Exporters desiring to submit bids for execution of projects abroad including service contract have been allowed to issue Corporate Guarantee in lieu of Bid Bond Guarantee, provided the amount of such guarantee shall not exceed 5% of the contract value.

Export on Elongated Credit Terms [Refer Para A. 11[1]]

Normally, proceeds of export of goods, other than those for which exporters have been permitted to offer commercial credit, have to be realised within six months from the date of shipment whichever is earlier (or 15 months from the date of shipment in respect of exports to Indian-owned warehouses established abroad with the permission of the Reserve Bank). In some cases, however, the overseas buyers may be seeking longer period for payment of proceeds of commodities which are normally exported from India on "cash" terms generally on the ground that remittances of proceeds are not permitted within 6 months or earlier by the buyers' country in view of its difficult balance of payments position. Exporters intending to export goods on elongated credit terms may submit their proposals giving full particulars through their banks to the concerned Regional Office of Reserve Bank for consideration.

Transfer of Documents [Refer Regulation 12 of FEM (Export of Goods and Services) Regulations, 2000[1]]

An authorised dealer may accept, for negotiation or collection, shipping documents including invoice and bill of exchange covering exports, from his constituent (not being a person who has signed the declaration).

Provided that before accepting such document for negotiation or collection, the authorised dealer shall-

(a) where the value declared in the declaration does not differ from the value shown in the documents being negotiated or sent for collection, or

(b) where the value declared in the declaration is less than the value shown in the documents being negotiated or sent for collection, require the constituent concerned also to sign such declaration and thereupon such constituent shall be bound to comply with such requisition and such constituent signing the declaration shall be considered to be the exporter for the purposes of these

1 These paras are as per Annexure to RBI Master Circular No. EC.CO.PCD. No. 29/15.02.76/2002-03, dated 24.1.2003.

Regulations to the extent of the full value shown in the document being negotiated or sent for collection and shall be governed by these Regulations accordingly.

Trade Discount [Refer Para C.3[1]]

Bills in respect of exports by sea or air which fall short of the value declared on GR/SDF Forms on account of trade discount may be accepted for negotiation or collection by authorised dealers only if the discount has been declared by exporter on relative GR/SDF Form at the time of shipment and accepted by Customs.

Advance Remittances against Export [Refer Regulation 16 and Para C.4[1]]

Exporters may receive advance payments (with or without interest) from their overseas buyers provided (a) the shipments are made within one year from the date of receipt of advance payment, (b) the rate of interest, if any payable does not exceed LIBOR+ 100 basis points and (c) the documents covering the shipment are routed through the authorised dealer through whom the advance payment is received.

Provided that in the event of the exporter's inability to make the shipment, partly or fully, within one year from the date of receipt of advance payment, no remittance towards refund of unutilised portion of advance payment or towards payment of interest, shall be made after the expiry of the said period of one year, without the prior approval of the Reserve Bank.

Where the export agreement provides for shipment of goods extending beyond the period of one year from the date of receipt of advance payment the exporter shall require the prior approval of the Reserve Bank of India.

The appropriations made against every shipment must be endorsed on the original copy of the inward remittance certificate issued for advance remittance.

Purchase of foreign exchange from the market for refunding advance payment credited to EEFC account may be allowed only after utilising the entire balances held in the exporter's EEFC accounts maintained at different branches/banks.

Certain Exports requiring prior approval [Refer Regulation 14]

A. Export of goods on lease, hire, etc.

No person shall, except with the prior permission of the Reserve Bank, take or sent out by land, sea or air any goods from India to any place outside

---

1 These paras are as per Annexure to RBI Master Circular No. EC.CO.PCD. No. 29/15.02.76/2002-03, dated 24.1.2003.

India on lease or hire or under any arrangement or in any other manner other than sale or disposal of such goods.

B. Exports under trade agreement/rupee credit etc.

(i) Export of goods under special arrangement between the Central Government and Government of a foreign state, or under rupee credits extended by the Central Government to Government of a foreign state shall be governed by the terms and conditions set out in the relative public notices issued by the trade Control Authority in India and the instructions issued from time to time by the Reserve Bank.

(ii) An export under the line of credit extended to a bank or a financial institution operating in a foreign state by the Exim Bank for financing exports from India, shall be governed by the terms and conditions advised by the Reserve Bank to the authorised dealers from time to time.

C. Counter Trade

Any arrangement involving adjustment of value of goods imported into India against value of goods exported from India, shall require prior approval of the Reserve Bank.

Part Drawings [Refer Para C.5[1]]

In certain lines of export trade, it is the practice to leave a small part of the invoice value undrawn for payment after adjustment due to differences in weight, quality, etc. to be ascertained after arrival and inspection, weighment or analysis of the goods. In such cases, authorised dealers may negotiate bills, provided—

(a) the amount of undrawn balance is considered normal in the particular line of export trade, subject to a maximum of 10 per cent of the full export value;

and

(b) an undertaking is obtained from exporter on the duplicate of GR/ SDF/ PP that he will surrender/account for the balance proceeds of the shipment within the period prescribed for realisation.

NOTE: In cases where exporter has not been able to arrange for repatriation of the undrawn balance in spite of best efforts authorised dealers, on being satisfied with the bona fides of the case, should ensure that the exporter has realised at least the value for which the bill

---

1 These paras are as per Annexure to RBI Master Circular No. EC.CO.PCD. No. 29/15.02.76/2002-03, dated 24.1.2003.

was initially drawn (excluding undrawn balances) or 90% of the value declared on GR/PP/SDF form whichever is more and a period of one year has elapsed from the date of shipment.

Reduction in Invoice Value on Account of Pre-payment of Usance Bills [Refer Para C. 11[1]]

Occasionally, exporters may approach authorised dealers for reduction in invoice value on account of cash discount to overseas buyers for prepayment of usance bills. In such cases authorised dealers may allow cash discount to the extent of amount of proportionate interest on the unexpired period of usance calculated at the rate of interest stipulated in the export contract or at the prime rate/LIBOR of the currency of invoice where rate of interest is not stipulated in the contract.

Reduction in Value [Refer Para C.12[1]]

If, after a bill has been negotiated or sent for collection, the amount thereof is desired to be reduced for any reason, authorised dealer may approve such reduction if satisfied about genuineness of the request provided:

(a) the reduction does not exceed 10% of invoice value;

(b) it does not relate to an export of commodities subject to floor price stipulations,

(c) the exporter is not on the exporters' caution list of RBI; and

(d) the exporter should be advised to surrender proportionate export incentives availed of, if any.

In the case of exporters who have been in the export business for more than three years, reduction in invoice value may be allowed without any percentage ceiling subject to the above conditions as also subject to their track record being satisfactory i.e. the export outstandings do not exceed 5% of the average annual export realisation during the preceding three calendar years. For the purpose of reckoning the percentage of outstanding export bills to average export realisation during the preceding three calendar years, outstandings in respect of exports made to countries facing externalisation problems may be ignored provided the payments have been made by the buyers in the local currency.

Write off of Unrealized Export Bills [Refer Para C. 18[1]]

(i) An exporter who has not been able to realise the outstanding export dues despite best efforts, may approach the authorised

1 These paras are as per Annexure to RBI Master Circular No. EC.CO.PCD. No. 29/15.02.76/2002-03, dated 24.1.2003.

dealer, who has handled the relevant shipping documents, with appropriate supporting documentary evidence with a request for write off the unrealised portion. Authorised dealers may accede to such requests subject to the undernoted conditions:

(a) The relevant amount has remained outstanding for one year or more;

(b) The aggregate amount of write off allowed by the authorised dealer during a calendar year does not exceed 10% of the total export proceeds realised by the concerned exporter through the concerned authorised dealer during the previous calendar year;

(c) Satisfactory documentary evidence is furnished in support of the exporter having made all efforts to realise the dues;

(d) The case falls under any of the undernoted categories:

   (i) The overseas buyer has been declared insolvent and a certificate from the official liquidator indicating that there is no possibility of recovery of export proceeds produced;

   (ii) The overseas buyer is not traceable over a reasonably long period of time;

   (iii) The goods exported have been auctioned or destroyed by the Port/Customs/Health authorities in the importing country;

   (iv) The unrealised amount represents the balance due in a case settled through the intervention of the Indian Embassy. Foreign Chamber of Commerce or similar organisation;

   (v) The unrealised amount represents the undrawn balance of an export bill (not exceeding 10% of the invoice value) remained outstanding and turned out to be unrealisable despite all efforts made by the exporter;

   (vi) The cost of resorting to legal action would be disproportionate to the unrealised amount of the export bill or where the exporter even after winning the Court case against the overseas buyer could not execute the Court decree due to reasons beyond his control;

   (vii) Bills were drawn for the difference between the letter of credit value and actual export value or between the provisional and the actual freight charges but the amount has remained unrealised consequent on dishonour of the bills by the overseas buyer and there are no prospects of realisation.

(e) The case is not the subject matter of any pending civil or criminal suit;

(f) The exporter has not come to the adverse notice of the Enforcement Directorate of the Central Bureau of Investigation or any such other law enforcement agency;

(g) The exporter has surrendered proportionate export incentives if any, availed of in respect of the relative shipments.

The authorised dealer should obtain document/s evidencing surrender of export incentives availed of before permitting the relevant bills to be written off. Authorised dealers are to put in place a system under which their internal inspectors or auditors carry out random sample check/percentage check of outstanding export bills to be written off.

(ii) Where there is no further amount to be realised against the GR/ SDF/ PP form covered by the write off, authorised dealer should certify the duplicate form, as under:

"Write off of..

(Amount in words and figures)

permitted in terms of paragraph C. 18 of Directions to Authorised Dealers.

Date Stamp & Signature of Authorised Dealer"

*Special Facility of "Write off of unrealised export bill to Status Holders

Status holder exporters, (viz. Export Houses, Trading Houses, Star Trading Houses, Super Star Trading Houses) and manufacturer exporters exporting more than 50 per cent of their production, and recognised as such by DGFT, may be permitted to "write off outstanding export bills upto an annual limit of 5 per cent of their average annual realisations (not turnover) during the preceding 3 calendar years. The limit of 5% will be cumulatively available in a year and will be subject to the following conditions:-

(i) The exporter should submit to the concerned authorised dealer a Chartered Accountant's certificate indicating-

* As per RBI Master Circular No. EC.CO.PCD. No. 29/15.02.76/2002-03, dated 24.1.2003.

(a) the export realisation in the preceding three calendar years and also the amount of "write off" already availed of during the year, if any.

(b) the relevant GR/SDF Nos. to be written off, Bill No., invoice value, commodity exported, country of export,

(c) the export benefits, if any, availed of by the exporter have been surrendered.

It is clarified that the following do not qualify for the "write off" facility:-

(a) Exports made to countries with externalisation problem i.e. where the overseas buyer has deposited the value of export in local currency but the amount has not been allowed to be repatriated by the central banking authorities of the country.

(b) GR/SDF forms which are under investigation by agencies like, Enforcement Directorate, Directorate of Revenue Intelligence, Central Bureau of Investigation, etc. as also the outstanding bills which are subject matter of civil/criminal suit. After the "write off" has been permitted authorised dealer may certify the duplicate forms as under:-

"Write off of...

(Amount in words and figures)

permitted in terms of AP (DIR Series) Circular No. 30, dt. April 4, 2001.

Date Stamp & Singnature of Authorised Dealer"

Change of Buyer/Consignee [Refer Para C.14[1]]

Prior approval of RBI is not required if after goods have been shipped they are to be transferred to a buyer other than the original buyer in the event of default by later, provided the reduction in value, if any, involved does not exceed 10% and the realisation of export proceeds is not delayed beyond the period of six months from the date of export. Where the reduction in value exceeds 10%, the conditions stipulated for reduction in value should also be satisfied.

It has been clarified vide AD (GP Series) Circular No. 28 dt. 30.12.1998 that authorised dealers may at the request of exporter allow change of tenor

1 These paras are as per Annexure to RBI Master Circular No. EC.CO.PCD. No. 29/15.02.76/2002-03, dated 24.1.2003.

of bills in respect of bills drawn on the original buyer or the alternate buyer. provided the revised due date of payment does not fall beyond six months from the date of shipment, if the change of tenor takes place before the original due date of payment of the bill.

Extension of Time Limit

In terms of Regulation No. 9 of the Foreign Exchange Management (Export of Goods and Services) Regulations, 2000 the export proceeds are required to be realised within a period of 6 months from the date of shipment. In the case of exports to a warehouse established abroad with the approval of Reserve Bank, the proceeds have to be realised within 15 months from the date of shipment. Where the export of goods or software has been made by a unit situated in a Special Economic Zone, the amount representing the full export value of goods or software shall be realised and repatriated to India with no prescription as to time-limit[1].

Where an exporter has not been able to realise proceeds of shipment within the prescribed period (i.e. 6 months from the date of exports) for reasons beyond his control, the exporter is required to apply to Reserve Bank of India in form ETX for extension of period of realisation

Authorised dealer who has handled export documents may extend without any reference to RBI, after obtaining an application from the exporter, the period of realisation beyond six months from the date of export, where invoice value does not exceed US $ 1,00,000 subject to the following conditions:

(i) the authorised dealer is satisfied that the exporter has not been able to realise export proceeds for reasons beyond his control;

(ii) the exporter submits a declaration that he will realise the export proceeds during the extended period;

(iii) the extension may be granted upto a period of 3 months at a time and while considering the extension beyond one year from the date of export the total export outstandings of the exporter should not be more than 10% of the average of export realisations during the preceding three financial years.

The ceiling of US $ 1,00,000 would not apply where the exporter has filed suits against the importer abroad. In such cases extension may be granted upto six months at a time, irrespective of the amount involved.

Cases which are not covered by the above instructions and cases

1 These paras are as per Annexure to RBI Master Circular No. EC.CO.PCD. No. 29/15.02.76/2002-03, dated 24.1.2003.

indicated below would require prior approval from the Regional Office of the Reserve Bank of India.

(i) where the export invoices are under investigation by Enforcement Directorate/Central Bureau of Investigation or other investigating agencies.

(ii) where invoice value exceeds US $ 1,00,000 (except in cases where the exporter has filed suits against the importer abroad).

Temporary Extension in the Prescribed Period of Realisation

As a temporary measure for a period of one year, w.e.f. 1.9.2001, exporters were allowed a period of 360 days from the date of shipment, for realisation and repatriation of full value of goods/software for exports to certain specified countries.

Manufacturers/exporters of certain specified products and having export contracts of Rs. 100 crores and above in value terms in one year have been allowed w.e.f. 1.10.2001, a period of 365 days from the date of shipment for realisation and repatriation of full value of the exports of the products specified.

Remittances Connected With Exports

Agency Commission on Exports [Refer para D 1[1]]

(i) Authorised dealers may allow payment of commission, either by remittance or by deduction from invoice value, on application submitted by the exporter. The remittance of agency commission may be allowed subject to the following conditions:

(a) Amount of commission has been declared on GR/SDF/PP/SOFTEX form and accepted by Customs authorities or Ministry of Information Technology, Government of India/EPZ authorities as the case may be. In cases where the commission has not been declared on GR/SDF/ PP/SOFTEX form, remittance thereof may be allowed after satisfying about the reasons adduced by the exporter for not declaring commission on Export Declaration Form provided a valid agreement/ written understanding between the exporter and/or beneficiary for payment of commission subsists.

(b) The relative shipment has already been made.

(ii) Authorised dealer may allow payment of commission by Indian

---

1 These paras are as per Annexure to RBI Master Circular No. EC.CO.PCD. No. 29/15.02.76/2002-03, dated 24.1.2003.

exporter's, in respect of their exports covered under counter trade arrangement through Escrow Accounts designated in U. S. dollar, subject to the following conditions:-

(a) The payment of commission satisfies the conditions as at (a) and (b) stipulated in paragraph above.

(b) The commission is not payable to Escrow Account holders themselves.

(c) The commission should not be allowed by deduction from the invoice value.

NOTE : Payment of commission is prohibited on export made by Indian partners towards equity participation in an overseas joint venture/ wholly owned subsidiary as also exports under Rupee Credit Route

Refund of Export Proceeds *[Refer para D 2[1]]*

Refund of export proceeds may be allowed by authorised dealers through whom the proceeds were originally received, provided such goods are re-imported into India on account of poor quality etc and evidence of re-import has been submitted. In all such cases, exporters should be advised to surrender the proportionate incentives availed of, if any, against the relevant export

Export Claims *[Refer para C 13[1]]*

Authorised dealers may remit export claims on application. provided the relative export proceeds have already been realised and repatriated to India and the exporter is not on the caution list of Reserve Bank. In all such cases of remittances. the exporter should be advised to surrender proportionate export incentive, if any, received by him.

Exchange Earners Foreign Currency (EEFC) Account Scheme

Under Regulation 4 of the Foreign Exchange Management (Foreign Currency Accounts by a Person Resident in India) Regulations, 2000 a person resident in India may open, hold and maintain with an authorised dealer in India, Exchange Earners Foreign Currency Account in the form of non-interest bearing current account only subject to following terms & conditions.

1. Limit up to which foreign currency may be credited to EEFC account

(1) An entity or a person specified in column 1 of the Table 'below

1 These paras are as per Annexure to RBI Master Circular No. EC.CO.PCD. No. 29/15.02.76/2002-03, dated 24.1.2003.

may credit to the EEFC Account an amount upto the limit specified in Column 2 thereof from out of the foreign exchange earnings specified in the sub-paragraph (1A) namely:

Entity or person	Limit (per cent)
1. A Status Holder Exporter (as defined in EXIM Policy in force)	100
2. A resident in India for professional services rendered in his individual capacity	100
3. 100 per cent Export Oriented Unit/s, Units in Export Processing Zone/Software Technology Park/Electronic Hardware Technology Park	70
4. Any other person resident in India	50

Provided that the Reserve Bank may, on application made to it and on being satisfied that it is necessary to do so, grant permission to hold higher percentage of inward remittance/payments in foreign exchange in the EEFC account

Explanation For the purpose of category (2) in column 1. "professional" shall mean

(i) Director on Board of overseas company

(ii) Scientist/Professor in Indian University/Institution

(iii) Economist

(iv) Lawyer

(v) Doctor

(vi) Architect

(vii) Engineer

(viii) Artist

(ix) Cost/Chartered Accountant

(x) Any other person rendering professional services in his individual capacity, as may be specified by the Reserve Bank from time to time

(1A) Following foreign exchange earnings are specified for the purpose of sub-paragraph (1) namely:

(i) inward remittance through normal banking channel, other than the remittance received pursuant to any undertaking given to the Reserve Bank or which represents foreign currency loan raised or investment received from outside India or those received for meeting specific obligations by the account holder;

(ii) payments received in foreign exchange by a 100 per cent Export Oriented Unit or a unit in (a) Export Processing Zone or (b) Software Technology Park or (c) Electronic Hardware Technology Park for supply of goods to similar such unit or to a unit in Domestic Tariff Area; and also payments received in foreign exchange by a unit in Domestic Tariff Area for supply of goods to a unit in Special Economic Zone (SEZ).

(iii) payment received by an exporter from an account maintained with an authorised dealer for the purpose of countertrade, in accordance with the approval granted in terms of Regulation 14 of the Foreign Exchange Management (Export of Goods and Services) Regulations, 2000:

(iv) advance remittance received by an exporter towards export of goods or services;

(v) payment received for export of goods and services from India, out of funds representing repayment of State Credit in U.S. dollar held in the account of Bank for Foreign Economic Affairs, Moscow, with an authorised dealer in India:

(vi) professional earning including director's fees, consultancy fees, lecture fees, honorarium and similar other earnings received by a professional by rendering services in his individual capacity.

(2) Except to the extent provided in sub-paragraph (1), no payment received in foreign exchange by the account holder from any other person resident in India, shall be credited to an EEFC account.

Explanation - For the purpose of the sub-paragraph (1), payment received through an international credit card for which reimbursement will be provided in foreign exchange may be regarded as a remittance through normal banking channels.

2. Permissible credits to EEFC account

Following credits may be made to an EEFC Account, namely —

(i) A portion of inward remittance/payment received by the recipient in foreign exchange subject to the provisions of paragraph (1);

(ii) Interest earned on the funds held in the account;

(iii) Recredit of unutilised foreign currency earlier withdrawn from the account;

(iv) Amount representing repayment by the account holder's importer customer, of loan/advances granted in terms of clause (iv) of Paragraph 3.

3. Permissible debits to the EEFC account

Following debits may be made to an EEFC Account, namely —

(i) Payment outside India towards a current account transaction in accordance with the provisions of the Foreign Exchange Management (Current Account Transactions) Rules, 2000 and towards a capital account transaction permissible under the Foreign Exchange Management (Permissible Capital Account Transactions) Regulations, 2000.

(ii) Payment in foreign exchange towards cost of goods purchased from a 100 per cent Export Oriented Unit or a Unit in (a) Export Processing Zone or (b) Software Technology Park or (c) Electronic Hardware Technology Park.

(iii) Payment of customs duty in accordance with the provisions of Export Import Policy of Central Government for the time being in force.

(iv) Trade related loans/advances, not exceeding US $ 3 million, by an exporter holding such account to his importer customer outside India, subject to compliance with the Foreign Exchange Management (Borrowing and Lending in Foreign Exchange) Regulations, 2000.

(v) Payment in foreign exchange to a person resident in India for supply of goods/services including payments for air fare and hotel expenditure.

4. Miscellaneous

(i) There is no restriction on withdrawal in rupees of funds held in an EEFC account. However, the amount withdrawn in rupees shall not be eligible for conversion into foreign currency and for recredit to the account.

(ii) Authorised dealer may issue cheque books of separate series with the superscription 'EEFC Account' to the account holders maintaining such accounts, and also satisfy himself while honouring the cheques that the payment made by the account holder by issue of a cheque is permissible under these Regulations.

(iii) It is further advised that all the EEFC accounts should be held in the form of non interest bearing current accounts only and no credit facility, whether funded or non-funded should be made available against EEFC balances.

20

Availing Facilities Under Export Import Policy, 2002-07

In order to promote exports from India, the Government has framed following special schemes.

I. Export Promotion Capital Goods Scheme

The scheme allows import of capital goods for pre-production, production and post-production including CKD/SDK thereof as well as computer software systems) at 5% Customs duty subject to an export obligation equivalent to 8 times of duty[1] saved on capital goods imported under the EPCG Scheme to be fulfilled over a period of 8 years reckoned from the date of issuance of licence. However, in respect of EPCG licences with a CIF value for Rs. 100 crore or more, the same export obligation shall be required to be fulfilled over a period of 12 years. The capital goods shall include spares, jigs, fixtures, dies and moulds. EPCG licence may also be issued for import of components of such capital goods required for assembly or manufacture of capital goods by the licence holder. Second hand capital goods upto 10 years old may also be imported under the EPCG scheme.

Spares for the existing plant and machinery may also be imported under the EPCG scheme subject to an export obligation equivalent to 8 times of duty saved to be fulfilled over a period of 8 years reckoned from the date of issuance of licence.

The scheme covers manufacturer exporters with or without supporting manufacturer(s)/vendor(s), merchant exporters tied to supporting manufacturer(s) and service providers.

A person holding an EPCG licence may source the capital goods from a domestic manufacturer instead of importing them. The domestic

1 Refer Customs Notification No. 55/2003-Cus. Dated 1.4.2003.

manufacturer supplying capital goods to EPCG licence holders shall be eligible for deemed export benefit.

Import of capital goods shall be subject to Actual User Condition till the export obligation is completed. The following conditions shall apply to the fulfilment of the export obligation-

(i) The export obligation shall be fulfilled by the export of goods capable of being manufactured or produced by the use of capital goods imported under the scheme. It may also be fulfilled by the export of same goods for which EPCG licence has been obtained, manufactured or produced in different manufacturing units of the licence holder/specified supporting manufacturer(s)/vendor(s). The export obligation under the scheme shall be, over and above, the average level of exports achieved by him in the preceding three licensing years for same and similar products except for categories mentioned in Handbook (Vol. 1). Alternatively, export obligation may also be fulfilled by exports of other goods manufactured or service provided by the same firm/company which has the EPCG licence. However, in such cases, the additional export obligation imposed under EPCG scheme shall be over and above the average exports achieved by the unit in preceding three years for the substitute products/services. This facility shall only be available to manufacturer exporters/ service provider.

(ii) The export obligation under the scheme shall be, in addition to any other export obligation undertaken by the importer, except the export obligation for the same product under Advance Licence, DFRC, DEPB or Drawback scheme.

Any firm/company registered with BIFR or any firm/ company acquiring a unit, which is under BIFR shall be allowed EO extension as per the rehabilitation package prepared by the operating agency subject to subsequent approval of BIFR. However, in cases where the rehabilitation package does not specify the EO extension period, a time period upto 12 years reckoned from the date of issue of licence would be permitted on merits of the case for fulfilment of export obligation.

Similarly, small-scale SSI units shall also be entitled for similar facility as per the rehabilitation scheme of the concerned State government. However, in cases where the State rehabilitation scheme does not specify the EO extension period, a time period upto 12 years reckoned from the date of issue of licence would be permitted on merits of the case for fulfilment of export obligation.

In the case of EPCG licences issued to agro units in the agri export zones, a period of 12 years reckoned from the date of issue of the licence would be permitted for the fulfilment of export obligation.

The licence holder under this scheme shall fulfil the export obligation over the specified period in the following proportions:

Period from the date of issue of licence	Proportion of total export obligation
1. Block of 1st and 2nd year	Nil
2. Block of 3rd and 4th year	15%
3. Block of 5th and 6th year	35%
4. Block of 7th and 8th year	50%

However, the export obligation of a particular block of year may be set off by the excess exports made in the preceding block of the year.

In respect of licences of Rs. 100 crores or more, or where the licence is issued to units in the notified agri export zone, the export obligation shall be fulfilled over a period of 12 years in the following proportions:

Period from the dale of issue of licence	Proportion of total export obligation
1. Block of 1st to 5th year	Nil
2. Block of 6th to 8th year	15%
3. Block of 9th and 10th year	35%
4. Block of 11th and 12th year	50%

An application for grant of an EPCG licence shall be made in Appendix 9 of the Handbook of Procedures alongwith the documents prescribed therein. Before clearance of capital goods through customs, the importer shall execute a bond in such form and for such sum and with such surety or security as may be specified by the Assistant or Deputy Commissioner of Customs binding himself to fulfil specified export obligation.

The licence holder shall submit a yearly report on the progress made in fulfilment of export obligation in Appendix 9A (or 9B for services rendered) of the Handbook of Procedures, duly certified by a Chartered Accountant/ Cost & Works Accountants, to the concerned licensing authority.

On being satisfied that the export obligations have been fulfilled, the licensing authority shall issue a certificate of discharge of export obligation to the EPCG licence holder and send a copy of the same to the customs authorities with whom BG/LUT has been executed.

II. Duty Exemption/Remission Schemes

Duty Exemption Scheme enables import of inputs required for export production. An advance licence is issued under the Duty Exemption Scheme. Duty Remission Scheme enables post export replenishment/ remission of duty on inputs used in the export-product. Duty Remission Scheme consists of (i) DFRC and (ii) DEPB. DFRC permits duty free replenishment of inputs used in the export product. The DEPB scheme allows drawback of import charges on inputs used in the export product.

Advance Licence

An Advance Licence is issued to allow duty free import of inputs which are physically incorporated in the export product (making normal allowance). In addition, fuel, oil, energy, catalysts etc. which are consumed in the course of their use to obtain the export product, may also be allowed under the scheme. Duty free import of mandatory spares upto 10% of the C.I.F. value of the licence which are required to be exported/supplied with the resultant product may also be allowed. Advance Licence can be issued for:

(i) Physical Exports

(ii) Intermediate Supplies

(iii) Deemed exports

Advance Licence is issued for duty free imports of inputs, subject to actual user condition. Such licences (other than Advance Licence for deemed exports) are exempted from payment of Basic Customs Duty, Additional Customs Duty, Anti-Dumping Duty and Safeguard Duly, if any.

Advance Licence for deemed exports shall be exempted from Basic Customs Duty and Additional Customs Duty only. However, in case of supplies to EOU/SEZ/EHTP/STP under such licences, anti-dumping duty and safeguard duty shall also be exempted.

Advance licences and/or materials imported thereunder shall not be transferable even after completion of export obligation.

Advance licences (including Advance Licence for deemed exports and intermediate supply) shall be issued with a positive value addition. However, for exports for which payments are not received in freely convertible currency, the same shall be subject to value addition as specified in Appendix 32 of the Handbook of Procedures.

Advance Licences shall be issued in accordance with the Policy and Procedure in force on the date of issue of licence and shall be subject to the fulfilment of a time bound export obligation as may be specified.

The facility of Advance Licence shall also be available where some of the inputs are supplied free of cost to the exporter. In such cases, for calculation of value addition, the notional value of free of cost inputs alongwith value of other duty-free inputs shall be taken into consideration.

An application for advance licence should be made in the form given at Appendix 10B of the Handbook of Procedures alongwith the documents specified therein.

Ministry of Finance, Deptt. of Revenue has issued Notification No. 43/2002-Cus. dated 19.4.2002, in respect of duty exemption on materials imported against an Advance Licence.

Advance Licence for Annual Requirement

Advance licence can also be issued on the basis of annual requirement for physical exports.

Export House, Trading House, Star Trading Houses and Super Star Trading Houses shall be entitled for the Advance Licence for annual requirement. However, if the status holders are holding the certificate as merchant exporter, they are also entitled to the Advance Licence for Annual Requirement provided they agree to the endorsement of the name (s) of the supporting manufacturer(s) on the relevant licence.

The entitlement under this scheme shall be upto 200% of the FOB value of export in the preceding licensing year. Such licence shall have positive value addition.

Min. of Finance, Deptt. of Revenue has issued Notification No. 56/2003-Cus. dt. 1.4.2003, granting exemption from basic customs duty and additional duty leviable on materials imported against Advance Licence for Annual Requirement.

Advance Release Order

An Advance Licence holder, holder of Advance Licence for Annual Requirement and holder of DFRC intending to source the inputs from indigenous sources/state trading enterprises/EOU/SEZ/EHTP/STP units in lieu of direct imports has the option to source them against the advance release order denominated in foreign exchange/Indian rupees. The transferee of a DFRC shall also be eligible for ARO facility. However, supplies may be obtained against the licence from EOU/EHTP/STP/SEZ units, without conversion into ARO.

An application for grant of ARO shall be made in the form given in Appendix 24 of the Handbook, to the Regional Licensing Authority concerned.

An ARO issued for the procurement of an individual item shall be automatically valid for procurement from one or more indigenous sources.

If an ARO is issued alongwith the Advance Licence, its validity shall be co-terminus with the validity of the Advance Licence.

Advance Licence for Intermediate Supply

Advance Licence may be issued for intermediate supply to a manufacturer-exporter for the import of inputs required in the manufacture of goods to be supplied to the ultimate exporter/deemed exporter holding another Advance Licence.

Advance Licence for Deemed Exports

Advance Licence can be issued for deemed exports to the main contractor for import of inputs required in the manufacture of goods to be supplied to the specified categories.

In addition, in respect of supply of goods to specified projects, an Advance Licence for deemed exports can also be availed by the sub-contractor or the main contractor to such project provided the name of sub-contractor(s) appears in the main contract. Such licence for deemed export can also be issued for supplies made to United Nations Organisations or under the Aid Programme of the United Nations or other multilateral agencies and paid for in foreign exchange.

For Customs duty exemption, please refer Notfn. No 47/2002-Cus dt. 22.4.2002

Duty Free Replenishment Certificate (DFRC)

Duty Free Replenishment Certificate is issued to a merchant-exporter or manufacturer-exporter for the import of inputs used in the manufacture of goods without payment of Basic Customs Duty and Special Additional Duty. However, such inputs shall be subject to the payment of Additional Customs Duty equal to the Excise Duty at the time of import.

(i) Duty Free Replenishment Certificate shall be issued only in respect of export products covered under the Standard Input Output Norms (SIONs) as notified by DGFT. However, DFRC shall not be issued in respect of SIONs which are subject to "actual user" condition or where the input is allowed with prior import condition or for import of Acetic Anhydride, Ephedrine and Pseudo Ephedrine.

(ii) Duty Free Replenishment Certificate shall be issued for import of inputs, as per SION, as indicated in the shipping bills. The validity of such licences shall be 18 months DFRC and/or the material imported against it shall be freely transferable.

(iii) The Duty Free Replenishment Certificate shall be subject to a minimum value addition of 25% except for items in gems and jewellery sector for which value addition as given in the Handbook shall be applicable.

(iv) The export products, which are eligible for modified VAT, shall be eligible for CENVAT credit. However, non-excisable, non-dutiable or non-CENVAT products, shall be eligible for drawback at the time of exports in lieu of additional customs duty to be paid at the time of imports under the scheme.

(v) The exporter shall be entitled for drawback benefits in respect of any of the duty paid materials, whether imported or indigenous used in the export product as per the drawback rate fixed by Directorate of Drawback (Ministry of Finance). The drawback shall however be restricted to the duty paid materials not covered under SION.

(vi) Duty Free Replenishment Certificate may be issued in respect of exports for which payments are received in non-convertible currency. Such exports shall, however be subject to value addition as specified in Appendix-32 of the Handbook.

DFRC may also be issued for supplies treated as deemed exports.

The exporter exporting under DFRC shall be required to give a declaration in the EP copy of the Shipping Bill indicating the serial number and product group of SION of the export product. In case of export of gold/silver/platinum jewellery and articles thereof. the wastage norms as per the Handbook, may be indicated on the EP copy of the shipping bill. However, in respect of certain specified products of Engineering, Electronics, Chemicals and Allied Products, Plastics, Textiles and Miscellaneous, the exporter is required to give declaration with regard to technical characteristics, quality and specifications in the shipping bill.

DFRC shall also be available for supplies mentioned in paragraph 82 of the Policy except for supplies made to DFRC holders. Such DFRC shall be issued with a single port of registration mentioned in paragraph 4.19 of the Handbook (Vol. 1) as per option of the applicant.

The CIF value of DFRC shall be arrived at after discounting 20% from the FOR value of supply. The FOR shall be calculated on the basis of the document mentioned in sub-paragraph (11) below. The application shall be accompanied by the following -

(i) A copy of the Invoice duly signed by the unit receiving the material and their jurisdictional excise authorities certifying the item of supply, its quantity, value and date of such supply. However in case of supply of items which are non-excisable or supply of excisable items to a unit producing non-excisable product (s), a Project Authority Certificate (PAC) certifying quantity, value and date of supply would be acceptable in lieu of excise certification.

Notwithstanding the above, in respect of supplies to EOU/ SEZ, a copy of ARE-3 duly signed by the Jurisdictional excise authorities certifying the item of supply, its quantity, value and date of such supply shall be furnished:

(ii) Payment certificate from the project authority in the form given in Appendix-12A of the Handbook (Vol. 1) In the case of Advance Licence for Intermediate Supplies/ deemed exports, supplies to the EOUs/ SEZs/ EHTPs/STPs, documentary evidence from the bank substantiating the realisation of proceeds from the Licence holder or EOUs/SEZs/ EHTPs/STPs, as the case may be, through the normal banking channel, shall be furnished in the form given at Appendix- 22A of the Handbook (Vol 1).

However realisation of export proceeds shall not be insisted upon if the shipments are made against confirmed irrevocable inland letter of credit and the same is certified in columns 5/6/ 7 of Appendix 22 A of the Handbook (Vol 1).

Export shipments under DFRC can be effected from any specified port The DFRC shall be issued with single port of registration, which will be the port from where the exports have been effected However, for import from a port other than the port of export, TRA shall be issued by the Customs authority at the port of export to the Customs authority to the port of import.

An application for grant of DFRC may be made to the licensing authority concerned in the form given in Appendix 10D of Handbook of Procedures alongwith the documents prescribed therein Such an application may be made by the Registered Office/Head Office or a branch Office or manufacturing unit of the eligible exporter Further, the application shall be filed only after realisation of export proceeds However, in case of exports against irrevocable Letter of Credit, application may be filed after exports The CIF value of DFRC shall be arrived at after discounting 20% from the FOB value of exports The FOB value shall be calculated on the basis of the bank realisation certificate.

The application for DFRC shall be filed within six months from the date of realisation reckoned from the last date of realisation in respect of shipments for which DFRC is being claimed However, in case of exports against irrevocable Letter or Credit, it shall be filed within six months from the date of exports/supply reckoned from the last date of exports/supply in respect of shipments for which DFRC is being claimed In respect of exports/supply against advance payment, DFRC shall be filed within six months from the date of exports against advance payment.

Wherever provisional shipment has been allowed by the customs authorities. DFRC against such exports shall be issued only after the release of the shipping bill by the Customs The time limit for filing of application in such cases shall be six months from the date of release of shipping bill or three months from date of realisation, whichever is later.

The applicant shall file one application relating to one export product from one port of export Where the same export product has been exported from different ports of registration, the exporter shall file more than one application for the same export product group.

For customs duty exemption on materials imported against DFRC, please refer Notification No 46/2002-Cus dt 22.4.2002.

Duty Entitlement Passbook Scheme (DEPB)

The objective of Duty Entitlement Passbook Scheme is to neutralise the incidence of Customs duty on the import content of the export product. The neutralisation shall be provided by way of grant of duty credit against the export product.

Under the Duty Entitlement Passbook Scheme (DEPB), an exporter may apply for credit, as a specified percentage of FOB value of exports, made in freely convertible currency The credit shall be available against such export products and at such rates as may be specified by the Director General of Foreign Trade by way of public notice issued in this behalf, for import of raw materials, intermediates, components, parts, packaging material etc.

The holder of Duty Entitlement Passbook Scheme (DEPB) shall have the option to pay additional customs duty, if any, in cash as well.

The DEPB shall be valid for a period of 12 months from the date of issue The DEPB and/or the items imported against it are freely transferable.

An application for grant of credit under DEPB may be made to the licensing authority concerned in the form given in Appendix-10C of Handbook of Procedures alongwith the documents prescribed therein Such application may be made by the Registered Office/Head Office or a branch office or manufacturing unit of the eligible exporter The FOB value in free foreign exchange shall be converted into Indian rupees as per the exchange rate for exports notified by the Ministry of Finance as applicable on the date of order of 'Let Export' by customs.

The application for obtaining credit should be filed within a period of six months from the date of exports or within three months from the date of realisation, whichever is later, reckoned from the last date of realisation/ exports, in respect of shipments, for which the claim has been filed.

An applicant may file one or more applications subject to the condition that each application shall contain not more than 25 shipping bills Such bills must relate to exports made from one Customs House only This limit shall not apply to the application filed through EDI mode.

The DEPB shall be issued with single port of registration i.e. the port from where the exports have been made.

It may be noted that no exports shall be allowed under DEPB scheme unless the DEPB rate of the concerned export product is notified.

Appendix 10A of the Handbook of Procedures prescribes the form regarding fixation of DEPB rates All applications for fixation of DEPB rates shall be routed through the concerned Export Promotion Council which shall verify the FOB value of exports as well as the international price of inputs covered under Standard Input Output Norms

For duty exemption, the Ministry of Finance has issued Notification No 45/2002-Cus dt 22.4.2002.

Jobbing, Repairing, etc. for Re-export

Import of goods, including those mentioned as restricted in ITC (HS) Classification but excluding prohibited items, in terms of paragraph 4.1.1. of the Policy supplied free of cost, may be permitted for the purpose of jobbing without a licence/certificate/permission as per the terms of notification issued by Department of Revenue from time to time In this regard, Min. of Finance, Deptt of Revenue has issued Notification No 32/97-Customs dt. 1.4.97. All goods so imported except the wastage shall be re-exported Minimum 10% value addition is to be achieved.

Back to Back Inland Letter of Credit

An Advance Licence holder, holder of Advance Licence for annual requirement and holder of DFRC may, instead of applying for an Advance Release Order avail the facility of Back to Back Inland Letter of Credit from the Banks For this purpose, the Advance Licence Holder and a DFRC holder may approach a Bank for opening an Inland Letter of Credit in favour of an indigenous supplier Before the opening of an L/C the Bank will ensure that necessary Bank Guarantee or Letter of Undertaking has been executed by the Advance Licence Holder and an endorsement to that effect has been made on the Licence However, execution of BG/LUT shall not be required against DFRC After opening the Inland Letter of Credit, the Bank shall make the endorsement specifying that the value of Advance Licence stands reduced by the value of inland L/C so opened on the (i) Exchange Control copy of the Advance Licence for Physical Exports/Deemed Exports/DFRC (11) Customs copy of the such Advance Licence

The licence shall be invalidated by the bank for direct import only in respect of the full quantity and value of the item being sourced indigenously

The non-negotiable copy of inland LC together with the photocopy of the Advance Licence duly carrying endorsements made by the bank shall be sufficient for the indigenous supplier to claim deemed export benefits LC issued against DFRC shall, however, be entitled only to benefit of Deemed Export Drawback, whereas LC for other categories shall be entitled to benefits of Deemed Export Drawback and Refund of Terminal Excise Duty.

Newcomers

In the case of newcomers, who have not exported in each of the preceding three licensing years, the Advance Licence shall be issued subject to furnishing 100% Bank Guarantee to Customs authority to cover exemption from Customs duty together with 15% interest Specific endorsement to this effect shall be made in the licence by the licensing authority.

III. Gem & Jewellery Export Promotion Schemes

Exporters of Gem and Jewellery are eligible to import their inputs by obtaining Replenishment (REP) Licence from the Licensing Authorities.

REP Licences are granted at the rate and tor the items mentioned in Appendix 26 of the Handbook of Procedures Such licenses may also be issued for import of consumables as per the details given in para 4.80 of Handbook of Procedures.

Exporters of gold/silver/platinum jewellery and articles thereof may import their essential inputs such as gold, silver, platinum, mountings, findings, rough gems, precious and semi precious stones, synthetic stones and unprocessed pearls etc in accordance with the procedure prescribed in the Handbook.

IV. Diamond Imprest Licence

Diamond Imprest Licence for import of cut & polished diamonds including semi processed diamonds, half cut diamonds, broken in any form, for mixing with cut & polished diamonds or for export as it is, may be issued for export of cut & polished diamonds Such licences shall carry an export obligation, which has to be discharged in accordance with the procedure specified in this behalf.

An exporter of cut & polished diamonds who is status holder may be issued a licence for import of cut & polished diamonds upto 5% of the export performance of the preceding year of cut & polished diamonds.

The export obligation against each consignment shall be fulfilled within a period of five months from the date of clearance of such consignment through Customs However, at no point of time, the importer shall be required to maintain records of individual import consignments nor will they be required to co-relate export consignments with the corresponding import consignments towards fulfillment of export obligation.

An application for Diamond Imprest licence for import of cut and polished diamonds including semi processed diamonds, half cut diamonds, broken in any form may be made to the licensing authority concerned as given in Appendix-25 of the Handbook (Vol. I), 2002-2007, in the prescribed form alongwith the documents prescribed therein[1]. In addition, the exporter shall furnish.

(i) Declaration giving the name and address of his bankers,

(ii) Certificate from his bankers to the effect that realisation of export proceeds against exports made by the exporter are not outstanding for a period of more than six months.

Holder of such Diamond Imprest Licence shall achieve a minimum value addition of 10% While discharging export obligation, the quantity of diamonds imported against such licence shall be accounted for in the caratage Cut and polished Diamonds exported for discharge of export obligation need not necessarily be the same as imported under this licence, as paragraph 4.4.16 of the Exim Policy permits mixing of these diamonds with other diamonds The holder of such Diamond Imprest Licence shall be eligible for import of such diamonds each not exceeding ¼ of a carat (25 cents) in weight These licences /goods imported against such licences shall be subject to actual user condition and will not be transferable even after completion of exports The entitlement for these licences shall be exhausted within the same year of its issuance and shall not be allowed to be carried forward to the next year.

Before clearance of the first consignment of import, the licensee shall execute, Legal Undertaking (LUT) with the concerned licensing authority. The duration of LUT shall be for a period of two years. The applicant may submit the LUT along with the application itself which may be accepted and such an acceptance may be endorsed on the back of the licence. The LUT shall be executed in the form given in Appendix 21 A of the Handbook (Vol. I), 2002-07.

In respect of Diamond Imprest Licence, issued under para 4.4.16 of Exim Policy, subsequently one more application for issue of the licence may also be considered, if 75% of the export obligation on the earlier licence has been fulfilled. However, a licence in the next year will be issued only if 75% of the export obligation on the subsequent licence has been fulfilled.

The Licensing Authority may grant extension in export obligation

1 As per Public Notice No. 3(RE-02)/2002-07, Dated 31.3.2002.

period for a period of four months against one or more consignment on payment of penalty of 1 % on the unfulfilled FOB value of export obligation with reference to CIF value of the imports made for which extension is being sought. Any request for extension beyond a period of four months can be considered only by a Committee headed by the Director General of Foreign Trade.

The cases of bonafide default in fulfilment of export obligation by an exporter who has obtained Diamond Imprest Licence may be regularised provided the exporter has paid customs duty along with 15% interest thereon to the Customs on the unutilised diamonds.

V. 100% Export Oriented Units and Units in STPs/EHTPs

Units undertaking to export their entire production of goods and services (except permitted DTA sales) may be set up under the Export Oriented Unit (EOU) Scheme, Electronic Hardware Technology Park (EHTP) Scheme or Software Technology Park (STP) Scheme. Such units may be engaged in manufacture, including repair, remaking, reconditioning, re-engineering and rendering of services. No trading units shall be permitted.

Facilities to 100% EOUs/STP/EHTP Units

Export Oriented Units enjoy the following benefits/incentives:

1. Can import or procure from the domestic sources, free of duty, all their requirements of capital goods, raw material, consumables, spares, packaging material, office equipments, DG sets etc.
2. No licences are required for import/domestic procurement.
3. Are exempted even from the anti-dumping duties.
4. Domestic procurement is free from variety of state levies including CST.
5. Are entitled for duty-free supply of furnace oil.
6. Are eligible for concessions in respect of payment of Income Tax.
7. Can utilize goods imported/domestically procured over a period of 3 years.
8. Can achieve NFEP cumulatively over a period of 5 years. Virtually no penal action for shortfalls during the first three years of operation. Requirement of minimum export performance also abolished.
9. Full freedom to sub-contract part of the production and production process in the domestic area. Gem and jewellery EOUs also permitted to sub-contract.

10. Can clear goods upto 50% of the value of exports in the domestic area on concessional duty. Sales beyond this limit can be made on full duty.
11. Can supply to other EOU/SEZ/EHTP/STP unit without payment of duty and such supplies are counted towards fulfilment of EP.
12. Supplies from the domestic area to EOU are allowed Deemed Export benefit.
13. Can procure duty-free inputs for supply of manufactured goods to advance licence holders.
14. Are exempted from industrial licensing for manufacture of items reserved for Small Scale Industry sector.
15. Are exempted from state trading regime except in limited cases.
16. Can club their exports with exports of their parent company for purposes of obtaining Trading House/Export House status.
17. Brand Promotion and Equity: Manufacturers/processors who have acquired quality status with specified certification from identified agencies are eligible for double weightage for recognition as status holder.
18. Can repatriate their profits freely without any dividend-balancing requirement.
19. Are permitted 100% Foreign Direct Investment through automatic approval route except for few sectors.
20. Agriculture/Horticulture processing EOUs may provide inputs and equipments to contract farmers in DTA to promote production of goods as per the requirement of importing countries.
21. Foreign bound passengers may take goods from EOUs to promote trade, tourism and exports.
22. Export/import of all products through post parcel/courier allowed.
23. Can sell all products including gems and jewellery through exhibitions and duty free shops or shops set up abroad.

VI. Special Economic Zones (SEZs)

Special Economic Zones (SEZs) is a specially delineated duty free enclave and shall be deemed to be foreign territory for the purposes of trade operations and duties and tariffs. Goods and Services going into the SEZ area shall be treated as deemed exports and goods and services coming into Domestic Tariff Area (DTA) from the SEZ shall be treated as if the goods are being imported.

SEZ units may be set up for manufacture of goods and rendering of services/ production/processing, assembling, trading, repair, remaking, reconditioning, reengineering including making of gold/silver/platinum Jewellery and article thereof or in connection therewith.

(1) SEZ units may export goods and services including agro-products, partly processed goods, sub-assemblies and components except prohibited items It may also export by-products, rejects, waste scrap arising out of the production process.

(2) SEZ unit may import/procure from the DTA without payment of duly all types of goods and services, including capital goods, whether new or second hand, required by it for its activities or in connection therewith provided they are not prohibited items of imports in the ITC (HS) However, any permission required for import under any other law shall be applicable Goods shall include raw material tor making capital goods for use within the unit The units shall also be permitted to import goods required tor the approved activity, including capital goods, free of cost or on loan from clients.

SEZ units may procure goods required by it without payment of duty, from bonded warehouses in the DTA set up under the Policy and from International Exhibitions held in India.

SEZ units may import/procure from DTA, without payment of duty, all types of goods for creating a central facility for use by units in SEZ The central facility for software development can also be accessed by units in the DTA for export for software.

Gem & Jewellery units may also source gold/silver/platinum through the nominated agencies.

SEZ units may also import/procure goods and services from DTA without payment of duty for, setting up, operation and maintenance of units in the Zone

(3) SEZ unit may on the basis of a firm contract between the parties, source the capital goods from a domestic/foreign leasing company In such a case the SEZ unit and the domestic/foreign leasing company shall Jointly file the documents to enable import/ procurement of the capital goods without payment of duty.

(4) SEZ unit shall be a positive net foreign exchange earner.

(5) The unit shall execute a legal undertaking with the Development Commissioner concerned and in the event of failure to achieve positive foreign exchange earning it shall be liable to penalty in

terms of the legal undertaking or under any other law for the time being in force.

(6) SEZ unit may export goods manufactured or software developed by it, though a merchant-exporter/status holder recognised under the policy or any other EOU/SEZ/EHTP/STP unit.

(7) Goods imported/procured by an SEZ unit may be transferred or given on loan to another unit, within the same SEZ which shall be duly accounted for, but not counted towards discharge of export performance.

(8) SEZ unit, including gem and jewellery units, may subcontract a part of their production or production process through units in the DTA or through other SEZ/EOU/EHTP/STP with the permission of the Customs authorities Subcontracting of part of production process may also be permitted abroad with the approval of the Development Commissioner.

(9) SEZ units may sell goods, including by-products and services, in the DTA on payment of applicable duties.

(10) Other Entitlements.

(i) Units set up in SEZs will be charged rent for lease of industrial plots and standard design factory buildings/sheds as per rates fixed from time to time.

(ii) Corporate tax SEZ units engaged in manufacturing and services will be eligible for entitlements in respect of payment of income tax as per the provisions of Income Tax Act

(iii) Exemption from service tax.

(iv) FOB Value of export of an SEZ unit can be clubbed with FOB value of export of its parent company in the DTA, or vice versa, for the purpose of according Export House, Trading House, Star Trading House or Super Star Trading House status,

(v) Foreign Investment Foreign Equity up to 100% is permissible for all manufacturing activities in Special Economic Zones (SEZs), under automatic route, except for the following activities:

(a) arms and ammunition, explosives and allied items of defence equipment, defence aircraft and warships,

(b) atomic substances,

(c) narcotics and psychotropic substances and hazardous chemicals,

(d) distillation and brewing of alcoholic drinks, and

(e) cigarettes/cigars and manufactured tobacco substitutes Sectoral norms as notified by the Government shall apply to foreign investment in services and trading activities

(vi) SEZ units may retain 100% of their export proceeds in their EEFC account.

(vii) Export value of goods, software and services by SEZ units may be realized and repatriated to India within 12 months from the date of export or within the time extended by Reserve Bank of India.

(viii) Software units may, in addition, also be allowed to use the computer system for training purpose (including commercial training) subject to the condition that no computer terminal shall be installed outside the Zone premises for the purpose.

(ix) Procurement of raw materials and export of finished products shall be exempt from Central levies.

(x) Exemption from industrial licensing for manufacture of items reserved for SSI sector.

(xi) State Trading Enterprises policy shall not apply to SEZ manufacturing units Export of iron ore shall however be subject to the decision of the Government from time to time Requirements of other conditions like minimum export price/ export in consumer pack as per Exim Policy shall apply in case the raw materials are indigenous and exported without further processing/manufacturing by the SEZ units Export of textile items shall be covered by bilateral agreements, if any Wood based units shall comply with the directions of Hon'able Supreme Court.

(xii) SEZ unit may install one tax machine at a place of its choice, outside the Zone, subject to intimation of its location to the concerned Customs/Central Excise authorities.

(xiii) SEZ units may, temporarily take out of the Zone duty free laptop computers and video projection systems for working upon by persons authorised by unit.

(xiv) SEZ units may install personal computers not exceeding two in number imported/procure duty free in the registered/ administrative office subject to the guidelines issued by Department of Revenue in this behalf.

(xv) For IT and IT enabled services, persons authorized by the software units may access the facility installed in the SEZ unit through communication links.

VII. Agri Export Zones

Units in Agriculture Export Zones are entitled to all the import facilities available for export of goods in terms of the provisions of the respective schemes discussed earlier in this Chapter

VIII. Service Providers

Service Providers are entitled to all the import facilities available for export of goods in terms of the provision of the respective Schemes discussed earlier in this Chapter.

IX. Status Holders

Status Certificate

Merchant as well as Manufacturer exporters, Service providers, Export Oriented Units (EOUs) / units located in Special Economic Zone (SEZ's) /Agri Export Zone (AEZs) / Electronic Hardware Technology Parks (EHTPs)/ Soft ware Technology Parks (STPs) shall be eligible for such recognition.

Export Performance Level

The applicant is required to achieve the prescribed average export performance level

Category	Average FOB / FOR value during the preceding l/2/3 licensing years, in Rupee's
Export House	45 crore
Trading House	300 crore
Star Trading House	1500 crore
Super Star Trading House	6000 crore

Note:

1. Units in Small Scale Industry/Tiny Sector/Cottage Sector/Units registered with KVICs or KVIBs/ Units located in North Eastern States, Sikkim and J&K/ Units exporting handloom, handicrafts, hand knotted carpets, silk carpets/exporters holding golden status/ exporters exporting to countries in Latin America and CIS/sub

Saharan Africa, units having ISO 9000 (series) / WHO GMP/ HACCP/SEI CMM level-II and above status granted by specified agencies shall be entitled for export house status on achieving Rs 15 crore FOB/ FOR during the current licensing year or during the preceding 1/2/3 licensing years The same threshold limit shall be applicable to the service exporters and agri exporters (other than grains) for obtaining Export house status

2. Export made on re-export basis shall not be counted for the purpose of recognition.
3. The exports made by a subsidiary of a limited company shall be counted towards export performance of the limited company for the purpose of recognition For this purpose, the company shall have the majority shareholding in the subsidiary company.

Special Strategic Package for Status Holders

The status holders shall be eligible for the following new/ special facilities.

(i) Licence/certificate/permissions and Customs clearances for both imports and exports on self-declaration basis,

(ii) Fixation of Input-Output norms on priority within 60 days,

(iii) Exemption from compulsory negotiation of documents through banks. The remittance, however, would continue to be received through banking channels;

(iv) 100% retention of foreign exchange in EEFC account;

(v) Enhancement in normal repatriation period from 180 days to 360 days.

(vi) Duty free import entitlement for status holders having incremental growth of more than 25% in FOB value of exports (in free foreign exchange) subject to a minimum export turnover of Rs. 25 crore (in free foreign exchange). The duty free entitlement shall be 10% of the incremental growth in exports. Such entitlement can be used for import of capital goods, office equipment and inputs for their own factory or the factory of the associate/supporting manufacturer/job worker. The entitlement/ goods shall not be transferable.

X. Deemed Exports

"Deemed Exports" refers to those transactions in which the goods supplied do not leave the country and the payment for such supplies is received either in Indian rupees or in free foreign exchange.

Categories of Supply

The following categories of supply of goods by the main/ sub-contractors regarded as "Deemed Exports", provided the goods are manufactured in India:

(a) Supply of goods against Advance Licence/Advance Licence for Annual Requirement/DFRC under the Duty Exemption /Remission Scheme.

(b) Supply of goods to Export Oriented Units (EOUs) or units located in Special Economic Zone (SEZs) or Software Technology Parks (STPs) or Electronic Hardware Technology Parks (EHTPs).

(c) Supply of capital goods to holders of licences under the Export Promotion Capital Goods (EPCG) scheme.

(d) Supply of goods to projects financed by multilateral or bilateral agencies/funds as notified by the Department of Economic Affairs, Ministry of Finance under International Competitive Bidding in accordance with the procedures of those agencies/funds, where the legal agreements provide for tender evaluation without including the customs duty.

(e) Supply of capital goods, including in unassembled/ disassembled condition as well as plants, machinery, accessories, tools, dies and such goods which are used for installation purposes till the stage of commercial production and spares to the extent of 10% of the FOR value to fertiliser plants.

(f) Supply of goods to any project or purpose in respect of which the Ministry of Finance, by a notification, permits the import of such goods at zero customs duty coupled with the extension of deemed exports benefits to domestic supplies.

(g) Supply of goods to the power projects and refineries not covered in (f above.

(h) Supply of marine freight containers by 100% EOU (Domestic freight containers-manufacturers) provided the said containers are exported out of India within 6 months or such further period as permitted by the Customs.

(i) Supply to projects funded by UN agencies.

(j) Supply of goods to nuclear power projects through competitive bidding as opposed to international competitive bidding.

The benefits of deemed exports shall be available under paragraph (a), (e), (f) and (g) only if the supply is made under the procedure of International Competitive Bidding (ICB).

Benefits for Deemed Exports

Deemed exports shall be eligible for any/all of the following benefits in respect of manufacture and supply of goods qualifying as deemed exports subject to the terms and conditions as given in Handbook (Vol.I):-

(a) Advance Licence for intermediate supply/ deemed export/DFRC.

(b) Deemed Exports Drawback.

(c) Refund of Terminal Excise duty.

XI. Garment Quota Policy

Quota policy for export of certain yarn fabrics and made up items from Cotton to U.S.A., EEC Member States, Sweden, Norway, Finland, Canada and Austria is announced by the Ministry of Textiles. Similarly quota policy for export of garments and knitwars to these countries is announced.

21

Availing Financial Incentives

Besides foreign exchange facilities and incentives under the Import Export Policy, 2002-07 a number of financial and fiscal incentives are also available to the exporters. In this chapter we shall briefly discuss various financial incentives. Fiscal incentives will be discussed in subsequent chapter.

Various financial incentives available to the exporters are as under:

I. Marketing Development Assistance (MDA)

Assistance under Marketing Development Fund is provided by the Government for stimulating and diversifying the export trade. It is available in respect of the following purposes:

(i) Market research, commodity research, area survey and research;

(ii) Export publicity and dissemination of information:

(iii) Participation in trade fairs and exhibitions;

(iv) Trade delegation and study teams;

(v) Establishment of offices and branches in countries abroad; and

(vi) Grants in aid to Export Promotion Councils and other approved organisations.

The Federation of Indian Exporters Organisation (FIEO) disburses MDA grants for the following four activities on behalf of the Ministry of Commerce:

(i) One person sale-cum-study tour (s) abroad;

(ii) Participation in fairs/exhibitions abroad;

(iii) Bringing out publications for use abroad; and

(iv) Advertising in foreign media.

Export Promotion Councils/Commodity Boards/APEDA/MPEDA also grant MDA assistance for the above type of activities in conjunction with FIEO.

MDA for other activities like opening of foreign offices, setting up of warehouses and after sales services, installations abroad, research and development work on products etc. is disbursed directly by the Ministry of Commerce, Udyog Bhawan, New Delhi-110 001.

II. Spices Export Promotion Schemes

Under these schemes the Spices Board develops the production and exports of value added spices through spice house certification, Spices Board Logo, Brand Promotion Scheme, Financial assistance for printing of brochure/ folders, assistance for packaging development, reimbursement of air freight/ courier charges for sending samples abroad etc.

III. Air Freight Subsidy on Horticulture and Floriculture Exports

In order to make exports of horticulture (i.e. specified fresh fruits, and specified fresh vegetables) and floriculture products competitive in the world market, the Government grants; air freight subsidy on selected fruits and floriculture items.

IV. New External Marketing Assistance Scheme for Jute

The scheme envisages grant of market assistance at the rate of 5-10% of the F.O.B. value realisation on export of specified diversified products. The benefit under the scheme is available to both manufacturer exporters and merchant exporters.

V. Financial Assistance Scheme for Agricultural, Horticulture and Meat Exports

The Agricultural Products Export Development Authority (APEDA) provides assistance upto 50 per cent of the cost of study subject to the ceiling of Rs. 2 lakhs per beneficiary lor undertaking feasibility studies and market surveys by growers, exporters and their organisations. The surveys may be conducted to find potential export markets/accessing market information and price trends, with respect to products, infrastructure requirements, etc. This assistance aims at encouraging exporters, growers and trade associations to develop their own market and information sources.

VI. Financial Assistance for Marine Products Exports

There are a number of financial assistance schemes to promote export production and marketing of products of the fisheries sector. These schemes, *inter alia*, cover all stages or aspects like farming quality control, development of production infrastructure and equipment, transportation and air freighting of samples.

VII. Market Access Initiative (MAI)

Financial assistance shall be available under the scheme to the export promotion councils, industry and trade associations and other eligible entities, as may be notified from time to time, on the basis of the competitive merits of proposals received in this regard for the following purposes which inter-alia includes:-

(i) Marketing studies on country product focus approach basis.

(ii) Setting up of common showrooms under one roof and warehousing facility in the identified centres on the basis of marketing studies in important cities abroad.

(iii) Participation in sales promotion campaigns through international departmental stores.

(iv) Publicity campaign for launching identified products in selected markets.

(v) Participation in international trade fairs, seminars, buyers sellers meet.

(vi) Promotion of select brands.

(vii) Transport subsidies for select agriculture products.

(viii) Registration charges for product registration abroad for pharmaceuticals, bio-technology and agro chemicals and testing charges for engineering products.

(ix) Inland freight subsidies for units located in North East, Sikkim and Jammu & Kashmir.

(x) Setting up of "business centre" in Indian missions abroad for visiting Indian exporters/businessmen.

VIII. Towns of Export Excellence

A number of towns in specific geographical locations have emerged as dynamic industrial locations handsomely contributing to India's exports. These "Industrial Clusters" rooted in history symbolise the bursting forth of the free market spirit and are essentially collective response to common problems of competitiveness. Some have become globally renowned manufacturing bases. It is necessary to grant recognition to these industrial cluster items with a view to maximize their export profiles and help in upgrading them to move up in the higher value markets.

A number of such industrial cluster towns are exporting a substantial portion of their products which are world class. For example, Tirupur is exporting 80% of its production of hosiery. A beginning is being made to consider industrial cluster towns such as Tirupur for hosiery, woollen blanket in Panipat, woollen knitwear in Ludhiana to be eligible for the following benefits:-

Common service providers in these areas shall be entitled for facility of EPCG scheme. The recognised associations of units will be able to access the funds under the Market Access Initiative scheme for creating focussed technological services. Further such areas will receive priority for assistance for identified critical infrastructure gaps from the scheme on Central Assistance to States mentioned in paragraph 3.1 of the Policy. The units in these notified areas would be eligible for availing all the EXIM policy schemes as per their choice and the provisions of those schemes shall stand relaxed to the extent provided in this paragraph in respect of such units.

Existing industrial clusters need upgradation of services and simplification of procedures. To achieve that purpose, it is proposed to bring about synergy and convergence of various schemes for development of cluster to improve the competitiveness of the units located there.

Selected towns producing goods of Rs. 1000 crore or more will be notified as Towns of Exports Excellence on the basis of potential for growth in exports. Proposal for strengthening infrastructure, simplifying rules & procedures and developing production infrastructure relating to design, R&D packaging, logistic support as well as to provide awareness and information about international marketing will be considered under the scheme.

IX. Special Focus on Cottage and Handicraft Sector

The small scale sector alongwith the cottage and handicraft sector has been contributing to more than half of the total exports of the country. The cottage and handicrafts sector, which mostly employs artisan and rural people, contributes significantly to this effort. In recognition of the export performance of this sector and to further increase its competitiveness, the following facilities shall be extended to this sector:

(i) The unit in this sector shall be eligible for funds from Market Access Initiative (MAI) scheme. Funds shall be earmarked for this sector in the MAI scheme. The funds shall be utilised for developing their website for virtual exhibition, among other activities;

(ii) Under the EPCG scheme, these units will not be required to maintain average level of exports as given in paragraph 5.4 (i) of the Policy;

(iii) These units shall be entitled to the benefit of export house status on achieving lower total export/deemed export performance of Rs. 15 crore during the preceding three licensing years. However, for new entrants, having exports of less than three years, such status may be granted on achieving the total exports of Rs.15 crore in the current or preceding one/two licensing years as given in paragraph 3.7.2 of the Policy; and

(iv) The units in handicraft sector shall be entitled to duty free imports of specified items upto 3% of FOB value of their exports.

22

Institutional Support for Exporters

A number of institutions in India are engaged in export promotion activities in their respective fields. Exporters should contact them for the necessary assistance.

1. Export Promotion Councils (EPCs) also known as registering authorities, a list of which is given in Appendix II.
2. Commodity Boards assisting the exporters in the same manner as the Export Promotion Councils.
3. Federation of Indian Export Organisations (FIEO), Punjab Haryana Chamber Building, 4/2 Siri Fort Institutional Area, New Delhi 110016, is an apex organisation coordinating and supplementing the export promotional activities of various organisations and institutions.
4. Indian Institute of Foreign Trade (IIFT), B-21, Industrial Area, South of IIT, New Delhi 110016, develops and organises new training programmes, research and market studies in the field of foreign trade
5. Indian Institute of Packaging (IIP), Plot No. 2, Macol Industrial Estate, P.B. 9432. Chakaia Andheri (E). Mumbai 400093, for improving the standard of packaging for various benefits.
6. Export Inspection Council (EIC), 11th Floor, Pragati Tower, 26 Rajendra Place, New Delhi 110008, provides sound development of export trade through quality control and pre-shipment inspection.
7. Indian Council of Arbitration (ICA), Federation House. Tansen Marg, New Delhi 110001, promotes the use of commercial arbitration in India.

8. India Trade Promotion Organisation (ITPO), Pragati Bhawan, Pragati, Maidan, New Delhi 110002 provides facilities concerning participation in fairs and exhibitions in India and abroad.

9. Chambers of Commerce & Industry, help in issuing certificate of origin and taking up specific cases of exporters to the Govt.

10. Bureau of Indian Standards (BIS), 9, Manak Bhavan. Bhahadur Shah Zafar Marg, New Delhi 110002 is engaged in standard formulation, certification marking and laboratory testing.

11. Export Directorate of Development Commissioner and Small Scale industries.

12. Scope Shipping Standing Committee functioning in the Ministry of Commerce, resolves the problems relating to quality, adequacy and cost of transportation problems faced by the exporters.

13. Textiles Committee, Textile Centre, Second Floor, 34 P D' Mello Road, Wadi Bandar, Mumbai 400009, carries pre-shipment inspection of textiles and market research for textile yarns, textile machines etc.

14. Marine Products Export Development Authority, World Trade Centre, MG Road, Ernakulam South, Cochin 682016, helps in the development of marine products meant for export with special reference to processing, packaging, storage and marketing etc.

15. India Investment Centre (IIC), Jeevan Vihar, 4th Floor, Parliament Street, New Delhi 110001, advises and assists Indian businessmen for setting up of industrial or other joint ventures abroad.

16. Freight Investigation Bureau assists in solving problems relating to freight rates, shipping space and regular shipping facilities etc.

17. Indian Govt. Trade Representative at various important cities in foreign countries assist Indian exporters regarding promotion of Indian products to the World Market.

18. Foreign Govt. Trade Missions in India help in marketing Indian products to their markets.

19. Directorate of Drawback in the Ministry of Finance fixes drawback rates of items exported. It also formulates the procedure and documents required for claim of duty drawback.

20. Board of Trade in the Ministry of Commerce provides of forum for ensuring continuous dialogue with trade and industry in respect of major developments in the field of international trade.

21. Office of the Director General of Foreign Trade (DGFT), New Delhi

is responsible for execution of the import and export policies of the Govt. of India. It has various subordinate offices in India.

22. Director General of Commercial Intelligence and Statistics (DGCIS), Council House Street, Kolkata 700001, is the primary agency for the collection, compilation and the publication of the foreign, inland and ancillary trade statistics and dissemination of various types of commercial information.

23. State Laison officers appointed by the State Governments develop export trade in goods produced in their States in consonance with the policies of the Central Government.

24. Niryat Bandhus are the nodal officers nominated by the states for export promotion work.

25. Air Cargo Task Force focuses attention and resolves problems faced by trade in the air freight industry.

26. Export Facilitation Committee set up by the Government, looks into the problems of generic nature faced by the exporters and which have not been resolved as a result of their interaction with the concerned agencies in the Ministry of Commerce or other Ministries/Departments.

Appendix I

Application Form For Allotment of Importer-Exporter Code (IEC) Number and Modification in Particulars of an Existing IEC No. Holder[1]

Note:

1. Please see paragraph 2.12 of the Policy and Paragraph 2.9 of the Handbook.
2. Please read the general instructions given at Appendix I before filling this application.

(For Office Use Only)

File Number .... Date .... IEC No. allotted ....

1. Application for (please tick)

   (A) Allotment of IEC No. ☐

   (B) Modification in particulars of existing IEC No. holder ☐

2. Name and address of the applicant (Registered office in case of limited companies and Head office for others) ....

   Pin ☐☐☐☐☐☐☐

3. Address of all the Branches/Divisions/Units/factories located in India and abroad.

   1. .... Pin ☐☐☐☐☐☐☐

   2. .... Pin ☐☐☐☐☐☐☐

   3. .... Pin ☐☐☐☐☐☐☐

   4. .... Pin ☐☐☐☐☐☐☐

4. E-Mail of the applicant : (for communication with DGFT) ....

---

1 Appendix 3 of Handbook of Procedure (Vol. 1), 2002-07.

5. PAN details:

   (a) Permanent Account Number: (PAN) ☐☐☐☐☐☐☐☐☐☐

   (b) Issuing authority: ....

6. (A) Date of birth of individual: (in case of proprietorships) ....

   (B) Date of incorporation: (in case of companies) ....

   (C) Date of formation: (In case of others) ....

7. In case the application is for modification in existing IHC, give:

   (a) Existing IEC No.: ....

   (b) Nature of modification required and details thereof: ....

8. Particulars of Fees Paid:

   (i) Bank Receipt / Demand Draft No. ....

   (ii) Name of Bank & Branch of issue ....

   (iii) Amount (in Rs.): ....

9. Details of Proprietor/Partner (s) /Director(s)) /Karta/Trustees to be given in the following manner:

   (a) Name : ....

   (b) Father's Name : ....

   (c) Residential address : ....

   (d) E. Mail address : ....

   (e) Telephone : ....

   (Note: Attach extra sheet wherever required)

10. In case of proprietorship, kindly indicate the total number and details of IEC (s) held by the proprietor ....
....
....
....

Declaration/Undertaking

1. I/We hereby declare that the particulars and the statements made in this application are true and correct to the best of my/our knowledge and belief and nothing has been concealed or held therefrom.
2. I/We fully understand that any information furnished in the application if proved incorrect or false will lender me/us liable for any penal action or other consequences as may be prescribed in law or otherwise warranted.
3. I/We undertake to abide by the provisions of the Foreign Trade (Development and Regulation) Act, 1992, the Rules and Orders framed thereunder, the Export and Import Policy Handbook of Procedures and any other documents issued under the Exim Policy.
4. I/We hereby declare that this application is made by me/us in the name of Registered/ Head office and I/we have not obtained or applied for Importer Exporter Code Number previously in this name from any office of the DGFT/Development Commissioner (Not applicable for existing IEC number holder).
5. I hereby certity that I am authorised to verify and sign this declaration as per Paragraph 9.9 of the Policy.
6. I/we hereby certify that none of the Proprietor/ Partner (s) / Director (s) /Karta/Trustees of the firm or company is a Proprietor/ Partner (s) /Director (s) /Karta/Trustees of the firm/ Company, which has come to the adverse notice of DGFT.
7. (Strike out whichever is not applicable).
   (a) The Proprietor/Partner (s) /Director (s) /Karta/Trustee, as the case may be of the firm/company is/are not associated as Proprietor/ Partner (s) /Director (s) /Karta/Trustee in any other firm/company which is in the caution list of RBI.
   (b) The Proprietor/Partner (s) /Director (s) /Karta/Trustee as the case may be of the firm/ company is/are associated as Proprietor/Partner (s) /Director (s) /Karta/Trustee in any other firm/company which is in the caution list of RBI.
8. (Strike out whichever is not applicable).
   (a) There is no non-resident interest in the firm/company and no non-resident investment with or without repatriation benefits has been made in the company.

(b) There is non-resident interest in the firm/company and no non-resident investment without repatriation benefits in the firm/ company is held with the general/specific permission of RBI (In case of specific RBI approval a self certified copy may also be furnished).

(c) There is non-resident interest in the firm/company and non-resident investment with repatriation benefits in the firm/ company is held with the specific permission of RBI (In case of specific RBI approval a self certified copy may also be furnished).

Photo of the Applicant duly attested by Bank	Signature of Applicant..
	Name..
	Designation..
	Official Address...
	Tele No...
	Residential Address...
Place :	....
Date :	E- Mail Address...

Documents to be enclosed with the application form

1. Bank Receipt (in duplicate) /Demand Draft evidencing payment of application fee in terms of Appendix 29.
2. Certificate from the Banker of the applicant firm (as per Annexure 1 to this form).
3. Two copies of Pass Port Size photographs of the applicant duly attested by the banker of the applicant.
4. A copy of Permanent Account Number issued by Income Tax Authorities duly attested by the applicant.

Note: Where the applicant declares that they are associated with firms/ companies caution listed by RBI they will be allotted IE Code No but with an additional condition that they can export only with RBI's prior approval and they should approach RBI for the purpose.

Annexure 1 to Appendix 3

Bank's Certificate

(To be issued on the official letter head of the Bank)

Ref. No. ....

To

....

....

(Name and address of the licensing authority)

Sir/Madam,

We certify that M/s ....
(Name and Address of the applicant)

are maintaining a Savings Bank Account/Current Account (tick whichever is applicable) No. .... with us since ....

Date: .... (Signature of the Banker)

Place: .... Name ....

Designation ....

(Official Stamp)

Appendix 1A

Profile of Exporter/Importer[1]

(For Official Use)

File No. .... Date ....

Note: To be submitted once alongwith the first application and to be submitted subsequently only in case of any change in the information already submitted. RLAs to enter this information in the computer so as to dispense with the need of repetitive declaration.

1. Name of the Applicant ....
2. Address of the applicant (Registered Office in case of limited companies, and Head Office for others) ....
....
....
....

   Tele No:................................

   Fax No:................................

   E-Mail Address.....................

3. IEC No. .... Date of Issue .... Issuing Authority ....
4. Nature of the concern, (please tick the appropriate column):

   Proprietorship ☐, Partnership ☐, Private Limited company ☐, Public Limited company ☐, HUF ☐, Trust ☐, Others ☐

5. Details of Proprietor/Partner (s) /Director (s) /Karta/Trustees to be given in the following manner:

   (a) Name ....

1 Appendix 2 of Handbook of Procedure (Vol. 1), 2002-07.

(b) Father's Name ....

(c) Residential address ....

(d) E-Mail address ....

(e) Telephone ....

(Note: Attach extra sheet wherever required)

6. Please tick the appropriate column.

(1) Manufacturer Exporter ☐

(2) Merchant Exporter ☐

(3) Service provider ☐

(4) Merchant cum Manufacturer ☐

(5) Trust ☐

(6) Others (please specify) ....

7. Status Code (Pl. tick the appropriate column)

Export House ☐, Trading House ☐, Star Trading House ☐, Super Star Trading House ☐, None ☐

Relevant Certificate No. ....

Issuing Date: ....

Valid upto: ....

8. RCMC No. .... Date of Issue ....

Valid upto .... Issuing Authority ....

Place: ....

Date: ......

Signature of the Proprietor/Partner (s) /...

Director (s) /Karta/Trustee ....

Name ....

Designation ....

Apppendix II

List of licensing authorities and their jurisdiction*

Sl. No.	Name & Address	Telegraphic/Tel./ Tlx/Fax No./E-Mail No.	Territorial Jurisdiction
1.	2.	3.	4.
		Head Quarter	
1.	Director General of Foreign Trade Udyog Bhavan, New Delhi.	CHIEF CONIMPEX **Tel:** 011-23011777 **Tlx** : 0131-66773 **Fax** : 011-23011779 011-23018613 **E-Mail:** dgft@ub.nic.in	Throught India
		Regional Licensing Authorities	
Northern Zone			
2.	The Joint Director General of Foreign Trade, Central Licensing Area, B. K. Roy Court, 6-7, Asaf Ali Road, New Delhi	**CONIMPEXTRA** **New** Delhi **Tel** : 011-23234935 011-23231694 **Tlx** : 031-61894 Fax. : 01-23234265	- Delhi, - Haryana, districts of (i) Faridabad (ii) Gurgaon - Uttar Pradesh, districts of namely (i) Meerut, (ii) Ghaziabad, (iii) Bulandshahar, (iv) Haridwar
3.	The Joint Director General of Foreign Trade, Udyog Bhavan, III Floor, Tilak Marg, Jaipur - 5.	CONIMPEXTRA Jaipur Tel : 0141-2380604/238259 Fax : 0141-2380604 E-Mail : jd dgft@raj.nic.in	Rajasthan.

1 Appendix 24 of Handbook of Procedure (Vol. 1), 2002-07.

1.	2.	3.	4.
4.	The Joint Director General of Foreign Trade, 6-IV-C, Green Field, Near Shakti Nagar Chowk, Ludhiana.	CONIMPEXTRA Ludhiana Tel : 0161-2430474/2401754 E-Mail : dgftldh@ ldh.nic.in	punjab excluding the districts of Amritsar and Roop Nagar (Roopar).
5.	The Joint Director General of Foreign Trade, 117/L/444 Kakadeo, Kanpur-208025. Tlx : 0325-261 Fax : 0512-2501344 E-Mail : jdgftkan@knp.nic.in	CONTIMPEXTRA Kanpur Tel : 0512-2250352 Tlx : 0325-261 Fax : 0512-2501344 E-Mail : jdgftkan@knp.nic.in	Uttar Pradesh excluding those areas which are under the jurisdiction of Jt. Director General of Foreign Trade (CLA), New Delhi, Varanasi, Moradabad and Panipat.
6.	The Joint Director General of Foreign Trade, B-38/1-A-2, Tulsipur, Mehmoorganj, Varanasi (U.P.) 0542-361907	CONTEMPEXTRA Varanasi Tel : 0542-362957 0542-361907	Districts of Varanasi, Mirzapur, Ghazipur, Azamgarh, Ballia, Deoria, Gorakhpur, Basti, Jaipur, Sonebhadra, Mau and Sidharthanagar.
7.	The Joint Director General of Foreign Trade, 110-111, Parvasnath Plaza, Majhola, Delhi Road, Moradabad-244103	CONIMPEXTRA Moradabad Tel : 0591-2488221 Fax : 0591-2487447 E-Mail : jdgftmbd@hotmail.com	Districts of Bijnaur, Moradabad, Rampur and Jyotiba Phuley Nager, in UP and Uttranchal excluding Haridwar
8.	The Jt. Director General of Foreign Trade, The Mall, C.B.R. Building, Amritsar-143001.	CONIMPEXTRA Amritsar Tel : 0183 : 2506403/2507403 Fax : 0183-2506403 E-Mail : rjdgftaser@hotmail.com	Amritsar District.
9.	The Jt. Director of Foreign Trade, Sector-35, D.S.C.O. 288, Chandigarh-160023	CONIMPEXTRA Chandigarh Tel : 0172-602314 Fax : 0172-648661 E-Mail : jdgcht@chd.nic.in	Himanchal Pradesh and Union Territory of Chandigarh as well as district of Roop Nagar (Roop) and Panchkula.

1.	2.	3.	4.
10.	The Jt. Director General of Foreign Trade, Model Town, Panipat (Haryana).	CONIMPEXTRA Panipat Tel : 0180-2650984/2651427 Fax. 0180 : 0180-2650710 E-Mail : jdgftpnp@yahoo.com	Haryana excluding districts of (i) Faridabad (ii) Gurgaon and (iii) Panchkula. Districts of Uttar Pradesh, (i) Saharanpur (ii) Muzaffarnagar
11.	The Jt. Director General of Foreign Trade 24/C, Gandhi Nagar, Jammu	Tel : 0191-535834 Fax. : 0191-535834 E-Mail : dgftjammu@yahoo.com	Jammu & Kashmir
Western Zone			
12.	The Jt. Director General of Trade, Central Govt. Offices, New Building, S.E. Wing, New Marine Lines Churchgare, Mumbai-400020	CONIMPEXTRA Mumbai Tel : 022-22016421 Tlx : 01185604 JCCI IN Fax : 022-22063438 E-Mail : zjdgft@dgftmum.bom.guj.nic.in	Maharashtra excluding the area which are under the Jurisdiction of Joint Director General of Foreign Trade (i) Pune, (ii) Daman, (iii) Dadra and Nagar Haveli.
13.	The Joint Director General of Foreign Trade, 'A' BlocK, 11th Floor, Govt. Multistoreyed Building, Lal Darwaja. Alhabad - 380001	CONIMPEXTRA Ahmedabad Tel : 0272 : 5506791/5506297 Tlx : 0272- 5506791/5506297 JCCI IN Fax : 0272-5506791 E-Mail : jdgftahd@fujl.fuj.nic.in	Gujrat State excluding the areas which are under the jurisdiction of Jt. DGFT Rajkot, Baroda, Surat and Development Commissioner KFTZ.
14.	The Joint Director General of Foreign Trade 'C' Block, PMT Commercial Complex, P.B. No. 1623, Pune-411042 Shankaresth Road, Swargate Pune-411037	CONIMPEXTRA Pune Tel : 020-4441577/4449598 Fax : 020-4441577 E-Mail : jdgftpune@hotmail.com	Districts of Maharashtra (i) Pune, (ii) Ahmed Nagar, (iii) Jalna, (iv) Beed, (v) Kolhapur, (vi) Latur, (vii) Nanded (viii) Osmanabad, (ix)Prabhani, (x) Ratnagiri, (xi) Sangli, (xii) Satara, (xiii) Solapur, (xiv) Sidhudurg (xv) Nasik.

1.	2.	3.	4.
15.	The Jt. Director General of Foreign Trade, Kuber Bhawan, 9th Floor, E-Block, Room No. 901, & 902, Kothi Compound, Vadodara - 390 001	Tel : 0265-2429368/2428789 Fax : 0265-2428789 E-Mail : jdgft@satyam.net.in	Districts of Gujrat (i) Vadodara, (ii) Kheda, (iii) Panchmahal (iv) Broach. Madhya Pradesh and Chhattisgarh
16.	The Jt. Director General of Foreign Trade, Office Building 'A' 3rd Floor, Nirman Sadan CGO Building, Behind Govt Press, 52-A, Area Hills, Bhopal - 462011	CONIMPEXTRA Bhopal Tel : 0755-2553323 Fax : 0755-2553303 E-Mail : dgftbpl@hotmail.nic.in	
17.	The Dy. Director General of Foreign Trade, Ashirwad Building, 18th June Road, Santa Inoz, Panjim-403001 (Goa)	CONIMPEXTRA Panjim Tel : 0832-224968 E-Mail : jdgftgoa@hotmail.com	Goa
18.	The Jt. Director General of Foreign Trade, Desai Building, Kavi Nanalai Marg, Bhupindra Road, Rajkot-360001.	CONIMPEXTRA Rajkot Tel : 0281-2227[illegible]30 Fax : 0281-2224185 E-Mail : jdgftraj@hotmail.com	The Districts of Gujrat (i) Saurashtra (excluding Kutch) (ii) Diu in the Union Territory of Daman and Diu.
19.	The Jt. Director General of Foreign Trade, Surat 634-636 Belgium Tower, Ring Road, Surat-395003. Eastern Zone	CONIMPEXTRA Surat Tel : 0261-2423381 Fax : 0261-2452216 E-Mail : dgftsur@fuj.nic.in	Districts of Gujrat (i) Surat, (ii) Valsad and (iii) Dangs.
20.	The Joint Director, General of Foreign Trade, 4 Esplanade East, Kolkata-700069.	CONIMPEXTRA Kolkata Tel : 033-22481228 Fax : 033-224858952 E-Mail : dgft@wb.nic.in	West Bengal, Sikkim, Tripura and Union Territory of Andaman and Nicobar.

1.	2.	3.	4.
21.	The Jt. Director General of Foreign Trade, Maitri Vihar, Link Road, Cuttack- 753012.	CONIMPEXTRA Cuttack Tel : 0671-2334034 Fax : 0671-2311596 E-Mail : jdgftctc@hotmail.com	Orissa.
22.	The Jt. Director General of Foreign Trade, R.B. Baruah Road, Guwahati-781024.	CONIMPEXTRA Guwahati Tel : 0361-562583 E-Mail : jdgftnel@sifu.com	Assam, Arunachal Pradesh, Nagaland and Manipur.
23.	The Jt. Director General of Foreign Trade, Biscoman Bhawan, (Ground Floor), Patna-800001.	CONIMPEXTRA Patna Tel : 0612-231326 0612-212052 E-Mail : jdgft@bih.nic.in	Bihar and Jharkhand
24.	The Dy. Director General of Foreign Trade, Morollo Building, Shillong, Meghalaya-790001. Southern Zone	CONIMPEXTRA Shillong Tel : 0364-223360 Fax : 0364-223360 E-Mail : jdgftshil@shilong.meg.nic.in	Meghalaya and Mizoram.
25.	The Joint Director General of Foreign Trade, 38 & 39, Whites Road Royapettah, Chennai-600014.	CONIMPEXTRA Chennai Tel : 044-28523317 Tlx : 041-6858 Fax : 044-28523529 E-Mail : acc@acc-ch.nic.in	Tamil Nadu Except the areas which are under the jurisdiction of (i) Jt. DGFT Madurai, (ii) Jt. DGFT Coimbatore, (iii) Jt. DGFT Pondicherry.
26.	The Joint Director General of Foreign Trade, C & E Wing, 6th Floor, Kendriya Sadan, 7th Main Road, II Block, Koramangla, 2nd Block Banglore-560034.	CONIMPEXTRA Banglore Tel : 080-5537213, 14, 15 Fax : 080-5537214 E-Mail : bngdgft@kar.nic.in	Karnataka.

1.	2.	3.	4.
27.	The Joint Director General of Foreign Trade, H.No.36/862-A Chittoor Road, (Opp. to SRVLP School), Eranakulam, Kochi-11.	CONIMPEXTRA Ernakulam Tel : 0484-377760 Fax : 0484-377760 PRO- 0484-375397 E-Mail : dgftchn@ker.nic.in	Kerala excepting the districts of (i) Trivandrum, Quilon and Pathanamiththitta (ii) Lakshdweep
27A.	The Joint Director General of Foreign Trade, No. 29, Shanthi Nagar Government Press Road, statue, Thiruvananthapuram 695001	Tel : 0471-335393 E-Mail : dgfttvm@kerala.nic.in	District of Kerala (i) Thiruvananthapuram (ii) Quilon (iii) Pathanamthitta
28:	The Joint Director general of Foreign Trade, Kendriya Sadan, i Floor, V Block, Sultan Bazar, Hyderabad-500195.	CONIMPEXTRA Hyderabad Tel : 040-4651598 Fax : 040-4651598	Andhra Pradesh excluding the areas in the jurisdiction of Jt. DGFT Vishakhapatnam.
29.	The Joint Director General of Foreign Trade, India Life Building (Annex), First Floor, Trichy Road, Coimbatore-641018	CONIMPEXTRA Coimbatore Tel : 0422-2300947 Fax : 0422-2300846 E-Mail : ddgft@kovai.tn.nic.in	Districts of Tamil Nadu (i) Coimbatore (ii) Nilgiris, (iii) Periyar, (iv) Salem, (v) Karur, (vi) Namakkal
30.	The Joint Director General of Foreign Trade, Plot No. 9 Kamarajar, Ist Main, II Cross Road, K.K. Nagar, Madurai-625001.	CONIMPEXTRA Madurai Tel : 0452-2586485 Fax : 0452-2586485. E-Mail : hgftmdu@yahoo.com	Districts of (i) Madurai, (ii) Quidi Milleh, (iii) Ramnad, (iv) Pasum Pon Thever Thirumaganar, Nellai Kattabomman, Chidambaranar and Kanyakumari.
31.	The Joint Director General of Foreign Trade, 205, Bharathi Street, Post Box No. 14 Pondicherry - 605001.	CONIMPEXTRA Pondicherry Tel : 0413-36311, 36216 E-Mail : jdgft@pond.ypon.nic.in	Union Territory of Pondicherry, Karaikal, Mahe, Yanam and Districts of Ramaswamy Padayatchiyar and South Arcot of Tamil Nadu

1.	2.	3.	4.
32.	The Joint Director General of Foreign Trade, Door No. 43-9-166, First Floor, T.S.N. Colony, Visakhapatnam-530016 (AP).	CONIMPEXTRA Visakhapatnam Tel : 0891-47146 E-Mail : jdgftvis@ap.nic.in	Districts of Andhra Pradesh (i) Srikakulam, (ii) Vizianagaram, (iii) Visakhapatnam, (iv) East Godavari, (v) West Godavari.
Soecial Economic Zones			
33.	Development Commissioner/ Jt. Development Commissioner/ Deputy Development Commissiner/ Asstt. Development Commissioner Andheri (East) Mumbai -400096	Seeprozone Mumbai Fax-022-8291385 E-Mail : dcsepz@bom.5vsnl. net.in dc@seepz.com	Units Situated in Santa Cruz SeZ and approved EOUs located in Maharashtra, Goa, Daman and Diu, Dadra and Nagar Havaii
34.	Development Commissioner/ Jt. Development Commissioner/ Asstt. Development Commissioner/ Gandhidam - Kutch	KAFTZ GAHDHIDHAM Fax : 02836 - 52250 E-Mail : kaftz@wilnetohline.net	Kutch district of Gujrat, Units situated in Kandla and Surat SEZs and approved EOUs located in Gujrat
35.	Development Commissioner/ Jt. Development Commissioner/ Deputy Development Commissioner/ Asstt. Development Commissioner National Highway 45, Tamabaram, Chennai- 600045	MSEZ CHENNAI Fax : 044-2368218 E-Mail : mepz@vsnl.com mepz@md5 - vsnl.net.in	Units situated in Madras Special Econimic Zone and approved EOUs located in Tamil Nadu, Andaman & Nicobar Islands, Union Territory of Pondicherry, excluding Mahe and Yanam.
36.	Development Commissioner/ Jt. Development commissioner/ Deputy Development commissioner/ Asstt. Development Commissioner Kakkanand, Coachin-682030	CSEPZONE Ernakulam Fax : 0484-422530 E-Mail : mepz@vsnl.com,	Units Situated in Coachin SEZ and approved EOUs located in Kerala, Karnataka, Lakshdwwp and Mahe.
.37.	Development commissioner/ Jt. Development commissioner/ Deputy Development commissioner/ Asstt. Development Commissioner/ Duvvada, Visakhapatanam-530046	VSEZ Visakhapatnam Fax : 0891-587352 E-Mail : vepz@ap.nic.in	Units situated in Visakhapatnam special Economic Zone and approved EOUs located in Andhra Pradesh and Yanam.

1.	2.	3.	4.
38.	The Development/Jt. Development Deputy Development/Assistant Development Commissioner, Noida Special Economic Zone, Noida Dadri Road, Phase II, Noida District, Goutam Budh Nagar-201305 (U.P.)	LIVWELL New Delhi Fax : 91-4562314 Fax : 91-456276 E-Mail : dcnepz@nda.vsnl.net.in and Chandigarh	Units situated in Noida special Economics Zones and 100%EOUs situated in Delhi, Uttar Pradesh, Uttranchal, Punjab, Haryana, Himachal Pradesh, Jammu & Kashmir, Rajasthan, Madhya Pradesh, Chattisgarh
39.	The Development/Jt. Development Deputy Development/Assistant Development Commissioner, Falta Special Economic Zone, 2nd MSO Building, Room No.4 Nizam Place, 234/4, A.J.C. Bose Road, Kolkata	SEZ Kolkata Tlx : 021592 FSEZ IN Fax : 033-2477923	Units situated in Falta special Econimic Zones and 100% EOUs situated in West Bengal, Orissa, Bihar, Jharkhand, Assam, Tripura, Manipur, Meghalaya Nagaland, Mizoram and Sikkim

Appendix III

Form of application for registration cum membership with export promotion councils†

Note: Please see paragraph 2.44 of the Policy and paragraph 3.12.02 of the Handbook (Vol.I).

For Official Use

File No.. Date ....

To,

The ....

....

....

(Name and Address of the Council)

Dear Sir,

Kindly register us as Merchant/Manufacturer/Merchant-cum-Manufacturer exporter of the export product(s) mentioned below:

1. Name of the applicant : ....

1A. E-Mail Address : ....

2. (i) Address of the applicant : ....
(Registered Offices in case : ....
of limited companies, and : ....
the head offices for others) : ....

(ii) Name and address of the : ....

† Appendix 4 of Handbook of Procedure (Vol. 1), 2002-07.

(iii) Name and address of the factory : ....

branches, if any : ....

*3. IEC No. .... Date of issue .... Issuing Authority ....

4. If the registration is required as a manufacturer exporter

SSI Registration/Industrial

Licence/IEM : No. .... Date ....

Issuing Authority ....

Others (specify) : ....

5. EH/TH/STH/SSTH Certificate No. .... valid upto ....

*6. Details of Directors/Partners/Proprietor/Karta to be given in the following manner.

(1) (a) Name : ....

(b) Father's Name : ....

(c) Residential Address : ....

(d) Telephone No. : ....

(2) (a) .... (3)(a) ....

(b) .... (b) ....

(c) .... (c) ....

(d) .... (d) ....

(4) (a) .... (5)(a) ....

(b) .... (b) ....

(c) .... (c) ....

(d) .... (d) ....

7. Name of export product(s) for

which registration is required : ....

8. I/We hereby solemnly declare that the above stated information is true and correct. I/We undertake, without any reservation to :

(a) abide by the terms of the registration certificate granted to us on all our exports :

---

1 Sl No. 3 and 6 are missing in the Govt. Publishing. They have been provided by the Nabhi's Board of Editiors as per previous Handbook.

(b) agree to abide by any code of conduct that may be prescribed;

(c) agree to abide by export floor price condition that may be stipulated by the Registering Authority :

(d) furnish without fail monthly returns of exports including Nil returns to the Registering authority by 15th day of the months following the quarter.

9. We further understand that our registration is liable to be cancelled in the event of breach of any of the undertakings mentioned above.

Yours faithfully,

(Signature)

Name ....

Address ....

Designation ....

Tele No. ....

Fax No. ....

Residential address ....

....

Place ....

Date ....

Documents to be enclosed with the application form

1. A self certified copy of the IEC Number issued by the licensing authority concerned.

2. A certificate from the bank in support of the applicant's financial soundness.

Apppendix IV

List of Export Promotion Councils/Commodity Board*

Sl. No.	*Name of the Export Promotion Council*	*Address of the Regd. Office of the Council*	*Address of the regional Ofices(s) of the Council*
1.	2.	3.	4.
1.	Agricultural and Processed Food Products Export Development Authority (APEDA)	3 Siri Institutional Area August Kranti Marg New Delhi-110016 Tel: (011)6513204 (011)6514572 (011)6534186 Fax : (011)6534870 Tlx : 82061 FEDA IN Grams : APEDA	12th Floor, Unit No. MVIRDC, Cuffe Parade World Trade Centre, Mumbai-400005 Tel : (022)2183106 (022)2189060 Fax : (022) 2189681 Tlx : 83737 APED IN 12/1/1Palace Cross Road, Bangalore 560020 Tel : (080)374244 Fax : (080) 3364560 Mayukh Bhawan, Bidhan Nagar, Kolkata 700091 Tel : (033)374244 Tlx : 0212222
2.	Apparel Export Promotion Council	15 NBCC Tower Bhikaji Cama Place New Delhi 110066 Tel : (011)6183351 (011) 6169394 (011)6169356 (011)6169357 Fax : (011)6188584 Tlx : 03172196/72442	4th Floor, sahyog Building, 58 Nehru Place New Delhi 110019 Tel : (011) 6416709 (011)6472533 Fax : (011)6487517 48 Community Centre Nariana Indl. Area Phase I, New Delhi 110028 Tel : (011)5790185 (011)5790187 (011)5798326 (011)5795309 Fax : (011)5790701 (011)5795309 Tlx. : 031 76247 AEPC IN 6 Community Centre Zamrudpur New Delhi 110048 Tel : (011)6460491 (011)6460492 (011)6218387 (011)6216963 Fax : 011-6480489 Tlx : 03171191 AEPC IN

1 Appendix 27 of Handbook of Procedure (Vol. 1), 2002-07.

1.	2.	3.	4.
			CFO 3&4 Tonk road, Nehru Place, Jaipur-302015 (Rajasthan) Tel : 518275, 518276 Fax : 518654 G 138 shastri Nagar, Jodhpur 34003 Tel : 0291 37652 Fax : 0291-37652, 0291-238015 Flat No. 112, Ground Floor, Pratap Colony, Model Gram Ludhiana (Punjab) Tel : 061 402697, 0161 207234 Fax : 0161 402697 12th Floor, Bajaj Bhavan, Nariman Point, Mumbai 400021 Tel : (022)2845479, (022)2045924 (022)2040174, (022)2853420 (022) 2853419, Fax : (022)2043178 Room No. 73-76, Cargo Complex Building, (ground floor) Sahar Village ville-Parle (East), Mumbai 400099 Tel : (022)8321327, Fax : (022)8213411 Karumuthu Centre IIIrd Floor, 498 Anna Salai, Chennai 600035 Tel. : (044)4343588, (044)4346848 Fax : (044)4346416 Tlx : (041)6626 AEPC IN No. 1 3rd Street, Indra Nagar, Off Avinashi road, Tripur 641603 Tamil Nadu Tel : (0421)743049, 748763, 749631 Fax : (0421)749630 Ist Floor, 5-10-19, Ritz Hotel Road, Saifabad, (Near Haga Bhawan/Police Control Room) Hyderabad Tel : 210372, Fax : 210378 42/1924, Vivail Building, K.K. Padmanabhan Road, Kochi-682018 Tel : (0484)391710, Fax : (0484)392907 2/2-B HOCHIMINH Sarani, Kolkata 700071 Tel : (033)2423911, Fax : (033)2422766

1.	2.	3.	4.
3.	Basic Chemicals, Pharmaceuticals & Cosmetics Export Promotion Council	Jhanshi Castle, 4th Floor 7 Cooperage Road, Mumbai 400039 Tel: (022)202 1288, (022)2021330 (022)2026684 Fax: (022) 2026684 Tlx: 011-84047 BCPC IN Grams: CHEMEXCIL	Kankaria Estate 9th Floor, 6 Little Russell St. Kolkata 700071 Tel: (033)2475562, Tlx: 021-5917 BCPC IN No. 23/1 & 2, 5th Main Road, 3rd Cross, Gandhi Nagar, Banglore-56009 Tel: (080)2269037, (080)2260446 Tlx: 08458430 BCPC IN Grams: CHEMEXCIL
4.	The Cashew Export Promotion Council of India	P.B. No. 1709, Chitoor Road, Ernakulam South, Coachin 682016 Tel: (0484)361459, (0484)369080 (0484)353357 Fax: (0484)370973 Tlx: (0885)6677 CEPC IN Grams: PROMOTION	
5.	Carpet Export Promotion Council	110-A/1, Krishna Nagar, (Gali No.5) Safdarjung Enclave, New Delhi 110029 Tel: (011)6102742 (011)6101024 Fax: 91-116165299 Grams: CARPCIL New Delhi.	Ist Floor, Kaleen Bhawan, Maryadpatti, Bhadohi 221401 (U.P.) Tel: 0541425975 Grams: CARPCIL BHADOHI
6.	Chemicals & Allied Products Export Promotion Ccouncil	"World Trade Centre" 2nd Floor, 14/1-B, Ezra Street Kolkata 700001 Tel: (022)2258216, (022)258217/19 (022)257079 Fax: 91-33-22551070 Tlx: 021-4368 Grams: CAPEXIL.	**Western Religion:** Commerce Centre, Block No. D-17, Tardeo Road, Mumbai - 400034 Tel: (022)4943410, (022)4960085 Fax: 91-22-4937665, Tlx: 011-75191 Grams: CAPEXIL

1.	2.	3.	4.
			Southern Region "Rasheed Mansion" 408 Anna Salai, Chennai 600006 Tel: (044)8292310 (044)8294713 Fax: 91-44-8295386 Grams: CAPEXIL **Northern Region** "Vandana Building" 4C, 4th Floor, 11, Tolstoy Marg, New Delhi-110001 Tel: (011)3356703/3711479/3752282 Fax: 91-11-3314486 E-Mail Address: capexiln@bol.net.in **Eastern Region** "Tobacco House" 1 & 2, Old Court House Corner, Kolkata 700001 Tel: (033)2207620 Fax: 91-332206945 Tlx: 021-4358 Grams: CAPEXIL.
7.	Coffee Board	1, Dr. Ambedkar Veedhi, Banglore 560001 Tlx: 08458281 Fax: 0802265557	
8.	Coir Board	Coir House M.G. Road, Ernakulam South Kochi 6822016 Tel: (0484)351788, (0484)351807 (0484)351954, (0484)354397 Fax: 0484 370034 Tlx: 08856363 Grams: COIRBOARD	8 Annexe Building cunningham Road, Banglore 560052 Tel: (080)268538 Gram: COIREGION.

1.	2.	3.	4.
9.	The Cotton Textiles Export Promotion Council	Engineering Centre, 5th Floor, 9, Mathew Road, Mumbai-400004 Tel: (022)3632910-13 Fax: (022)3632914 Tlx: (011)75466 TCIL Grams: TEXPROCIL	Cecil Court 26, Mahakavi Bhushan Marg, (Near Regal Cinema) Mumbai 400039 Tel: (022) 2021477, (022)2021522, (022)2027221 Fax: (022)2022510 Fax: (022)202510 No. F, II Floor, 'Mount Chambers' 758 Mount Road, Madras 600002 Tel.: 0448525486, Fax: (044)8521205 Tlx: 0416315 TCIL 101, Ashoka Estate 24 Barakhamba Road, New Delhi 110001 Tel: 011-3316168, Fax: 011 371904 Tlx: 03161331 TCIL Jaldarshan Housing Society Opp. Natraj Cinema Ashram Road, Ahmedabad 380009 Tel: 079 409323, Tlx: 0121 6362 TCIL 14/1B Ezra Estate, World Trade Centre, Kolkata 700001 Tel: 033 : 254541 Tlx: 021 4426 TXIL 'Jayanthi', IInd Floor, 48-A, S.S. Moorthy Street, Tuticorin - 628002 (T.N.) Tel: 24587, Tlx: 0434-323 TCIL IN Export Documentation Centre Building Wellington Island Cochin North End 682003 Tel: (0484)666521 Tlx: C/o. 8856802 2nd Floor, 593 Cross Cut Road, Gandhipuram Coimbatore 641012 Tel: 235587, Fax: 855-640 SIMA IN

1.	2.	3.	4.
			Air Cargo Complex Sanganer Airport, Jaipur 302011 Tel: 0141 550020 Tlx: C/o. 0363-232 FASH IN 10/293 Bungalow Road, congress Bhavan Ichalkaranji Dist. Kolhapur-416115 Tel: 22193 'Mayur Complex' 20 Plaaniappa Street Erode 638009 Tel: C/o. 77901, Tlx: 8502219 Air Cargo Complex International Airport Authority of India, Near Mumbai Airport Sahar Village, Mumbai 400057 Tel: (022)8324094
10.	Electronics and Computer Software Export Promotion Council (ESC)	PHD House, 3rd Floor, Ramakrishna Dalmia Wing, Opp. Asiad Village, New Delhi 110016 Tel (011) 6965103, (011)6964463 Fax: (011)65106312 (011)6583412 E-Mail: esc@giasd101.vsnl.net.in	
11.	Engineering Export Promotion Council	World Trade Centre 1st Floor, 14/1B Ezra Street, Kolkata 700001 Tel: (033)250514 (033)254631 Fax: 0091 033 254659	Centre 1, 12th Floor World Trade Centre, Cuffe Parade, Mumbai 400005 Tel: (022)2186655, (022)2186656, (022)2186660 Fax: 0091-22-218 0119 Tlx: 11-83037 Grams:OCEANBORNE Surya Kiran (4th Floor), 19 Kasturba Gandhi Marg, New Delhi 110001 Tel: (011)3314171, (011)3314174 Fax: 0091 113317795 Tlx: 3161669

1.	2.	3.	4.
			Grams: ENEXPROM Maalavika Centre, 3rd Floor, 144/145 Kodambakkam High Road, Madras 600034 Tel: (044) 8277501,(044)8276007, (044)8264972 Fax: 0091 448270491 Tlx: 418293, Grams: OCEANBORNE
12.	Federation of Indian Export Organisations (FIEO)	PHD House, 3rd Floor, Opp. Asian Games Village, New Delhi 110016 Tel: (011)6851310, (011)6851312 (011)6851314, (011)6851315 Fax: 91116863087, 6967859 Tlx: 03173194 Grams: APEXLINK E-Mail: fieodel@fieodel fieodel.cmc.net.in fieo@giasd101.vsnl.net.in	World Trade Centre No. 1. 11th Floor, Cuffe Parade Mumbai 400005 Tel: (022)2185093, (022)2183354 Fax: 91222183875 Tlx: 91222183875 01182984 FIEO IN Grams: FIEOWEST E-Mail: fieowr@giasbm01.vsnl.net.in Spencer Plaza Unit No. 706, 7th Floor, 769 Anna Salai, Chennai 600002 Tel: (044)8522427, (044)8521861 Fax: 91448524767 Tlx: 0418692 Grams: APEXLINK E-Mail: fieosr@giasmd01.vsnl.net.in Express Tower, 6th Floor, 42A Shakespeare Sarani (Junction) of Rawdon St. and Shakespeare Sarani, Kolkata 700071 Tel: (033)2406398, (033)2405076 Fax: 910332470364 Tlx: 02174401 E-Mail: fieoer@gems.vsnl.net.in

1.	2.	3.	4.
13.	The Gem & Jwellery Export Promotion Council	Diamond Plaza 5th Floor, 391-A, Dr. D.B.Marg, Mumbai 400004 Tel: (022)3856916, (022)3821806 (022) 3821801 Fax: (022)3868752 E-Mail: gjepc@vsnl.com	F-3, Jhandewalan Flatted Factories Complex, Rani Jhansi Road, New Delhi 110055 Tel: (011)3515395, (011)3614197 Fax: (011)3675274 Rajasthan Chamber Bhavan M.I.Road Jaipur-302003 Tel: (0141)565731, (0141)568029 Fax: (0141)567921 E-Mail: gjepccjp@jpl.Dot.net.in 626-628, Belgium Towers, 6th Floor, Ring Road, Surat 395001 Tel: 0261435008 Ankur Plaza 3rd Floor 52, G.N.Chetty Road T. Nagar Chennai 600017 Tel: 044-8276188, 044-8226686 E-Mail: gjepcsr@vsnl.com Unit No. 1F Ist Floor, 4 Ho Chi Minh Sarani Kolkata 700071 Tel: 033-2823630, 033-2823629 E-Mail: gjepcer@vsnl.com
14.	Export Promotion Council for Handicrafts	Plot No.1 Pocket 6&7 Sector-C, LSC Vasant Kunj, Delhi-110070 Tel: (011)6135256-58 Fax: 91-11-6135518-19 Tlx: 031-72315 EPCH IN Grams: CRAFTCIL E-Mail: epch@vsnl.com	
15.	The Handloom Export Promotion Council	34 Cathedral Garden Road, Nungambakkam, Chennai 600034 Tel: (044)8278879 (044)8276043 Fax: 0091(044)8271761	1004, 10th Floor Padma tower-1,5, Rajindra Place, New Delhi 110008 Tel: (011)5826965 Fax: (011)5826966, Tlx: 3166670 E-Mail: hepcrond@vsnl.com

1.	2.	3.	4.
		E-Mail: hepccatp@vsnl.com	15-A, Mama Paramanand Marg Opera House Mumbai-400004 Tel. Fax.: 91-22-3672921 E-Mail: hepcromu@mantraonline.com
16.	The Indian Silk Export Promotion Council	62, Mittal chambers, 6th Floor, Nariman Point,, Mumbai-400021 Tel: (022)2027662 (022)2025866 Fax: (022)2874606 E-Mail No. insepc@bom2.isnl.net.in	16 National Park, Lajpat Nagar IV, New Delhi-110024 Tel: (011)6216272 Fax: (011)6430685 Tlx: 03170175
17.	Council for Leather Exports	"Leather Centre" 53, Raja Muthiah Road, Chennai-600003 Tel: (044)589098 (044)580834 Fax: (044)588713, (044)587083 Grams: LEXPROCIL E-Mail: Cle@giasmd01.vsnl.net.in	15/238 Civil Lines P.O. Box No. 198, Kanpur-208001 Tel: (0512)311247 (0512)318053 Fax: (0512)311247 Grams: LEXPORT 11/4, World Trade Centre-I Cuffe Parade, Mumbai-400005 Tel: (022)2184060 Fax: (022)2151207 Flat No. 6G & 6H. "Gopala Towers" Rajindra Place, New Delhi-110008 Tel: (011)5752760 Tlx: 31-65935 CLED IN "Moti Jug House" Ground Floor, i, Auckland Place, Kolkata 700017 Tel: (033)2407270, Fax: (033) 2474543 Grams: REOLEXPORT Agra Extension Centre Block No. 26/2/4, Shop No. 112, Sanjay Place. Agra-282002 Tel: 352619

1.	2.	3.	4.
18.	The Marine Products Export Development Authority	P.B. No. 1663 MPEDA House, Panampilly Avenue Kochi 682036 Tel: (0484)311979 (0484)311901 Fax: 00910484313361 Tlx: 08856648 Cable: MARINE	6th Floor, Regent Chambers Jamnalal Bajaj Marg, Nariman Point, Mumbai-400021 Tel: (022)2831399, (022)2834354 Fax: 022 2834354 Tlx: 0115707 Cable: MARINE AUTHORITY 4-B Maruti Building, 12 Loudoun Street, Kolkata 700017 Tel: (033)2475908, (033)2471181 Tlx: 0212698 Cable: MARINE AUTHORITY Thoufeeq Complex Ravipuram, M.G. Road. Coachin-682016 Tel: (0484)350518, (0484)350562 Tlx: 08856657 Cable:MARINE AUTHORITY No. 10, Sambantham St. G.N.Chetty Road, T. Nagar, Chennai 600017 Tel: (044)8277490 Tlx: 0417234 Cable: MARINE AUTHORITY Sukhshanti Bldg. Ist Floor, Bhidiya, Veraval-362269 Gujrat Tel: 0287621429 Fax: 0287621429, Tlx: 0163203 Cable: MARINE AUTHORITY Door No. 13-1-15, Ward No. 13 Ist Floor, Kelle Court Panje, Mangesh Rao Road, Hampankutta Manglore 575001 Tel: 0824440360, Fax: 0824440360 Tlx: 0832231

1.	2.	3.	4.
			Cable: MARINE AUTHORITY Mira Flores, Ist Floor, Near Gomantak Press St. Inez, Panaji 403001 Goa Tel: (0832)224283, Fax: (0832)224283 Tlx: 0194312, Cable: MARINE AUTHORITY Srihari, Parameswara Nagar, Quilon 691001 Tlx: 0886281 Cable: MARINE AUTHORITY 487-9, Rama Talkies Road, Ist Floor, Srinagar, Visakhapatanam 530016 Fax: 0891552077 Telex: 0495392 Cable: MARINE AUTHORITY Thiruvarul, 24, Chidambara Nagar, 2nd Street, Tuticorn 628008 Tel: (0466)22602 Fax: (0466)22602 Tlx: 0434247 Cable: MARINE AUTHORITY (Paradeep) Plot No. 695/696, G Block, BJB Nagar, Bhubaneswar 751014 Tel: (0674)430724 Tlx: 06756285 Cable:MARINE AUTHORITY Trade Promotion Office, 101, Nirmal Tower, Barakhamba Road, New Delhi 110001 Tel: (11)3719126, Fax: (11)3310582 Tlx: 03162265, Cable: COMPEDA

1.	2.	3.	4.
19.	Overseas Construction Council of India	Commerce Centre (7th Floor), Tardeo Road, Mumbai-400034 Tel: (022)4943243 (022)4942344 Fax: 0091224943243 E-Mail: g-occi/s= Council/p=gems.vssnl.net.in Internet: occi.council@ gems. vssnl.net.in.	(Principal Office) H118, (11th Floor) Himalaya House, 23, Kasturba Gandhi Marg, New Delhi 110001 Tel (011)3327550 (011)3722425 Fax: 91-11-2212936 E-Mail: #occi@giasd1 01.vsnl.net.in
20.	The Plastics and Linoleums Export Promotion Council	Centre1,Unit1, 11th Floor World Trade Centre Cuffee Parade, Colaba Mumbai 400005 Tel: (022)2184474 Fax: 91-22-2184810 Tlx: 011-83940 PLXL IN Cable: PLEXCOUNCIL E-Mail/INTERNET: plexcon@giasbml.vsnl.in	Rasheed Mansion 622, Anna Salai Chennai-600006 Tel: (044)8278620, Fax: 91-44-8265744 Tlx: 41-634 PLXL IN Cable: LEXCONCIL World Trade Centre 14/1B Ezra Street Kolkata-700001 Tel: (033)254548, Fax: 91-33-258946 Tlx: 21-4014PLXL IN Cable: PLEXCOUCIL
21.	The Rubber Board	Shastri Road P.B. No. 1122 Kottayam 686002 Tel: (0481) 571-231, (0481) 571-231 (0481) 571-235, (0481) 571-236 (0481) 571-361 Fax: 91-481-571380 Tlx: 888-205 RUBR IN Cable: RUBBER BOARD	
22.	Shellac Export Promotion Council	14/1B, Ezra Street, World Trade Centre, Kolkata-700001	

1.	2.	3.	4.
		Tel: 25-4556 Fax: 033-248 4046/IF & 033-248 2070/IF-384	
23.	The Sports Goods Export Promotion Council	IInd Floor, 1-E/6, Swami Ram Tirath Nagar, (Jhandewalan Extn). New Delhi-110055 Tel: (011) 525695 Fax: 011-7532147 Cable: PRINCILEX	10, Shakti Nagar, Jalandhar-144001 Tel: (91)181-203734, Cable: Princilex
24.	Spices Board	Sugandha Board N.H.By-pass P.B. No. 2277 Palarivattrom.P.O. Coachin-682025, Phone:0484-333610-616, 347965 Fax: 0484-331429, 334429 E-Mail: 1. Spicesboard@vsnl.com E-Mail: 2. Mail@indianspices.com Website: w.w.w.indianspices com	(1) A-111 Defence Colony, New Delhi-110024 Tel:011-4611510, 4623597 Fax: 011-4621359 E-Mail: sbrodel@giasd101.vsnl.net.in (2) 195-A-Park Street Kolkata-700017 Phone: 033-2804304 Fax: 033-2479736 Email:sbroacal@gias101.vsnl.net.in (3) Unit No. 1 Plot No.9 & 10 Banking Complex Bldg-11, Near Commodity Exchange Sector-19-A, Vashi, Mumbai-400703 Phone: 022-7653093 Fax; 022-765116 E-Mail: rosbom@bom2.vsnl.net.in (4) 25 (old No. 13) First Floor, Second Street, East Abhiramapuram, Mylapore, Chennai-600004 Phone: 044-4991448 Fax: 044-4997474 E-Mail:sbrochn@vsnl. com

1.	2.	3.	4.
			(5) Kurangani Road, Bodyinayakanur-626513 Phone/Fax: 0456-21397 E-Mail: sbadbodi@sancharnet.in (6) 6th Bye Lane, Rajgarh Road Guwahati-781003: Phone: 036154617 (7) P.B.No. 85, Diesel Power House Road, Gangtok-737101 Phone: 03592-22904 Fax: 03592-22230 E-Mail: sbrogtk@dte.vsnl.net.in (8) 14-A Old Vasavi Nagar, Kharkana, Trimulgherry P.O., Secunderabad-500015 Phone: 040-7740436 Fax: 040-7744835 E-Mail: spiceboard@satyam.net.in (9) 22/1, Rest House Road, Banglore-560001 Phone: 080-5320354: Fax: 080-5320354 (10) 6, Ground Floor, Chidambaram Nagar 5th Street, Tuticorin 628008 (11) Plot No. 423, Sahid Nagar Bhuneshwar- 751007 (12) C/o. Office of the Directorate of Horticulture, PB No. 030, Aizol- 796001, Mizoram. Phone: 0389-322809 (13) 2, Ramvadi Society, Nirnay Nagar Road Chandlodie. P.O., Ahmedabad-382481 Phone: 7536684 (14) D/S, 1115 Sector-D, LDA Colony, Kanpur Road, Lucknow-226012 Phone: 0522-432009

1.	2.	3.	4.
25.	The Synthetic & Rayon Textiles Export Promotion Council	'Resham Bhavan' 78 Veer Nariman Rd. Mumbai-400020 Tel: (022) 2048797 (022)204890 (022)2824662 Fax: 91-22-2048358 Tlx: 11-83703 SEPC IN Gram:SYNRAYCIL E-Mail: SRTEPC-MUM @400.nicgw. nic. in	PHD House 4th Floor, Phase II Opp. Asian Games village New Delhi 110016 Tel: 011-6854760 Fax: 91-11-6854049 Tlx: 011-73058 PHDC-IN Khallelic Centre (Alsa Mall) No. 10, 3rd Floor, Montiety Road, Chennai-600008 Tel: 044-8553837/8554236 Fax: 91-44-8553555 Tlx: 041-7327 PEST IN Block No. 3 E Resham Bhavan Lal Darwaja Surat 395003 Tel: 0261423184 Fax: 91-261-421756
26.	Tea Board	14 Biplabi Trailokya Maharaj Sarani (Brabourne Road) Kolkata-700001 Tel: (033)25-1411 Fax: 033-2251417 Tlx: 021-4527 Cable: TEABORD	Azad Bhawan (3rd Floor) 4E/14, Jhandewalan Extn. New Delhi-110055 Tel: (011)52-4338 Telex: 031-62896 "Resham Bhawan" 78, Veer Nariman Road Mumbai-400020 Tel: (022)2041699 No.3 Blacker's Road (3rd Floor) "Vijaya Complex' (Mount Island Chennai-600002 Tel: (044)840640 Indra Gandhi Road, Willingdon Island Coachin-682003 KERLA Tel: (0484) 66-6523 (0484)666648 Tlx: 04846284

1.	2.	3.	4.
			"G.B.Road" P.O. Kunjaban Agartata-799001 Tripura Tel: (038)22-4182 "SHELWOOD" Coonoor-643101, Nilgiris, South India Tel: 0853-213 Club Road, P.O.Silchar-788001 Dist: Cachar (Assam) Tel: (03842)32518 College Road, Kottayam-686001 Kerla Tel: (0481)567319 Fax: 0481-567391 "Pradhan Bhawan" Hakimpura, Silguri, Darjeling Tel: (0353)420579 Fax: 0353-420579 Nehru Park, Jorhat-785001 Assam Tel: (0376) 320501 U.N.Bezbarua Road, Silkpukhuri Guahati-781003 Assam Tel: (0361)54-7969, (0361)54-2974 Telex: 235-2416, Fax: 0361-547969 S.A.S. House (2nd Floor), Flat No. 4, 6B, Sapru Marg, Lucknow-226001 Tel: (0522)-224960 Ganesh Ghat, Holding No.1782,P.O. Tezpur-(784001 Dist. Sonitpur (Assam) Tal:(03712) 20144 Mission Road, Palampur-176061 Kangra, Himanchal Pradesh Tel: (01894)30524 Fax: (01894)30524 Jasbhai F Patel Building (3rd Floor), Chock Katra Ahuwalia, Amritsar-143001, Punjab, Tel: (0183)551627, (0183)558515, (0183)543660 Fax: (0183)228138

1.	2.	3.	4.
27.	Tabacco Board	Srinivasa Rao Thota, G.T. Road. P.B.No.322,Guntur 522004 Andhra Pradesh. Tel: 230399, Fax: 0863 354232 Tlx: 471264 TOBD IN Gram: TOBX IN	Directorate of Auctions 1/19, IIIrd Cross, 4th Floor, Unity Building Annexe C.S.I. Compound, Banglore 560027 Tel: (080)2236599, 080 2225075 Tlx: 28458437 H. No. 10-4-1/5, Behind Chacha Nehru Park, Masav Tank, Hyderabad 500028 Tel: (040)317503, (040)319989 B/4141, Safdarjung Enclave New Delhi-110029 Tel: (011)610190
28.	Wool & Woollens Export Promotion Council	612/714 Ashok Estate, 24 Barakhamba Road, New Delhi-110001 Tel: (011)3315512, (011)3312305 Fax: (011)3314626 Cable : WARMTH	Churchgate Chambers 7th Floor, 5 New Marine Lines, Mumbai-400020 Tel: (022)2624680, Fax: (022)2624651 Cable:WOLLENS 704/3, (Gurdev Nager), Pakhowal Road, Ludhiana 141001 Tel: 0161-35842, Fax: 0161-405169 Cable: EXPROCIL Municipal Commercial Complex (Bharathiar Memorial Building), Hall No.2, 1st Floor, Avanashi Road, Tripur-641602 Tel: 0421-700316
29.	The Powerloom Development and Export Promotion Council (PDEXCIL)	16, 1st Floor, Mittal Chamber, Nariman Point, Mumbai-400021 Tel:(022)2846518/19 Fax: (022)2846517 E-Mail: Pdexcil.Pdepc@gems.vsnl.net.in Webside: w.w.w.pdexcil.org	

1.	2.	3.	4.
30.	Jute Manufacturers Development Council	3A, Park Plaza, 71 park Street, Kolkata-700016 Phone: 2172107, 2172540, 2263438 Fax: 2172456 E-Mail: jmdc@giasc101.vsnl.net.in	
31.	Export Promotion Council (EPC) for EOUs/SEZ Units	B-4, Pal Mohan Mansion, 26/34, East Patel Nagar, New Delhi-110008. Tel: (011)25787325/25819237 Fax: (011)25819237 E-Mail: ceu@vsnl.com	

Apppendix V

Select Trade Directories Published Abroad

Name of Director	Publisher's Address
1	*2*
1. International Directory of Importers - Europe 2 Volumes (Importers of various items in European countries)	Blytamann International (International Marketing Data) 195, Dry Creek Road, Healdsubrg - California 95448, USA.
2. International Directory of Importers - North America (Importers of various items in U.S.A. Canada)	– do –
3. International Directory of Importers - Middle East (Importers of Various items in Middle East)	– do –
4. International Directory of Importers - asia Pacifc (Importers of various items in Asia/Pacific)	– do –
5. International Directory of Importers - South Central America (Importers of various items in South American Countries)	– do –
6. International Directory of Importers - Africa (Importers of various items in U.S.A.)	– do –
7. United States Importers & Exporters Directory (Importers of various items in U.S.A,)	The Journal & Commerce 445, Marshal Street, Phillipsburg New Jersey 08865 U.S.A.
8. World Business Directory Volume- 1, 2, 3, 4 (Information on more than 100,000 Business Involved in International Trade)	World Trade Centre Assianc. 1, World Trade Center Suite 7710, NY. 10048 New York, Published by Gala Research International Ltd. UK.
9. Commercial Directory of Southern africa	AC Braby Publishing House, 12 Caversham Road, P.O. Box 1426, Pinetown 3600 NATAL RSA.

1	2
10. Business Directory of Honkong (Mfrs./Suppliers/ Agents/Importers in Hongkong)	Current Publication Ltd., G.P.O. Box 9848, 1501, Enterprise Building, 228 Queen's Road Hongkong.
11. Saudi Arabian Trade Director	Riyadh Chamber of Commerce and Industry.
12. Kompass – Australia – Belgium & Luxembourg – Denmark – Finland – France – F.R.G. – Hongkong – Ireland – Italy – Indonesia – Korea – Malaysia – Morocca – Netherlands – Norway – Singapore – Slovakia – Spain – Sweden – Switzerland – Taiwan – U.K. (Addresses of Mfrs./Suppliers/Agents/Distributors/ Wholesalers/importers)	Kompass Deutchland Verlagsund Vertriebsellschaft Gmbh. Postfach 964 D-7800 Freiburg Federal Republic of Germany
13. Commercial Reports	Indian Missions Abroad.

1	2
14. Asian Trade Directory (ASTRAD) (Australia, Indonesia, Japan, Korea, Maiaysia, Phillippines, Singapore, Taiwan, Thailand	Compiled with the Association.
15. Standard Trade Index Japan (Manufacturers/Importers and Exporters of all products)	The Japan Chamber of Commerce & Industry, 2.2 Marunouchi, 3-Chome, Chiyoda-ku Tokyo, Japan
16. Japan Trade Directory	Jetro (Japan External Trade Organisation (Publications Department) 2-5, Toranaman, 2-chome, Japan.
17. Ghana Business Directory	Ghana Natioal Chamber of Commerce.
18. The Business Directory of the new independent States (The former USSR)	National Market Research Institute Moscow, Russia.
19. Directory of Thai Chamber of Commerce and Industry (List of Thai Chambers of Commerce Members - Product-wise	The Thai Chamber of Commerce 150, Raja Bopit Road, Bangkok, Thailand.
20. Korean Business Directory (Manufacturers/Suppliers/Agents/Importer)	The Korea Foreign Trade Association 159-1, Sam Sung Dong, Kang Nam Gu-Seoul, South Korea.
21. Australian Register of mfrs. Exporters and Importers (Importers address Product-wise)	Who's Where Publishers Pty.POB 1250, North Sydeny, NSW 2060 Australia.
22. British Importers - 2 Volumes (Product-wise/Firm-wise (Importers address Procuct-wise)	Trade Research Publications, 6, Beech Hill Court, Berkhamsted-herts Hp4 2PR UK.
23. Exporters & Importers - The Republic of China (Exporters Importers and Manufacturers)	China External Trade Dev. Council (CETRA), 4-8th Floor, 333, Keelung Road, Sec.I Taipei Tiwan.
24. Taiwan Buyers Guide (Buyers Product-wise)	China Productivity Center, 11th Floor, 210-26 Tun HWA N. Road Taipei, Taiwan.
25. Pakistan Trade Directory (Exporters/Importers)	The Lahore Chamber of Commerce & Industry 11, Share Aiwan-E-Tijarat, POB No. 597 Lahore, Pakistan.

1	2
26. Yellow Pages of Pakistan	US Publishers (Pvt) Ltd. 13C, Mohhammed Ali Housing Society, Karanchi, Pakistan
27. Directory of Indonesian Importers & Exporters	World Export Promotion Center, Singapore.
28. Sharjah Commercial Directory	Sharjah Chamber of Commerce & Industry POB 580, Sharjah, UAE.
29. National Pink Pages Commercial Directory, UAE	AL FAJR, PO Box 505 Abu Dhabi, UAE.
30. Dubai Commercial Directory	Dubai Chambers of Commerce & Industry, PO Box. No. 1457, Dubai, UAE.
31. RAPID CATALOG Directory of Czech and Slovak Enterprises	Czechoslovakia Advertising Agency RAPID Praha1.
32. DCCI Trade Directory	The Dhaka Chambers of Commerce & Industry, 65-66 Motijheel Commercial Area Dhaka 1000.
Product Directory for Overseas Importers	
1. The International Directory of Importers:- – Apparel & Clothing – Furniture & Home Furnishings – Floor Coverings, Carpets & Rugs – Leather Goods, Footwear & Travel accessories – Drugs & Pharamaceuticals – Electronic & Computer Components & Parts	International marketing Data.
2. Asian Leather Directory	Asia Pacific Directories Ltd. POB 30972, 13/F, Park Commercial Center 6-19, shelter Street, Causbay, Hongkong
3. Carpet Annual (Importers/Exporters, Agents & Representatives)	Been Business Information Services Ltd. POB 20, Sovereign Way, Tonbridge, Kent TN9, IRO
4. International Leather Guide	– do –
5. Directory of the Furnishing Trade	– do –

Appendix VI

List of Indian Trade Periodicals Containing Names & Addresses of Importers

Periodical	Frequency	Publisher
1. Apparel The Clothiers Digest	– Monthly	– Clothing Manufacturers Association
2. Apparel Fortnightly	– Fortnightly	– Apparel Export Promotion Council
3. Chemexil Export Bulletin	– Monthly	– Basic Chemicals, Pharmaceuticals & Cosmetics EPC
4. Capxil Home Bulletin	– Monthly	– Chemicals & Allied Products EPC
5. Elsoftex Newsletter	– Monthly	– Electronics & Allied Products EP
6. Engineering Export News	– Fortnightly	– Engineering Export Promotion Council
7. Texprocil Data	– Monthly	– Cotton Textile EPC
8. Handloom Export	– Monthly	– Handloom Export Promotion Council
9. Silknet	– Weekly	– Indian Silk EPC
10. Indian Synthetic & Rayon	– Twice a year	– Synthetic & Rayon Textile EPC
11. Srtepo Newsletter	– Fortnightly	– Synthetic & Rayon Textile EPC
12. Wool & Woollens of India	– Quarterly	– Wool & Woollen EPC
13. Plexconcil Bulletin	– Monthly	– Plastics & Linoleums EPC
14. Indian Shellac	– Monthly	– Shellac Export Promotion Council
15. Leathers	– Monthly	– Council for Leather Exports
16. Coir News	– Monthly	– Coir Board
17. Monthly Bulletin of Coir Exports	– Monthly	– Coir Board
18. Indian Coffee	– Monthly	– Coffee Board

19. Indian Tea News	– Monthly	– Tea Board
20. Rubber Board Bulletin	– Monthly	– Rubber Board
21. Spice India	– Monthly	– Spices Board
22. Spices Market Weekly	– Monthly	– Spices Board
23. Export Inspection Journal	– Monthly	– Export Inspection Agency
24. ASSOCHAM Bulletin	– Monthly	– ASSOCHAM
25. Economic Trends	– Quarterly	– FICCI
26. Business Trends	– Weekly	– FICCI
27. FIEO News	– Fortnightly	– FIEO
28. Indian Trade Journal	– Weekly	– DGCI&S
29. Indian Shipping	– Monthly	– Indian National Shipowner's Association
30. Indian Jute	– Monthly	– JMDC
31. Jute News	– Monthly	– JMDC
32. Foreign Trade Bulletin	– Monthly	– Indian Institute of Foreign Trade
33. Monthly Newsletter IIC	– Monthly	– Indian Investment Center
34. The Indian Sea Foods	– Monthly	– MPEDA
35. Trade, Commerce & Industry	– Monthly	– Indian Merchants Chamber
36. Indian Export Bulletin	– Monthly	– ITPO
37. Bombay Chamber Fortnightly	– Monthly	– Bombay Chamber of Commerce

Goods Falling In More Than One Chapters of ITC(HS) Classification

Code	Items Description	Policy	Nature of Restriction
0001	All forms of wild animals including their parts and products	P	Not permitted to be exported.
0002	Exports of certain textile products of Cotton, wooll and manmade fibres and blends which are subject to MOU's /Agreements between India and Canada or EEC or USA as the case may be.	F	Subject to the conditions notified by the Government from time to time.
0003	Dress materials/ readymade garments fabrics/textile items with imprints of excerpts or verses of the Holy Quran	R	Exports permitted under licence.
0004	Military store as specified by Director General of Foreign Trade	F	No Objection Certificate from the Department of Defence Production and Supplies, Ministry of Defence, New Delhi, Except the items as specified at S.No.1 of Appendix 1 to Schedule 2 of ITC (HS) Classification of Exports and Imports 2002-2007
0005	Special Chemicals, Organisms, Materials, Equipments & Technologies as specified in Schedule-2 Appendix 3 of this book	P/R/F	Exports governed as per the conditions indicate in Appendix-3. Further where no specific conditions as at category 2 to 7 are enumerated, licence shall be required.
0006	Samples of goods included in Schedule 2 of this book	F	Samples of goods including those in Schedule 2 of this book, except all prohibited items, and all items specified in Appendix 3 to Schedule 2 (SCOMET)[1], restricted items, items at code 2901. 9303 and 9907, as well as subject to provisions contained in the Hand Book of Procedures (Vol.I) 2002-2007.
0007	Exhibits of goods included in Schedule 2 (SCOMET)	F	Exhibits of goods including those in Schedule 2 of this book, except all prohibited items as well as all items under category 0, 1 and 2 in Appendix 3 to Schedule 2 (SCOMET) items at code 2901, 9303 and

R-Restricted; F-Free; P-Prohibited; S-State Trading Enterprises.

1 Text not reproduced.

Code	Items Description	Policy	Nature of Restriction
9907,			as well as subject to provisio contained in the Hand Book Procedures (Vol.I) 2002-20(
0008	Any other items whose exports are regulated by a Public Notice issued by the Director General of Foreign Trade in this behalf.	R	Exports permitted under licence.

Goods Falling Within Specific Chapters of ITC (HS) Classification

	Live Animals		
0101	Horses-Kathiwari, Marwari and Manipuri breeds	R	Exporters permitted under licence.
0102	Cattle and buffaloes including their germplasm	R	Exporters permitted under licence.
0106	Exotic birds except the following species of exotic birds, policy of which is indicated against each	P	Not permitted to be exportec
	(i) Albino budgerigars (ii) Budgerigars (iii) Bangali finches (iv) White finches (v) Zebra finches	F	Subject to pre-shipment inspection for entries at S.No. (i) to (v) in column 2 Exports permitted under license.
	(vi) Jawa sparrow	R	A certificate from the Chicf Wild-life warden of the concerned State from where exotic bird (Jawa Sparrow) have been procured to the effect that the birds to be exported are from Captive Bre Stock. Exports if allowed sha be subject to pre-shipment inspection and CITES certificate.
0106	Camel	R	Exports permitted to be exported.

	Meat and Edible Meat Offal		
0201	Beef	P	Not permitted to be exporte
0201 0202 0206	a) Meat of Buffalo (both male and female) including heart, liver, tongue, offals, kidneys and other organs, except gonads and reproductive organs	F	Free, subject to conditions a below for entries at (a), (l and (c) of Column 2 a) The export of Chilled and Frozen Meat shall be allowed subject to the provision specified in the Gazette Notification on Raw Meat (Chilled and Frozen) under Export (Quality Control and Inspection) Act, 1963.
0204 0206	b) Meat of Indian sheep including heart, liver, lungs, brain, tongue, kidneys and other organs		

R-Restricted; F-Free; P-Prohibited; S-State Trading Enterprises.

1 Text not reproduced.

Code	Items Description	Policy	Nature of Restriction
0204 0206	c) Meat of Indian Goat including heart, liver, lungs, brain, tongue, kidneys and other organs.		b) Export of meat or Offals (excluding gonads and reproductive organs) of buffalo may be allowed on production of a certificate from the designated veterinary authority of the State, from which the meat or offals emanate, to the effect that the meat or offals are from buffaloes not used for breeding and milch purposes. c) Export of canned meat products shall be subject topreshipment inspection either by the State Directorate of animal Husbandry or Directorate of Marketing and inspection Government of India in accordance with either the standards prevalent in the exporting country or standards prescribed under the Meat Food Products Order, 1973 of Export (Quality Control and Inspection) Act, 1963 or orders made thereunder. d) The export of offals (excluding gonads and reproductive organs) of buffalo shall be allowed subject to the same conditions as specified for the export of Meat of Buffalo on Raw meat (Chilled and Frozen) under Export (Quality Control and Inspection) Act, 1963.
	Fish and Crustaceans, Molluscs and other Aquatic Invertebrates		
0301	Marine products	F	Subject to preshipment quality inspection as may be specified by the Government through a Notification
0302	Fresh and Frozen silver	R	Exports permitted under licence.
0303	pomfrets of weight less than 300 gms		

R-Restricted; F-Free; P-Prohibited; S-State Trading Enterprises.

Code	*Items Description*	*Policy*	*Nature of Restriction*
0303	Beche-de-mer of sizes below 3 inches	R	Exports permitted under licence.
0307	Sea shells, excluding polished sea shells and handicrafts made out of sea shells, of all species, except those of the undermentioned species the export of which shall not be allowed in any form	R	Exports permitted under licence.
	(i) Trochus niloticos	P	Not permitted to be exported for
	(ii) Turno species	P	the entires at Sl. No.(i) to (v) in
	(iii) Lambis specis	P	Column 2.
	(iv) Tridacna gigas	P	
	(v) Xancus pyrus		
	Products of Animals origin		
0506	Human skeletons	P	Not permitted to be exported
0506	(i) Bones and bone products (excluding bone meal), horn and horn products, (excluding horn meal), hooves and hoof products (excluding hoof meal) when exported to the European Union.	F	Export allowed subject to production of a certificate from Chemicals and Allied Products Exports Promotion Council (CAPEXIL) regarding producttion process in respect of the exported item.
	(ii) Export of Bones and bone prodpucts including Ossein and Gelatine intended to be used for Human consumption, meant for European Union.	F	Export allowed subject to approval of establishment of production and issue of Health Certificate by CAPEXIL in respect of the exported item
0505	Peacock Tail Feathers including handicrafts and articles made thereof	P	Not permitted to be exported.
0511	Manufactured Articles and Shavings of Shed Antlers of Chital and Sambhar	P	Not permitted to be exported.
	Edible Vegetables and Certain Roots and Tubers		
0703	(a) Onions (all varieties other than Banglore Rose onion and Krishnapuram onions)	STEs	Export permitted through specified STEs under quota released from time to time and conditionalities as notified through Public Notices/Notifications by DGFT
	(b) Bangalore Rose onion and Krishnapuran onions	STEs	Export through KAPPEC, AP MARKFED and KSCMF subject to conditions laid down by DGFT from time to time

R-Restricted; F-Free; P-Prohibited; S-State Trading Enterprises.

Code	*Items Description*	*Policy*	*Nature of Restriction*
0711	Onion as a apart of assorted vegetables	F	Export allowed up to 20 Kg. per consignment by air.
	Cereals		
1006	Rice Basmati	F	a) Exports allowed subject to registration of contract with the APEDA, New Delhi. b) Exports of empty printed gunny bags with Markings indicating the product being Indian Basmati Rice, in whatever manner, are not permitted except when exported alongwith the consignments of Basmati Rice, in which cases also, the same shall not exceed 2% of the total number of filled gunny bags of Basmati Rice being exported.
1006	Paddy (of Basmati Rice in husk)	F	a) Export allowed subject to registration of contracts with the APEDA, New Delhi. b) Export of empty printed gunny bags with Marking indicating the product being Indian Basmati Paddy, in whatever manner, are not permitted except when exported alongwith the consignments of Basmati Paddy, in which case also, the same shall not exceed 2% of the total number of filled gunny bags of Basmati Paddy being exported. c) In case of unbagged Indian Basmati Paddy being exported in bulk or in bags of 50 kgs or above, the exports of empty printed gunny bags with Markings indicating the product being Indian Basmati Paddy, in whatever manner, shall also be permitted to the extent of actual requirements considering the total quantity of the consignment and the sizes of the empty bags being exported.

R-Restricted; F-Free; P-Prohibited; S-State Trading Enterprises.

Code	Items Description	Policy	Nature of Restriction
Oil Seeds and Oleginous Fruits; Miscellaneous Grains, Seeds and Fruit; Industrial or Medicinal Plants; Straw and Fodder			
1201 to 1214	Seeds and planting materials, except the following;	F	Exports freely permitted subject to a declaration in the form of an affidavit from the exporter that the seed being exported is not Breeder or Foundation or Wild variety seeds and indicating the source of procurement
	(i) Cashew seeds and plants	R	Exports permitted under licence for all the entires from (i) to (xvi) in Column 2
	(ii) Jute Seeds	R	
	(iii) Egyptian clover (Barseem) Trifolium alaxtum seeds	R	
	(iv) Nux vomica seeds/ bark/ leaves/ roots/ and powder thereof	R	
	(v) Onion Seeds	R	
	(vi) Seeds of ornamental plants (wild variety)	R	
	(vii) Paddy seeds (wild variety)	R	
	(viii) Pepper cutting or rooted cuttings of pepper	R	
	(ix) Red sanders seeds (Pterocarpus santalinus)	R	
	(x) Rubber Seeds	R	
	(xi) Russa grass seeds and tufts	R	
	(xii) Seeds of all forestry species	R	
	(xiii) Sandal wood seeds (Santalum album)	R	
	(xiv) Saffron seeds or corms (planting material for saffron)	R	
	(xv) Wheat seeds (wild variety)	R	
	(xvi) Neem seeds	R	
1202	Groundnuts (Peanuts)	F	Exports to European Union allowed subject to compulsory registration of contracts with APEDA, alogwith controlled aflatoxin level certificate given by agencies/laboratories nominated by APEDA

R-Restricted; F-Free; P-Prohibited; S-State Trading Enterprises.

Code	Items Description	Policy	Nature of Restriction
*1207	Niger Seeds	STEs	Export through TRIEFD (to all permissible destinations other than USA) in accordance with the directions issued by the DGFT from time to time. For export of Niger seeds to USA, the following STEs may undertake exports directly or may register qualified exporters to whom permits may be granted for undertaking export of Niger seeds, subject to conditionalities as notified: (1) The National Agricultural Co-operative Marketing Federaltion of India (NAFED (2) The Dhara Vegetable Oil & Foods Company Ltd. (3) The Madhya Pradesh State Cooperative Oil Seeds Grower Federation Ltd. (4) The Karnataka State Agricultural Produce Processing and Export Corporation, and (5) Bihar and Andhra Pradesh Government Nominated Agencies.
1209	Seeds of all trees (excluding seeds of all forestry species), hedges, ornamental plants and flowers and vegetable seeds other than onion seeds	F	Exports permitted subject to a declaration in the form of an affidavit from the export that the seed being exported is not Breeder or Foundation or Wild variety seeds and indicating the sources of procurement.
1211	Plants and plant portions obtained from the wild, and their cultivated varieties not covered under schedule 2 Appendix 2 of this book, except for the extracts and derivatives, including value added herbal formulations of such plants for which these conditions shall not apply.	F	(a) Export of plants and plant portions obtained from the Wild will be allowed on production of a no Objection Certificate from Regional Deputy Director (Wild Life), or the Chief Conservator of Forests or the Divisional Forests Officers of the State concerned from where these plants and plant, portions have been procured.

R-Restricted; F-Free; P-Prohibited; S-State Tradir g Enterprises.

Code	Items Description	Policy	Nature of Restriction
			(b) The export of plants and plant portions of the cultivated varieties will be allowed subject to production of a certificate of cultivation from the Regional Deputy Director (Wild Life), or the Chief Conservator of Forest or the Divisional Forest officers of the State concerned or when cultivated in Non-forest areas, the District Agriculture Officer or the District Horticulture Officer concerned provided that, forest/wild life officials shall continue to issue transport permits and CITES permit when cultivation certificates are issued by DAO, DHO. (c) In respect of Plan Species Covered under CITES, a CITES Permit for export will also be required. (d) Exports allowed only through the ports of Mumbai, Kolkata, Coachin, Delhi, Chennai, Tuticorin and Amritsar.
1211	All items of plants included in Appendix I and Appendix II of the Convention on International Trade in Endangered Species (CITES), wild orchid as well as, plants as specified in Schedule 2 Appendix 2 of this book.	P	Not permitted to be exported. Revision of procedure for procurement certificate when cultivated in non-forest areas at Appendix 2 is notified alongwith.
1211	Sea weeds of all types, including G-edulis but excluding brown sea weeds and agarophytes of Tamil Nadu Coast origin in processed form	R	Exports permitted under licence.
1212	Brown sea weeds and Agrophytes excluding G-edulis of Tamil Nadu coast origin in processed form.	F	Exports allowed subject to quantitative celling as may be notified by DGFT from time to time

R-Restricted; F-Free; P-Prohibited; S-State Trading Enterprises.

Code	*Items Description*	*Policy*	*Nature of Restriction*
	Lac, Gums, Resins and Other Vegetable Saps and Extracts		
1301	Shellac and all forms of lac	F	(a) Registration with Tribal Cooperative Marketing Development Federation of India Ltd or Shellac Export Promotion Council (b) Production of quality certificate from Shellac Export Promotion Council
1301	Gum Karaya	STE	Export through the Tribal Cooperative Marketing Federation of India Limited (TRIFED), New Delhi
	Vegetable Plainting Materials; Vegetable Products not elsewhere specified or included		
1404	Cotton Linters	F	Deleted. It is now free for exports.
	Animal or Vegetable Fats and Oils and their Cleavages Products; Prepared Edible Fats; Animal or Vegetable Waxes		
1503	Tallow, fat and/or oils of any animal origin excluding fish oil	P	Not permitted to be exported
	Residues and Waste from the Food Industries; Prepared Animal Fodder		
2306	Deoiled groundnut cake containing more than 1% oil and groundnut expeller cakes	R	Exports permitted under licence
2302	Fodder, including wheat and rice straw	R	Exports permitted under licence
2302	Rice bran, raw and boiled	R	Exports permitted under licence
	Salt; Sulphur; Earths and Stone; Plastering Materials, Lime and Cement		
2505	Sand and soil	R	Exports permitted under licence.
2601	Iron ore However, export of the following types of iron ore are freely permitted except (d) and (e) which are permitted for export by STEs mentioned in column 4	STE	Export through MMTC Limited
	(a) Iron ore of Goa origin when exported to China, Europe, Japan, South Korea and Taiwan, irrespective of the Fe content;	F	

R-Restricted; F-Free; P-Prohibited; S-State Trading Enterprises.

Code	*Items Description*	*Policy*	*Nature of Restriction*
	(b) Iron ore of Redi origin to all markets, irrespective of the Fe content;	F	
	(c) All iron ore of Fe content upto 64%	F	
	(d) Iron ore concentrate prepared by benefications and or concentration of low grade ore containing 40 per cent of less of iron produced by Kudremukh Iron Ore Company Limited	STE	Kudremukh Iron Ore Company Limited, Bangalore
	(e) Iron ore pellets manufactured by Kudremukh Iron Ore Company Limited out of concentrates produced by it.	STE	Kudremukh Iron Ore Company Limited, Banglore
	(f) Rejects of iron ore chips and like generated from the manufacturing process after using imported raw material subject to the following conditions: (i) The quanity of export of such rejects shall not be more than 10% of the imported raw materials i.e. pellets (ii) The size of the rejected pellets chips (fines) shall be less than 6 mm.	F	
2602	Manganese Ores excluding the following: Lumpy/blended Manganese ore with more than 46 per cent Manganese	STEs	Export through (a) MMTC Limited (b) Manganese Ore India Limited (MOIL) for manganese ore produced in MOIL mines
2602	Lumpy/blended manganese ore with more than 46% manganese	R	Exports permitted under licence
2610	(a) Chrome ore other than (i) beneficated chrome ore fines/ concentrates (maximum feed grade to be less than 42% Cr_2O_3) and (ii) those categories of Chrome ores mentioned in (b) to (d) below as permitted through STEs.	R	Exports permitted under licence other than categories at (b) to (d) below
	(b) Chrome ore lumps with Cr_2O_3 not exceeding 40 per cent	STE	Export through MMTC Limited
	(c) Low silica friable/fine ore with Cr_2O_3 not exceeding 52 per cent and Silica exceeding 4 per cent	STE	Export through MMTC Limited

R-Restricted; F-Free; P-Prohibited; S-State Trading Enterprises.

Code	*Items Description*	*Policy*	*Nature of Restriction*
	(d) Low Silica Friable/fine Chromite Ore with Cr_2O_3 in the range of 52-54% and slica exceeding 4%	STE	Export through MMTC Limited
2614	Rare Earths, ores concentrates and compounds of monazite	R	Export permitted under licence.
2617	Other minerals containing the following substances as accessory ingredients including: (i) Samerskite (ii) Uraniferrous allanite Radium ores and concentrates	R	Export permitted under licence.
2618	Granular sillimanite produced by Indian Rare Earths Limited, Mumbai and Kerala Minerals and Metals Limited, Kollam	*Deleted*	Deleted: It is now free for exports.
	Minerals fuels; Minerals Oils and Products of their Distillation; Bituminous Substances; Minerals Waxes		
2709	Petroleum Products namely:		
2710	Crude oil	STE	Export through Indian Oil Corporation Limited
	(a) Kerosene	F	Export allowed subject to obtaining NOC from Ministry of Petroleum and Natural Gas
	(b) Liquefied Petroleum Gas (LPG)	F	Export allowed subject to obtaining NOC from Ministry of Petroleum and Natural Gas
	Organic Chemicals		
2901	Organic chemicals as below: (a) Acetic Anhydride (b) Poly Brominated Biphenyls (c) Poly Chlorinated Biphenyls (d) Poly Chlorinated terpheyls (e) Tris (2,3 Di-bromopropyl) phosphate (f) Crocidolite (g) Ephedrine and its salts/Pseudoephedrine and its salts (h) 1-Phenyl-2 Propa-none & 3,4-Methyl-enedioxphenyl-2-Phropanone (i) Methyl Ethyl Ketone & Potassium Permanganate	F	(a) No Objection Certificate from the Department of Chemicals and Petrochemicals, Ministry of Chemicals and Fertilizers, New Delhi in respect of items (b) to (f) in column (2) (b) No Objection Certificate from Narcotics Commissioner of India, Gwalior in respect of items (a), (g), (h) & (i) in column (2)

R-Restricted; F-Free; P-Prohibited; S-State Trading Enterprises.

Code	*Items Description*	*Policy*	*Nature of Restriction*
2902	Chemicals included in Annesxures A and B to the Montreal Protocol on substances that deplete the ozone Layer as specified in Schedule 2 Appendix 4 of this book	P/R	Exports permitted under licence subject to the condition that the export is made to a country which is a party to the 'Montreal Protocol on substances that Deplete the Ozone Layer'. However, export to countries which are not Parties to the Montreal Protocol is prohibited Revised Appendix 4 is notified alongwith.
	Pharmaceutical Products		
3002	Whole human blood plasma and all products derived from human blood except gamma globulin and human serum albumin manufactured from human placenta and human placental blood; Raw placenta; Placental blood plasma	R	Exports permitted underlicence except for individual case of export of samples for diagnostic/therapeutic prescription purposes on recommendation of a Doctor.
	Fertilisers		
3102 3103	Chemicals Fertilizers, all types, including super-phosphate except as at (a) below for which condition-alities are specified (a) Own manufactured DAP/SSP.	R	Manufacturers of DAP and SSP as listed at Appendix 5 shall be allowed to export their own manufactured DAP/SSP subject to: (i) Information to Department of Fertilizer about quantity of export alongwith a self declaration certificate with a certificate issued by statu-tory auditors that no concession/subsidy has been claimed for intended exports. (ii) Production of the above declarations/certification as (i) above to custom authorities as well.
3104	Muriate of Potash (MoP) except as stipulated at column 4	R	Exports permitted, freely by di-rect importers of MOP, out of quantity of import made during last six months.
3105	Micronutrient fertilizers and mixtures thereof containg NPK, excluding those specified in Sched-ule 1, Part A 1 (f) of Fertilizers (Control) Order, 1985	R	Export permitted under licence

R-Restricted; F-Free; P-Prohibited; S-State Trading Enterprises.

Code	*Items Description*	*Policy*	*Nature of Restriction*
Essential Oils and Resinoids; Perfumery, Cosmetic or Toilet Preparations			
3301	Sandalwood oil	F	Subject to Quantitative ceilings and conditionalities as may be notified by the Director General of Foreign Trade from time to time
Raw Hides and Skins (Other than Furskins) and leather			
4104 to 4107	Finished leather all kinds	F	Subject to the definition of finished leather, notified by DGFT from time to time
4302	Clothing leather fur suede hair, hair-on suede/shearing suede leather	F	As defined in ISI norms 8170
Wood and Articles of Wood; Wood Charcoal			
4401	Wood and wood products in the form of logs, timber, stumps, roots, bark, chips, powder, flakes, dust, pulp and charcoal except sawn timber made exclusively out of imported logs/timber (subject to conditions specified at code 4402)	P	Not permitted to be exports.
4402	Sawn Timber made exclusively out	F	(i) The Export would be of imported logs/timber of all the confined to the species which species of wood other than CITES has been imported; Appendix I & II species, (ii) The importer and exporter will be the same party/firm and the import and export will have to be effected from the same port. The scheme will be operational only from the ports of Mumbai, Kolkata, Chennai, Visakhapatanam, Kandla, Mangalore and Tutucorin. (iii) The export of sawn products derived from imported logs shall not exceed 60% of the imports in volume terms; (iv) The value addition of such exports shall be not less than 30%.

R-Restricted; F-Free; P-Prohibited; S-State Trading Enterprises.

Code	Items Description	Policy	Nature of Restriction
			(v) The Saw Mill of the exporter, where imported timber is sawn shall be registered with the State Forest Department and shall be located away from the forest area in a location approved by the Conservator of Forests of the State Government; (vi) The exporter must undertake exports within a period of 6 months from the date of import; (vii) The export contracts shall be registered with the Chemicals and Allied Products Export Promotion Council (CAPEXIL) who will monitor them to ensure that the scheme is not abused. (viii) The laws and rules framed by the Central Government and the State Government regulating timber in transit shall be followed by the exporters.
4403	Sandalwood in any form, but excluding:	P	Not permitted to be exported
	(i) Finished Handicraft products of sandalwood;	F	
	(ii) Machine finished sandalwood products	F	
	(iii) Sandalwood Oil	F	Subject to Quantitative ceilings and conditionalities as may be notified by the Director General of Foreign Trade from time to time.
	(iv) Sandalwood De-oiled Spent Dust	R	Exports permitted under licence. Subject to conditionalities as may be notified by the Director general of Foreign Trade from time to time.
	(v) Those forms of sandalwood as specified	R	Exports permitted under licence Subject to conditionalities as may be notified by the Director General of Foreign Trade from time to time.

R-Restricted; F-Free; P-Prohibited; S-State Trading Enterprises.

Code	*Items Description*	*Policy*	*Nature of Restriction*
4403	(a) Red Sanders wood in any form, whether raw, processed or unprocessed, except at (b) below	P	Not permitted to be exported
	(b) Value added products of Red Sanders wood	R	Exports permitted under licence subject to (i) Only value added products such as Extracts, Dyes, Musical Instruments and parts of Musical Instruments, made from redsanders wood, procured from legal sources, shall be allowed for exports. (ii) Applications for export licences should be accompanied by attested copies of certificate of origin issued by the Principal Chief Conservator of Forest of the State from where the stocks were procured, giving details of the date of procurement from legal sources and quantities procured. A Certificate of the current position of stock so procured and available with the applicant given after physical verification of the stocks, by the authority nominated for the purpose by the Principal Chief Conservator of Forests, should also accompany application for export licence. (iii) The applications shall be considered on merits for issue of Export Licence, which shall be subject to any other conditions such as MEP, quantity ceilings requirements under CITES, ect. as may be prescribed from time to time.

R-Restricted; F-Free; **P-Prohibited; S-State Trading Enterprises.**

Code	Items Description	Policy	Nature of Restriction
	Pulp of Wood or of other Fibrous Cellulosic Materials; Waste and Scrap of Paper or Paperboard		
4707	Waste paper	R	Exports permitted under licence
	Silk		
5001	Only pure races of Silk worms; silkworm seeds, and silk worm cocoons	R	Exports permitted under licence
5003	Mulberry Silk waste not carded or combed	F	Deleted
	Vehicles other than Railway or Tramway rolling stock, and parts and accessories thereof		
8703	Vintage motor cars, parts and components thereof manufactured prior to 1.1.1940	R	Exports permitted under licence
8711	Vintage Motorcycle, parts and components thereof manufactured prior to 1.1.1940	R	Exports permitted under
	Arms and Ammunition; Parts and Accessories thereof		
9303	Arms and ammunition viz., muzzle loading weapons and breach loading or bolt action weapons such shot guns, revolvers, pistols and their ammunition	F	(a) Licence under Arms Act and Rules framed thereunder; (b) Certificate from the Archaeological Survey of India certifying that the firearms to be exported are not antiques/rare specimens nor manufactured in India prior to 1956; and (c) Firearms to be exported shall bear appropriate marks of identification and prooftests.
	Miscellaneous Goods		
9907	Replicas of antique weapons	F	Certificate from the District Magistrate concerned/ Commissioner of Police under whose jurisdiction

R-Restricted; F-Free; P-Prohibited; S-State Trading Enterprises.

Code	*Items Description*	*Policy*	*Nature of Restriction*
			the replica has been manufactured and has been rendered innocaus.
9904	Condoms	F	No Objection Certificate from Ministry of Health and Family Welfare.

R-Restricted; F-Free; P-Prohibited; S-State Trading Enterprises.

ALL FOLLOWING PROJECT REPORTS ARE READILY AVAILABLE

- Khandsari Sugar & Imfl
- Lactic Acid From White Sugar By Fermentation Process
- Lactose & By Products Processing From Milk
- Liquid Glucose And Its Bye Products
- Macroni And Vermicilli
- Malt Extraction From Barley
- Mango Processing (Mango Pulp, Juice & Slices)
- Mayur Brand Type Chewing Tobacco
- Mineral Water
- Milk Preservation & Marketing To Whole Sellers (Inpouch Packing By Uht Technology)
- Milk Processing And Packaging Of Milk Products
- Milk Products (Casein, Lactose, Ghee & Whey Powder)
- Milk Toffee
- Mini Flour Mill
- Mini Sugar Plant
- Misri (Pearl Sugar Candies)
- Modern Rice Mill
- Murabba
- Mustard Oil Extraction & Refining
- Mutton Tallow
- Namkeen Industry (Bhujia, Chana Chur Etc.)
- Namkeen (Kurkure Type Snack Food
- Namkeen With Kurkurre Type Snack Food
- Namkeen & Sweets
- Non-Basmati Rice From Paddy
- Oleoresin, Essential Oil, Dyes & Powder Of Spices
- Oleoresin Extraction From Diptero-Carput Turminatus And Pinus Khasyana
- Oleoresin Extraction From Chilli
- Pan Masala With Packing In Pouches And Tin Cans
- Pan Masala, Tobacco, Zarda & Kimam
- Packaged Drinking Water
- Packaged Coconut Water (Coco Jal)
- Paneer From Milk
- Pappad Plant
- Papain From Papaya (Papaya Latex)
- Pectin From Mango Peel Pectin From Apple Pomace
- Phyto Tea (Herbal Tea)
- Pickles And Sauces
- Pickles Murabba Etc. (Veg. & Non. Veg.Pickles)
- Piggery Meat Process
- Pine-Apple Juice Preparation & Packaging
- Potato Chips/Waffers
- Potato Powder
- Pouch Filling & Packaging Of Edible Oil & Ghee
- Poultry Feed
- Processed Foods & Spices (Eou)
- Processed Readymade Food
- Processing Of Fruits & Vegetables
- Puree, Paste, Juice And Ketchup From Khajoor (Dates)
- Rabbit Farming

EIRI
We Create Industrialists

- Rasgullas Making & Canning In Metal Cans
- Ready To Eat Processed Cooked Food
- Ready To Eat Retort Packed Food
- Ready To Eat Snack Food (Crax, Roll & Ball Type)
- Rice & Corn Flakes
- Rice Noodles
- Roasted/Salted/Masala,Cashew Nuts, Almonds & Peanuts
- Roller Flour Mill (Atta, Suja And Maida)
- Salt Licks For Cattle
- Sattu
- Sausages Food Casing
- Soft Drinks (Cold Drinks)
- Soft Drinks Essences
- Soft Drinks (Non Carbonated) Mango,Licchi, Pineapple Flavours Frooti Type In Tetrapack)
- Softy Ice Cream Cones (Fully Automatic)
- Soft/Cold Drinks (Cola, Orange, Lemon Etc. Flavours)
- Soyabean Products
- Soyabean Bariyan
- Soya Milk & Paneer
- Spices/Masala With Formulae
- Spices And Namkeen (Integrated Unit)
- Snack Food (Kurkure Type)
- Starch & Allied Propduct From Broken Rice
- Strawberry Cultivation & Processing
- Sugarcane Juice Preservation
- Sugar Cubes From Cane Sugar
- Sugar Plant
- Supari (Sweet) – Betel Nut (Synthetic)
- Sweet Aroma Betel Nut
- Synthetic Tallow
- Tamarind Juice Powder
- Tamarind Juice Concentrates
- Tea & Coffee Processing & Packaging
- Toffees, Golies, Candy (Hard Boiled)
- Tomato Products
- Tomato Ketchup, Tomato Puree And Tomato Juice (Tomato Products)
- Trading Business Of Spices & Pan Masala
- Tuity Fruity
- Vermicilli (Including Roasted Vermicilli)
- Virgin Coconut Oil
- Vodka From Potatoes
- Walnut Processing
- Wine, Brandy, Whisky &Champagne
- Wine From Dates
- Yeast From Molasses
- Zarda, Kimam No. 60,90,120,160,240,300 & 400 (Tobacco)
- Zarda Kimam And Tobacco
- Zarda-Zafrani (Babachhaptype)

GUMS AND ADHESIVES

- Acrylic Adhesive
- Adhesive (Different Types)
- Adhesive (Fevicol Type)
- Adhesive For Stickers
- Adhesive Based On Vinyl Acetate
- Adhesive Based On Polyurethane
- Adhesive For Band Aid (Johnson & Johnson Type)
- Adhesive Industries (Laminated, Sticker,Ddl & Other Types)
- Adhesive For Gasket (Liquid/Paste)
- Araldyte Type Adhesive
- Alkyd Resin
- Bopp Self Adhesive Tapes
- Cyanoacrylate Adhesive
- Ester Gums
- Fevicol Type Adhesive
- Guar Gum
- Gum Bottle (Pvc)
- Gum For Pasting Labels
- Leather To Leather Adhesive
- Liquid Adhesive For Corrugated Boxes
- Office Paste
- Poly Amide Resin
- Pressure Sensitive Adhesive
- Pvc Indulation Tapes
- Printing Gums (Guar Gum Based)
- Rubber Adhesive
- Self Adhesive Labels
- Starch And Dextrin Based Afhesive
- Surgical Adhesive Plaster
- Synthetic Rubber Adhesive
- Synthetic Adhesive For Decorative Laminate Bonding
- Tapioca Starch Adhesive
- Vinyl Ester Adhesive
- Vulcanising Adhesive Formulation Vulcanizing Rubber Solution/Cement For Automobile Tyre
- Urea Formaldehyde Resin
- Water Based Latex Adhesive

Contact EIRI
for required Project report apart from this list.

Market Survey Cum Detailed Techno Economic Feasibility Report on all Projects are available Contact.
"ENGINEERS INDIA RESEARCH INSTITUTE", 4449, Nai Sarak (D), Main Road, Delhi-110006 (India)
Ph. : 09811437895, 9811151047, 91-11-23918117, 23916431, 23947058, 64727385, 45120361
E-mail : eiriprojects@gmail.com, eiribooks@yahoo.com • website: www.eiri.in, www.eiriindia.org • www.eiribooksandprojectreports.com

ALL FOLLOWING PROJECT REPORTS ARE READILY AVAILABLE

LEATHER & LEATHER PRODUCTS

- Handmade Leather
- Leather Auxillaries & Chemicals
- Leather Dyes
- Leather Washers
- Leather Board From Leather Waste
- Leather For Upholstry(Sofa)
- Leather Finishing Lacquer (Nitrocellulose Lacquer For Leather)
- Leather Garments
- Leather Goods
- Leather Shoes
- Leather Shoe & Chappal
- Leather Suitcases, Briefcases & Travelling Bags
- Leather Goods And Garments
- Leather Garments, Shoe & Chappal
- Leather Pigment Used For Colouring Of Leather
- Leather Tanning
- Leather Tanning & Garments (Eou)
- Sheep Skin Pickling Plant
- Shoe Upper
- Sport Shoes (Plastic)

MISCELLANEOUS PRODUCTS

- Agarbatti (Insence Stick)
- Abrasive Paper
- Agarbatti (Mosquito Repellent)
- Agarbati Bamboo Stick
- Agarbatti Synthetic Perfumery Compound
- Air Freshner(Odonil Type)
- Air Taxi
- Amusement Park
- Anodic Aluminium Label
- Aquaculture Prawn Farming (100% Eou)
- Aqua Culture Shrimp Farming (100% Eou)
- Artificial Flowers
- Artificial Jewellery
- Asbestos Yarn
- Ash Trays For Maruti Vehicle
- Air Bubble Packaging
- Asphaltic Roofing Sheet (Metal Components)
- Automatic Book Binding
- Alkyd Resin
- Apple Juice Concentrate
- Ball Point Pen Fefills (Jotter Type)
- Bank Branch Building
- Banquet Hall
- Bio-Coal Briquettes From Agriculturalcellulose Waste
- Boot Cream/Polish
- Buffing & Polishing Compound
- Brass Badges By Etching
- Briquetted Fuel From Agro Waste
- Briquetting Of Lignite Coal
- Buffalo Horn Tip, Hoof
- Banquet Hall
- Button
- Calcined Petroleum (C.P) Coke
- Canvas Shoes
- Canvas Shoes, Jungle Boots
- Carbon Brush, Brush Holder & Slip Ring
- Cement Sheets With Coir Fibre & Other Segments
- Ceramic Tiles (Glazed) By Double Firing/Heating
- Children Recreation Centre
- Coal Briquettes
- Cold Storage & Ice
- Cold Storage For Fruits And Vegetables
- Compressor (Hermetic) For Air Conditioner
- Costume Jewellery/Imitation Jewellery
- Decorative Laminated Sheet (Sunmica)
- Dental Colleges
- Diamond Cutting & Exports
- Drinking Straw From Propylene
- Engineering College
- Engineering College, Management Institute, Cbse School, Hostel (Boys And Girls), Medical College With Hospital And Research Institute
- Electropolishing On Gold Jewellery (Gold Ornaments)
- Entertainment Club
- Fashion Technology Institute
- Fast Food Parlour
- Fast Food (Instant Food & Fast Food Parlour)
- Fire Extinguishers (Soda Acid Type)
- Fish Net
- Floriculture (Cut Flower Rose) With Green House
- Floor Covering Sheet
- Film Studio (Video)
- Flush Door, Chip Board, Wood Wool & Other Insulating Boards
- Gas Detectors Of L.P.G
- Gems Manufacturing
- Glass Bottle By Scrap
- Glass Jars Manufacturing Plant For Packaging Of 50, 100, 150, 200 Grams Coffee Packaging
- Goat & Sheep Farming
- Gold Electroplating
- Gold Jewellery (E.O.U)
- Gold Plated Silver Jewellery & Cutlery
- Granite Slab And Tiles
- Granite Mining
- Green House
- Hard Chromium Plating
- Health Club And Beauty Parlour Cum Hair
- Saloon With Sona Bath
- Health Club Cum Beauty Parlour Training Institute
- Horn Tip,Hoove Button
- Hospital

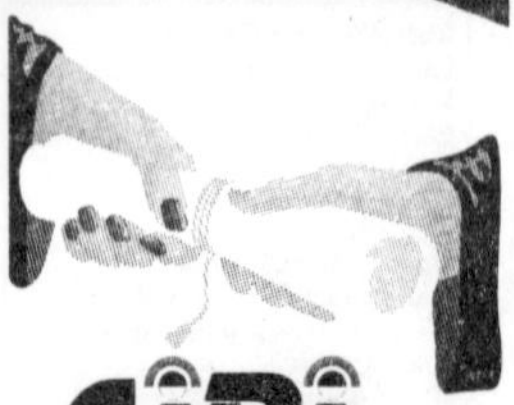

EIRI

Is fully capable to prepare any Project Report of your Choice

- Hospital (100 Beds)
- Hospital (200 Beds)
- Ice Making Plant
- Imitation And Costume
- Jewellery (Necklace, Earrings Ear Top Etc.)
- Initmate Scent Chemicals From All Types Of Flavour
- Investment Casting
- Jute, Coir, Glass Rope/ Sutli
- Jute Twine
- Jute Bags From Yarn Without Spinning Process
- L.P.G Bottling Plant
- L.P.G Regulator (Domestic Purpose)
- Laminated Particle Board & Hard Board
- Laminated Safety & Toughened Glass
- Leasing & Hire Purchase
- Lichen (Charila)
- Manila Ropes
- Medical College
- Medical University
- Metal Pretreatment Chemicals Powder, Coating Chemicals
- Match Unit From Waxed Paper
- Medium Density Fibre Board
- Melamine Crockery
- Mineral Water
- Mini Cement Plant
- Mirror Silver, Golden, Pink, Black & Smokes
- Modern Advt. Agency With Dtp & Film Studio
- Motel/Small Hotel
- Multi Colour Printing
- Multi Purpose Cold Storage And Dehydration And Canning Of Fruits And Vegetables
- Multi Storey Commercial Complex Alongwith Residential And Delux Flats For Foreign Tourists & Revolving Restaurent At The Top
- Multiple Lamination Industry
- Mushroom Growing And Processing (By Deep Freezing Method)
- News Paper Printing
- Nickel Lined Industrial Screen
- Non Coking Coal To Coking Coal
- Nursing Home
- Offset Colour Printing Press (Six Colour)

Market Survey Cum Detailed Techno Economic Feasibility Report on all Projects are available Contact.
"ENGINEERS INDIA RESEARCH INSTITUTE", 4449, Nai Sarak (D), Main Road, Delhi-110006 (India)
Ph. : 09811437895, 9811151047, 91-11-23918117, 23916431, 23947058, 64727385, 45120361
E-mail : eiriprojects@gmail.com, eiribooks@yahoo.com • website: www.eiri.in, www.eiriindia.org • www.eiribooksandprojectreports.com

EDIBLE OILS, ESSENTIAL OILS, LURICATIING OILS, GREASES, VEGETABLE OILS, WAXES, CAMPHOR, PERFUMES & PERFUMERY COMPOUNDS AND REFINED OILS ETC.

ALL FOLLOWING PROJECT REPORTS ARE READILY AVAILABLE

PAINT, ENAMEL, SOLVENTS, THINNERS, INKS & VARNISH
PAINT, ENAMEL, SOLVENTS, THINNERS, INKS & VARNISH

- Acrylic Emulsion Paints
- Acrylic Cement Paint (Dry Powder)
- Aluminium Paint
- Automobile Paints
- Ball Point Pen Refill Ink
- Bituminious Road Emulsion
- Bitumen
- Bituminious Felts For Water & Damp Proofing
- Bituminious Road Emulsion Rapid Medium & Slow Setting
- Buffing & Polishing
- Cement Paint For White & Grey Cement
- Dispersant
- Dry Distemper
- Dry Distemper & Cement Paint
- Duplicating Ink Black For Gestner Duplicator
- Emulsion Paints (Water Based)
- Hammertone Paint
- Insulating Varnish & Wire Enamel
- Iron Oxide Pigments
- Insulating Varnish (Poly Vinyl Butyral Based, Ffc Grade)
- Lime Colour (Cement Colour)
- Synthetic Red Oxide For Floorings
- Solvent & Thinners
- Marking Inks (Water Proof)
- Metal Naphthanate (As Drier For Paints)
- N.C.Putty
- Offset Printing Ink
- Oil Bound Distemper Paint
- Paint Brushes
- Paint Manufacture For Rolling Coating Of Aluminium And Steel Coil
- Paint Removers
- Paint Industry
- Paint & Varnish
- Picture Varnish
- Powder Coating Paint
- Printing Inks (Offset,Flexo & Roto Gravure)

- Primer Paint & Enamel Paint
- Putty & Water Proofing Paint
- Printing Inks (Flexo-Graphic Ink)
- Putty (Metal Casement)
- Red Oxide Primer (Anti Corrosive)
- Refrectory Paint (Graphite Based)
- Screen Printing Inks
- Silk Screen Printing Ink Formulation For Plastic, Paper, Cloth
- Stamp & Pad Ink
- Stoving Paint
- Spirit Soluble Maleic Resin
- Texture Paint
- Thinners And Its Allied Products
- Toner Ink
- Varnish Thinner (Solvent)
- Vacuum Metallizing Lacquers
- Wood Primer

PHARMACEUTICAL, DRUGS, AYURVEDIC/HERBAL COSMETICS & MEDICINES, HOMOEOPATHIC MEDICINES, HOMOEOPATHIC MEDICINES, DISPOSABLE SYRINGE, DENTAL COLLEGE & FINE CHEMICALS ETC. MEDICINES, HOMOEOPATHIC MEDICINES, DISPOSABLE SYRINGE, DENTAL COLLEGE & FINE CHEMICALS ETC.

- Aromatic Pills
- Alumina From Bauxite
- Aspirin
- Ayurvedic Pain Balm Ointments
- Ayurvedic Churan And Tablets
- Ayurvedic Tablets (Hajmola Type)
- Ayurvedic/Herbalpharmacy
- Ayurvedic Sherbats
- Ayurvedic Products
- Bulk Drugs (E.O.U)
- Blood Bags
- Calcium Gluconate
- Capsule, Tablet & Injection With Modern Instruments
- Cashew Feni
- Chloroquinone Phosphate (Bulk Drugs)
- Clinical Thermometer
- Dental Clinic
- Dental College
- Dental Grade Eugenol
- Dextrose Monohydrate, Liquid Glucose
- Dehydrated Onion & Onion Powder
- Dextrose Powder (Anhydrous From Starch)
- Dextrose Saline Solution
- Distillery (I.M.F.L)
- Disposable Needles For Syringes
- Disprin
- Distilled Water
- Empty Hard Gelatine Capsules
- Fairness Cream
- Filling & Packing Of Capsules
- Glucose - D - Powder
- Glycerine
- Hair Colour Mate (Formulations And Process Only)
- Herbal Cosmetics
- Herbal Shampoo
- Herbal Shampoo And Cream
- Herbal Hair Oils (Ayurvedic)
- Homoe & Bio-Medicines With Mother Tincture
- Homoepathic Medicines
- Hypodermic Needles
- I.V. Fluids
- Ibuprofen
- Infusion & Transfusion Sets (I.V. Set)
- Injectable For Pharmaceuticals
- Injection Ampoules Packaging Box
- Integerated Surgical Cotton
- Ice Making Plant
- Ice & Cold Storage
- Lactose & By Products Processing From Milk
- Lichen (Jatamansi Charila)
- Liquid Glucose And Its By-Products
- L-Lysine Monohydro Chloride
- Liquid Glucose From Potatoes
- Medical College
- Methanol (Hpcl Grade)
- Nicotine From Tobacco Waste
- Ointment-Ayurvedic (Yellow & White)
- Pharmaceutical And Food Grade Gelatine
- Pharmaceutical Industry (Tablets, Capsules, Liquid, Gel, Ointment Powder Injectable)
- Pharmaceutical Unit (Eou) With Formulations, Injectables, Etc.
- Pyridine & Derivatives
- Salt (Iodized Salt)
- Saline & Injection Water
- Saline Water & Dextrose Solution (I.V.Fluid In Plastic Bottles)
- Sorbitol
- Starch (Maize)
- Surgical Adhesive Plaster
- Surgical Bandages
- Surgical Gloves
- Surgical Cotton
- Surgical Cotton And Bandage
- Synthetic Camphor Powder
- Tablets & Capsules
- Tissue Culture
- Tincture From Rectified Spirit
- Trimethopime
- Veterinary College With Hospital
- Veterenary Medicines (Only Formulations)
- Vitamin 'C', Sorbitol' Anhydrous Dextrose, Starch

Market Survey Cum Detailed Techno Economic Feasibility Report on all Projects are available Contact.
"ENGINEERS INDIA RESEARCH INSTITUTE". 4449, Nai Sarak (D), Main Road, Delhi-110006 (India)
Ph. : 09811437895, 9811151047, 91-11-23918117, 23916431, 23947058, 64727385, 45120361
E-mail : eiriprojects@gmail.com, eiribooks@yahoo.com • website: www.eiri.in, www.eiriindia.org • www.eiribooksandprojectreports.com

ALL FOLLOWING PROJECT REPORTS ARE READILY AVAILABLE

- Alluminium Printing Plate For Offset Printing Machine
- Aluminium Foils
- Aluminium Wire And Rods
- Brass And Aluminium Hinges
- Hard Anodizing On Aluminium
- Pilfer Proof Caps
- Piston Assembly (Aluminium Alloy)
- Pressure Die Casting (Aluminium)
- Paper Coated Aluminium Wire
- Pressure Cooker

FISH FARMING AND FISHERY PRODUCTS

- Aquaculture Prawn Farming (Fresh Water)
- Chitin & Chitosan From Prawn Shell Waste
- Chemicals From Prawn Fish Head
- Developing Trout Fish Preservation & Storage And Marketing Infrastructure
- Fish Farming
- Fish Canning And Pouching
- Fish Processing (Blast Freezing Process)
- Fish Net
- Fish Oil Soap
- Fish Meal
- Hdpe Fishing Net
- Plastic Milk Crate And Plastic Fish Crate
- Trout Fish Farming, Canning & Preservation With Aqua Feed Manufacturing (Integrated Complex)

SURGICAL AND DISPOSABLE MEDICAL PRODUCTS

- Ayurvedic/Herbal Pharmacy
- Blood Bags
- Bandage Cloth Weaving On Power Loom
- Crepe Bandage
- Disposable Surgical Caps & Masks
- Dextrose Saline (I.V.Fluid) In Plastic Bottle
- Dextrose Saline (I.V.Fluid)
- Disposable Needles For Syringes
- Disposable Plastic Syringes
- Diagnostic Centre
- Electronics Blood Pressure Measuring Instument
- Hospital Cum Nursing Home
- Homeopathic Medicines
- I. V. Fluids (Ffs Technology)
- I.V. Set-Cannula
- Intravenous
- Medical College
- Plastic I.V. Bottles

- Plaster Of Paris Bandages
- Pharmaceuticals (Tablet, Capsule, Syrups And Ointments)
- Repacking Of Medicines
- Surgical Cotton & Bandage
- Surgical Examination Gloves
- Surgical Bandage
- Surgical Adhesive Tape On Cloth Surface
- Surgical Methylated Spirit
- Sodium Phosphate Enema
- Vetenary Medicines

ALCOHOL, BEER, IMFL, COUNTRY LIQUOR, WINE & OTHER RELATED PROJECTS

- Alcohol From Rice Straw
- Alcohol From Molasses
- Alcohol From Potatoes
- Alcoholic Beverages And Vinegar From Coconut Water
- Alcoholic Drinks From Ethyl Alcohol By Mixing Of Various Flavours (Flavoured Alcoholic Beverages)
- Beer Plant (E.O.U.)
- Country Liquor
- Cider Plant
- Ethanol (Biofuel)
- Grape Wine
- Herbal Beer
- Mineral Water (Packed In Bottles, Glasses, Jars)
- Rectified Spirit For Potable Alcohol
- Industrial Alcohol & Medical Alcohol
- Rectified Spirit From Rice/Paddy Straw
- Indian Made Foreign Liquor
- Imfl (Whisky) From Potatoes
- Octalol (Octyl Alcohol) From Molasses
- Potable Beer (Alcoholic) Based On Potato & Barley/Malt
- Vodka From Potatoes
- Whisky
- Wine From Dates

ENGINEERS INDIA RESEARCH INSTITUTE
EiRi

PULP, PAPER, STRAW/GREY BOARD, KRAFT PAPER,PACKAGING, PAPER CARRY BAG, PAPER FROM AGRO WASTE & STATIONERY ETC.

- Ammonia Paper
- Automatic Book Binding
- Adhesive (Fevicol Type)
- All Pin & Gem Clips
- Ball Pen
- Ball Pen Refill Ink
- Ball Pen Ink Remover
- Carbon Paper
- Card Board
- Carbon Less Paper
- Cellphane Paper
- Computer Continuous Stationery
- Computer Forms & Security Printing Press
- Corrugated Board & Box (Printed & Laminated)
- Corrugated Board And Boxes From From Card Boards
- Corrugated Cartons From Plain Papers
- Corrugated Paper
- Corrugatred Packing & Material (Bulb & Tubes Packing)
- Desk Top Publishing
- Defoaming Agent For Paper Plant
- Drinking Straw Paper
- D.T.P Cum Offset Press
- Egg Trays From Pulp
- Ecg Paper
- Exercise Note Book, Register And Pad
- Flexographic Ink
- Greeting Card By Offset Press
- Hand Made Paper Filter Paper
- Hard Board
- Hard Board From Bagasse
- Injection Ampoules Packaging Boxes
- Insulatiing Paper
- Kraft Paper
- Kraft Paper From Bagasse
- Laminated Packaging Paper With Printing
- Lamination & Coating On Paper
- M.G. Paper From Waste Paper
- Mill Paper From Waste Paper
- Mill Board From Rice & Wheat Straws
- Mill Board From Waste Paper
- Mini Paper Plant From Sisal
- Mini Paper Plant
- Multi Wall Paper Sacks
- News Paper For Children
- News Print Paper From Rice Straw/Bagasse
- News Paper Childrens
- News Print Paper

Market Survey Cum Detailed Techno Economic Feasibility Report on all Projects are available Contact.
"ENGINEERS INDIA RESEARCH INSTITUTE". 4449, Nai Sarak (D), Main Road, Delhi-110006 (India)
Ph. : 09811437895, 9811151047, 91-11-23918117, 23916431, 23947058, 64727385, 45120361
E-mail : eiriprojects@gmail.com, eiribooks@yahoo.com • website: www.eiri.in, www.eiriindia.org • www.eiribooksandprojectreports.com